Ivy Compton-Burnett and English Domestic Novel

In the Same Series

Fictional Theories and Three Great Novels
Asha Kumar

Virginia Woolf and Anita Desai
Asha Kanwar

The Novels of Kamala Markandaya and Ruth Jhabvala
Rekha Jha

The Novels of Virginia Woolf
B. Sudipta

The Novels of Graham Greene
P.N. Pandit

Ivy Compton-Burnett and English Domestic Novel

T. Asoka Rani

PRESTIGE

Published by
PRESTIGE BOOKS
New Delhi 110 008

1995

ISBN: 81-85218-60-9

Photo Typesetting by
Pivot Computers
4559, Nai Sarak
Delhi 110 006

Printed at
Mehra Offset Press
New Delhi 110 002

Contents

To
my father

Sri T. M. Reddy

Preface

Domesticity denotes fondness for home and family life. When such domesticity permeates a novel, that novel can be said to answer to the description of a 'Domestic Novel' on the analogy of a 'Domestic Drama.' A Domestic Novel deals with the stark realities of everyday life within the framework of a household. Its compelling attraction lies in the depiction of the domestic atmosphere and in the handling of personal relationships within the domestic setting. Oliver Goldsmith's *The Vicar of Wakefield*, whether or not by a set design, happens to be the first benign comedy of English domesticity. Its theme dealing with the intricacies of the home and the hearth no doubt caught the public attention, but it could not gain instant recognition as a Domestic Novel. Though Fanny Burney originated the simple novel of home life, it was in Maria Edgeworth that the form of Domestic Novel found a major proponent. After Jane Austen, who gave it a shape and content, the Domestic Novel suffered a setback, despite the efforts of some not-so-well-known writers, till the 1840s when, after a long exile, it resurrected itself. In the twentieth century, both men and women novelists, under the influence of Darwin, Marx and Freud, dealt with bigger issues like politics, religion, science, philosophy and war. Ivy Compton-Burnett, standing apart from them, devoted herself to the exploration of domestic relationships with unflinching dedication in all the twenty novels to her credit. She achieved a remarkable measure of success and made a commendable contribution to the English fiction.

Ivy Compton-Burnett did not get the attention she deserved from Indian scholars and critics. Her novels were labelled as 'Pure' having kept political, religious, historical, philosophical and such other factors strictly outside their purview. Unlike the conventional writers who glorified domestic life, she turned the search-light on to the impure aspects of domestic life and, turning inside out the Victorian family, she ruthlessly exposed the dirt behind the veneer of respectability. This she repeated with a vengeance in everyone of her twenty novels—no mean contribution, by any standard, to the English literature.

Attracted by the sheer sincerity of her approach in the Domestic tradition, I was tempted to make an honest effort in a critical assessment of the entire gamut of her literary output. I am greatly indebted to Prof. M. Radhamani Gopalakrishnan for her guidance and to the Prestige for bringing out this book expeditiously and so elegantly.

T. ASOKA RANI

List of Abbreviations

BS	*Brothers and Sisters*
DD	*Darkness and Day*
DOL	*Dolores*
DS	*Daughters and Sons*
EB	*Elders and Betters*
FF	*A Family and a Fortune*
FHF	*Father and His Fate*
GG	*A God and His Gifts*
HH	*A House and its Head*
HIH	*Heritage and its History*
LF	*Last and the First*
MF	*Mighty and their Fall*
MS	*Mother and Son*
MSMS	*Manservant and Maidservant*
MW	*Men and Wives*
MWTM	*More Women than Men*
PC	*Parents and Children*
PM	*Pastors and Masters*
PP	*Present and the Past*
TWTW	*Two Worlds and their Ways*

INTRODUCTORY

The expression 'Domestic Novel' has not yet gained wide currency unlike its counterpart, 'Domestic Drama' in English. Ernest Baker uses it freely to refer to novels of Ivy Compton-Burnett, Charlotte Smith and other works of fiction with domestic life as their focal points. 'Domestic Fiction,' 'Fiction of Home Life' and similar descriptions have been employed by critics like George Sampson and Diana Neill to denote novels of this kind. Hilary Spurling describes Ivy Compton-Burnett's works as 'Domestic Novels.'

The origin of the world 'domestic' is from Latin 'domesticus' meaning 'of the house and home' or 'family affairs.' Domesticity stands for devotion to home and family life. A Domestic novel deals with the realities of everyday life and its compelling attraction lies in the depiction of the atmosphere and in the handling of personal relationships within the domestic setting.

In the field of drama, the term 'Domestic Drama' had already gained wide currency by the sixteenth century. Domestic tragedy in the hands of Heywood and Dekker was "a tragedy of the common people, ordinarily set in the domestic scene, dealing with personal and family relationships rather than with large affairs of state, presented in a realistic fashion, and ending in a tragic or otherwise serious manner."[1]

Certain social, political and literary conditions of the Elizabethan Age facilitated the emergence of the Domestic Drama towards the close of the sixteenth century. The new rising middle classes occasioned a demand for a new kind of drama dealing with their problems in everyday life. Playwrights had to take note of the existence of these middle classes who were developing an identity of their own. Domestic Drama is defined as: "A serious play, generally realistic in style, with its protagonist drawn from the lower or middle classes and its action concerned with personal or domestic matters, rather than high politics."[2] Plays like *Arden of Feversham*, *The Miseries of Enforced Marriage*, *A Warning for Fair Women*, *A Yorkshire Tragedy* and *A Woman Killed with Kindness* are concerned with serious domestic problems of the middle classes. Dekker and Heywood achieved great success as domestic dramatists who set aside the convention that tragedy was concerned only with the disasters of kings and queens. They proved that the emotional conflicts in the household of an ordinary person are ideal themes for drama, and that they are, in fact, all the more appealing to the audience who could identify themselves with the problems of characters who were closer to them in social status. *Arden of Feversham* (1590) of anonymous authorship dealt with an intense tragedy figuring ordinary people. *A Woman Killed with Kindness* (1603), a highly popular domestic tragedy written by Heywood, portrayed the emotional tensions arising out of certain incidents which have not so far been considered as subjects for literature. The momentary lapse of a woman from marital fidelity, handled in a subtle and subdued manner both by her husband in the play and by the playwright in his art, is taken to the very height of tragic intensity, without a single character being subjected to death. The wife's death in the end comes as a note of relief because it is more self-induced than caused by external agency.

A group of dramatists including Drayton, Dekker, Johnson and Heywood worked under Henslowe and continued to serve the public demand by producing the new kind of domestic drama to their tastes. Since the eighteenth century, dramatists have slowly but increasingly developed the awareness of the literary potential in general and tragic potential in particular in themes of domestic origin.

The rise of the novel coincides with the rise of the middle-classes. In 1688, the Glorious Revolution finally destroyed the feudal pretensions of the Stuarts and inaugurated the political and social dominance of middle-class commercial interests. In the earlier days, the Elizabethans wrote prose fiction, but nothing akin to a novel as per its recognized genre. All the familiar forms—romances, horror tales, stories of domestic life—were there in embryo, but undeveloped, with little characterization and incoherent or improbable plots. Through a series of slow and gradual changes, in response of changes of interest and taste of the newly emerging middle-class reading public, the modern novel came into being in the eighteenth century. At the beginning of the eighteenth century, drama was highly popular. But long before its end, it was the novelist who reigned supreme. The middle-classes were better off, better educated, and more leisured. They now formed the bulk of those who read for enjoyment. Reading was more popular than theatre-going. Thus, while domestic drama was born consequent to the emergence of the middle-classes, the novel was born due to the demands from the politically and socially evolved middle-classes, now ready for prose fiction.

The stream of sentimentalism rose in the first half of the eighteenth century, when Samuel Richardson (1689-1761) created the sentimental novel. With his novels *Pamela* (1740) and *Clarissa* (1748), he made sentimental fiction highly popular. His contribution to fiction was the analysis of emotion and motive and introspection in the widest sense. Following his tradition, a flood of sentimental fiction was let loose in England. It was enormously widened, deepened and accelerated by Laurence Sterne (1713-68). Sensibility, in the hands of Richardson, acquires tragic seriousness whereas Sterne is capable of adding humour to its pathos. He opened a new field of humour which is gentle and devoid of satire. His style, though looking grotesque with its digressions, parentheses, dashes and eccentricities of punctuation, is the perfect expression of his mind. He was an expert in distinguishing nuances of feeling and in subtle expression of character.

The advent of the Domestic novel can be traced to the publication of Goldsmith's *The Vicar of Wakefield* (1776). Oliver Goldsmith (1728-74) tamed and domesticated the pastoral romance. S. Diana Neill points out the significance of the novel: "*The Vicar of Wakefield* was important as the first masterpiece of domestic fiction; its real theme was the home and the hearth."[3] Ernest A. Baker is also of the view that *The Vicar of Wakefield* "is an idyll, the benign comedy of simple domesticity."[4]

In this novel, Goldsmith draws a picture of quiet, fire-side family-life such as no one before, or perhaps since, has drawn. The novel is devoid of melodramatic action. The humour is gentle and tolerant, without touches of either satire or obscenity. It cannot be put into the category of propaganda fiction; for the author recommends nothing more remarkable than family affection and Christian good will.

> we loved each other tenderly, and our fondness increased as we grew old. . . . We had an elegant house, situated in a fine country, and a good neighbourhood. The year was spent in a moral or rural amusement; in visiting our rich neighbours, and relieving such as were poor. We had no revolutions to fear, nor fatigues to undergo; all our adventures were by the fireside, and all our migrations from the blue bed to the brown.[5]

As there is little suspense or excitement in the plot, the reader's interest is held by the characters. The absence of ideology means that the story is not dated by contemporary notions. It is a simple chronicle of a good man's fortitude in the face of worldly pressures. Goldsmith gives a detailed description of a quiet home in the country-side. He commences with a description of the Primrose family emphasizing their love for one another. He concludes his story with the Vicar sitting by a cheerful fireside, surrounded by his family. Thus he creates an impression that happy and innocent domesticity is the main appeal of the novel.

The birth of the Domestic Novel was purely accidental. Goldsmith's contribution itself was inadvertent. Walter Allen explains: "*The Vicar of Wakefield* survives almost in spite of Goldsmith's own intentions. We read it as a domestic idyll, . . . But this was not quite how Goldsmith meant us to see his novel. . . . What he achieved was something very different from what he intended; instead of the near-tragedy of a man who brought himself and his family to ruin he produced something very much like a fairy tale, an idealized picture of rural life."[6]

The subject Goldsmith intends to deal with in this novel, apart from family affection, is the common subject of the times, the problem of arbitrary and irresponsible power. He wants to work on a table at the expense of sentimental optimism with implicit trust in goodness and honesty. His aim is to satirize the Vicar's unworldliness, foolish optimism and unbounded benevolence, the very qualities which are responsible for the sufferings of the family. The wisdom of Mr. Burchell has to rescue him and his family from ruin. He begins the novel with the idealized picture of the Vicars—happy, affectionate and contented. Then the scene changes to one of prolonged suffering. And then, as at the touch of a wand, they are rewarded and restored to peace and happiness. This sudden reversal of catastrophe is unconvincing and incredible. Baker comments: "Goldsmith started in one direction, lost his way before he had gone far, and presently found himself going, without being able to stop, in a direction entirely opposite. The idyll was to have been a comic idyll, a bitter-sweet pastoral, the bitterness concealed in the irony."[7] This may, be perhaps, due to the fact that Goldsmith was one of the novelists who cared least for realism. Robert C. Rathburn affirms: "Oliver Goldsmith in *The Vicar of Wakefield* (1766) tried to write a philosophic tale in the quixotic vein, but his sentimental Irish streak betrayed him into producing a pastoral idyll instead."[8]

Fanny Burney (1752-1840) who can be called "the originator of the simple novel of homelife,"[9] is a major figure in the advent of Domestic novel. In this respect, her importance as the forerunner of Jane Austen is undisputed. She has no moral or utilitarian preoccupation and in this she differs from most of her contemporaries. Some of the novelists of the time are in the direct line of their predecessors. She breaks with sentimentalism and shows to her contemporaries, simpler modes of telling a domestic story and also of other interests than by crude sentimentalism. With Fanny Burney, feminine point of view began to be felt in the field of fiction. "In *Evelina* Fanny Burney writes the first English novel of home life."[10] This novel is about the entrance of a young girl into society. Her second novel *Cecilia* (1781) is a story of love and family pride. Her recurring theme is a young girl's impressions of the society, her mistakes, and her discovery of love which, after some misunderstandings owing to her innocence, ends in marriage. She is the first writer to elevate the ordinary embarrassments in a girl's life to the level of the main theme of a novel. Her world is dominated by the quest for marriage. The society which she describes minutely, values fine clothes more than true love.

Fanny Burney is scathing when she comes to expose the pretensions of the regular who aspire to be elegant and genteel. Miss Branghton has a way of veiling her vulgarity when she loudly acclaims her own good taste with the remark: "For my part," said Miss Branghton, "I like it because it is not vulgar."[11] In all her novels, she emphasizes and illuminates the gap between generations: "the young are rash, and the aged are mercenary; their deliberations are never in concert, their views are scarce ever blended; one vanquishes, and the other submits."[12]

Fanny Burney has the skill of capturing the idiosyncrasies of manners and tone which help to bring a character alive. This aspect of her genius receives praise from Dr. Johnson when he says: "Oh, you little character-monger, you!" The greatest tribute comes from George Sampson when he says: "Macaulay just saluted her as the first English novelist of her sex; he forgot that she was the first English novelist of her kind, without respect of sex."[13]

Domestic novel which evolved in the later half of the eighteenth century could not gain instant popularity. While Fanny Burney's novels show the natural advantages of women writers for delicate domestic comedy, the sentimental novels of Henry Mackenzie and Gothic novels of Horace Walpole (1717-97), Clara Reeve (1729-1807), William Backford (1760-1844), Ann Radcliffe (1764-1823) and Matthew Lewis (1775-1818) reveal the growing taste of writers and readers uniformly for strong appeals to the emotions.

In conscious reaction against the domesticity of Richardson, Horace Walpole wrote his Horror or Gothic novel, *The Castle of Otranto* (1764). The Gothic novel is essentially the offspring of the novel of sensibility. Its sources are to be sought in the novels of sensibility by two French novelists writing in English, A.F. Frevost d'Exiles (1697-1763) and Baculard d'Arnaud (1716-1805). Their novels contain a good part of the material that was soon to be successfully utilized in Gothic novels.

Horace Walpole included in his novels the glamour of the past and the excitement of the supernatural. He allowed fantasy to have a free play at the cost of realistic characters and convincing dialogue. Yet, it influenced and inspired many talented writers of the time. This occasioned Michael Stapleton to comment thus: "Fanny was using the material of everyday and making it absorbing; in doing this she was giving the novel a direction which had been suggested by Richardson in parts of Sir Charles Grandison. She was to be followed by Jane Austen."[14]

Charlotte Smith (1749-1806), who comes before Jane Austen, also "wrote domestic fiction having a family resemblance to Richardson's modified by what she learned from Fanny Burney."[15] Her first novel *Emmeline, The Orphan of the Castle* (1788) belongs to the type of Fanny Burney's *Cecilia* with reminiscences of Richardson's *Clarissa*. The selfless and dutiful *Emmeline* rejects her wealthy suitor thinking her birth illegitimate. Later, finding that she is the legitimate daughter, she marries her steadier and obstinate lover at that time. Her next two novels, *Ethelinde* or *The Recluse of the Lake* (1789) and *Celestina* (1791) mark her skilful presentation of mountainous and rural beauties respectively. *Desmond* (1792) presents a virtuous wife who flees from her contemptible husband but comes back to nurse him while dying. She marries her noble lover only after completing her year of mourning. Her next novel, *The Old Manor House* (1793) is not purely domestic in nature. Baker observes that it represents "domestic fiction, branching off into intrigues and adventures."[16] Her handling of domestic problems indicates the popularity of domestic themes having been handled by Fanny Burney till recently. However, unlike Fanny Burney, Charlotte Smith shows an awareness of industrial revolution and its effects. After experimenting with the then popular Gothic themes for a while, she reverts to domestic theme in *The Banished Man* (1794). Afterwards, she switches over to full-blooded romance in *Montalbert* (1795). Her last novel, *The Young Philosopher, Nature his Law and God his Guide* (1798) is also not domestic in nature. It recounts the tale of an idealist, a disciple of Rousseau, who is driven to seek a better way of living in the American backwoods.

Maria Edgeworth (1767-1849) too finds her right medium in the domestic novel. She shows greater vivacity and a more genial breadth than Fanny Burney. Her fiction is didactic, and thus adds another dimension to domestic fiction. However, the moralist in her is quite often defeated by her liveliness and keen sense of character. Fanny Burney introduces an element of sensation by giving faint glimpses of vice and horror in the lower classes, though her main object is to ridicule the absurdities of those who ape their betters or of the crazes and affectations rampant in a more elevated sphere. Maria Edgeworth too does in no way overlook the poorer classes in her Irish stories, but she treats them as though she is one of their superiors, at best as a charitable observer, and never, even in her imagination, as one among them. Her first significant regional novel, *Castle Rackrent* (1800) and other Irish stories *Ormond* and *The Absentee* made her highly popular. Her earliest English novel, *Belinda* (1801) examines the question of how a woman ought to live. *Belinda* is like Elinor of Jane Austen's *Sense and Sensibility*—virtuous, sensible and reasonable—and likewise refuses to be ruled by prudential calculations of money. "Like Jane Austen, Miss Edgeworth believed strongly that both sexes could and should be rational."[17] Her notion that wife is not a slave forms the theme of *The Modern Griselda* (1805). *Helen* (1834), her next novel, exposes the fashionable society women who do not hesitate to ruin their friends' lives for selfish motives. Elizabeth Gaskell was so highly impressed by the central situation of this novel, that her own novel, *Wives and Daughters*, came to be based on the same theme.

It was Jane Austen (1775-1817) who perfected the domestic novel. Baker observes: "Miss Edgeworth and Miss Austen found their right medium in the domestic novel, that form of the novel of manners the general scheme of which had evolved and come into chief favour during the last half-century."[18] He refers to the domestic novel as a form of 'the novel of manners' because of the close attention paid in the delineation of characters in minute details. It is due to Fanny Burney's success in this respect that Dr. Johnson had called her "the character-monger." Jane Austen achieved great success with the form, despite the self-imposed limitation of the scope of her works. On the analogy of domestic tragedy, fiction which may be termed 'domestic comedy' forms an integral part of domestic novel in English: "basing her plots on courtship and marriage, she initiated one of the greatest and most characteristic traditions of the English novel, that of familiar domestic comedy."[19]

The term "cup-and-saucer school" was applied to the fiction of both Fanny Burney and Jane Austen.[20] This expression denotes the intimate connection between the themes of their choice and the gross realities of everyday life symbolized by cups and saucers.

Jane Austen's advent was during the heyday of sentimental novels in England. Readers were moved to tears over Richardson and shuddered over Mrs. Radcliffe, but were at home with the historical novels of Walter Scott. Jane Austen, however, broke away from that tradition and following the foot-steps of Goldsmith and Fanny Burney, gave the novel a new dimension by writing on matters of everyday life: "from Fanny Burney, she may well have learned how much could be achieved in the novel of home life, and how well worthwhile was the chronicling of such 'small beer.'"[21] She even refines upon Fanny Burney. She introduces into her novels characters and incidents from the everyday life of the middle- class. Though Fanny Burney also depicts home life, she deals only with aristocracy, whereas Jane Austen's province is restricted to middle-class. Her life amid middle-class country society provides her with the opportunity of knowing intimately the world of social pretension and of ambition, of balls and of visits and speculations about marrying and giving in marriage. In the daily routine of visits, shopping, sewing and gossip, she finds the raw material for her novels. The world which her books present is essentially the eighteenth century middle-class world in its habits, tastes and appearance. Unlike Maria Edgeworth, she does not seek to instruct her readers. Nor does she, like Elizabeth Gaskell, confine herself to social problems. She never strays beyond her family circle. She writes to her niece that "3 or 4 Families in a Country Village is the verything to work on . . ."[22] Writing to her nephew, J. Edward Austen, she gracefully acknowledges her narrow and limited range: "the little bit (two inches wide) of ivory on which I work with so fine a Brush, as produces little effect after much labour."[23] Also when invited by Prince Regent's Chaplain to write a historical romance, she replies that such a novel "might be much more to the purpose of profit or popularity than such pictures of domestic life in country villages as I deal in. . . . No, I must keep to my own style and go on in my own way."[24] This confinement to domestic novel is no small achievement. Her masterpieces of domestic fiction prove that feminine sensibility is in many ways best suited to reveal the intricacies of personal relationships.

Jane Austen began as a satirist of the current sentimental mode—that romantic view of life which trusts the dictates of the heart. *Northanger Abbey*, which treats this sentimental love superficially, is a direct assault on Gothic or horror novels. *Sense and Sensibility* analyzes with profundity the contrast between a woman who submits herself to the guidance of commonsense and one who follows impulse. The theme of *Pride and Prejudice* is announced in its original title—"First Impressions"—and such 'impressions' are not to be trusted but must be corrected by experience and after-thought. In the last three novels there is very little preoccupation with sentimentalism. *Mansfield Park* presents the antithesis between worldliness and idealism. *Emma*, her most thoughtful comedy, is a study in the self-deception of vanity. *Persuasion*, more definitely a love story than its predecessors, brings out the contrast between true love and prudential calculations.

"It is a truth universally acknowledged, that a single man in possession of a good fortune must be in want of a wife."[25] This opening sentence of *Pride and Prejudice* illustrates the fact that Jane Austen's novels, like those of Fanny Burney and others are pre-occupied with the business of marriage. The novels and much of her other writing focus attention on the experiences of young women as they move through love to marriage. It is so because she is fundamentally concerned with the world of women, and in this world, the question of marriage is of unique importance. A large proportion of the population was affected by the crisis in marriage and the matter excited increasing public concern. The dominance of women among the reading public prompted these authors to write on themes germane to their interests.

Jane Austen elevated the status of the domestic novel. She proved that the trivialities of domestic life, if carefully observed and critically and faithfully portrayed, would become literature of perennial value.

Before and around Jane Austen's time, two novelists of Scotland, Elizabeth Hamilton (1758-1816) and Mary Brunton (1778-1818), wrote domestic novels, though qualitatively they stand no comparison to those of Jane Austen.

Elizabeth Hamilton has the distinction of producing the first Scottish domestic novel, *The Cottagers of Glenburnie* (1808), which is also a didactic story. Her skill in faithful presentation of the speech and manners of rustic life deservedly gets a word of praise from E.A. Baker when he says: "this realism, of dialogue especially, became a tradition in the Scottish peasant novel."[26] Her works include *Memoirs of Modern Philosophers* (1800) and *Translation of the Letters of a Hindoo Rajah* (1796). Mary Brunton exaggerates virtues and vices in all her three novels, *Self-Control* (1811), *Discipline* (1814) and the unfinished *Emmeline*.

Jane Austen's influence, to some extent, is discernible in the novels of Catherine Grace Gore, published in eighteen thirties. She attempts to follow Jane Austen in her novel, *Mothers and Daughters*. Novels written between 1825 and 1850, which deal with the upper-class marriage market and fashionable life, are said to belong to the 'Silver-fork School.'[27] *Mothers and Daughters* is a silver-fork novel and reveals how it was difficult for young girls in that society to get married. It gives a depressing picture of women struggling hard for an establishment. Her other novel, *Mrs. Armytage or Female Domination* (1836) condemns female domination. Mrs. Gore, through this story of a bossy and dominating widow, implies that only loving and homely type of women deserve respect. Commenting on Jane Austen's influence on another novel, *Mrs. Armytage*, A.W. Ward and A.R. Waller observed: "shows a fitness and justice that make it comparable to the work of Jane Austen, though it is quite unlike that work in its gravity, its didactic tone and its use of incident."[28]

Susan Ferrier (1782-1854) follows Miss Edgeworth's pattern of comedy with greater variety in her three novels, *Marriage* (1818), *The Inheritance* (1824) and *Destiny* (1831). What Miss Edgeworth does for Irish life, Miss Ferrier does for Scottish. Ian Jack points out: "Susan Ferrier has been called the Scots Jane Austen and . . . her attitude to the novel had a good deal in common with that of her great contemporary."[29] Michael Stapleton also expresses the same view: "The author of three novels of Scottish life, she has something in common with Jane Austen though, unlike her great contemporary, she is quite explicit in her comment."[30] Her theme is always the importance of a young woman's choosing the right husband and the harm caused by unwise marriages.

Her strong dislike of the fashionable world is evident from her three novels. She contrasts the decent and moral Scots with worldly Londoners. In both *Marriage* and *Destiny*, she elucidates the fortunes of two girls brought up in separate homes. In each case, one girl is beautiful but selfish and makes a fashionable marriage which breaks down eventually. The other girl, though not beautiful, is good and is rewarded with a successful marriage. The capability of women to correct themselves if they go wrong is implied in *The Inheritance*. Gertrude falls in love rashly, spends money lavishly and commits mistakes which, however, she bitterly regrets later. Her impeccable lover, Lyndsay, waits patiently for her reformation and marries her. Susan Ferrier believes in the perfect equality of men and women. Like Charlotte Bronte and Anne Bronte, she too stresses that a woman need not worship the man she loves.

Mary Russell Mitford (1787-1855), like Ferrier, belongs to the period of revival of Romanticism. Like her, Mary Mitford "belongs by temperament and method to the later eighteenth century, to the school of manners of which Fanny Burney was a pioneer, and Jane Austen the mistress craftswoman."[31] Miss Mitford produced no novels, but wrote a series of charming sketches of rural life depicting the village, Three Mile Cross, near Reading, in *Our Village: Sketches of Rural Life, Character and Scenery* (1819-32).

Emily Eden (1797-1869) wrote a domestic tale in her *The Semi-attached Couple*, disclosing the jealousy and pangs and friction between a couple. Clarence L. Barnhart writes: "she wrote two gently satirical novels, *The Semi-detached House* (1859) and *The Semi-attached Couple* (1860), which have been paid the high compliment of being compared to Jane Austen."[32]

Catherine Crowe (1800-1876) was a pioneer of the lowliest sort of domestic fiction, though it was the sensationalism in *The Adventures of a Maid Servant* (1841) that enthralled her readers.

The change of lifestyle that came about towards the close of the eighteenth century generally helped the women novelists like Fanny Burney, Maria Edgeworth, Susan Ferrier and Jane Austen in their literary output. Greater refinement and a quieter taste of life replaced the coarse brutality of the earlier period and this proved to be of advantage to the women novelists.

John Galt (1779-1839) "is one of the pioneers of the domestic novel that played so important a part in Victorian fiction."[33] *The Ayrshire Legates* (1821) and *The Entail* (1823) are his novels dealing with home life, though of inferior quality. His novels resemble those of Susan Ferrier, but, unlike her, he deals with a class of people not so affluent.

During the days of Jane Austen, a French critic, de Bonald, analyzed the reasons for the accepted English eminence in the realm of novel, in his *Du Style et da la Litérature* (1806). Ian Watt remarks: "He took it for granted that the novel was essentially concerned with private and domestic life; what could be more natural, therefore, than that a distinctively commercial bourgeois and urban society which laid so much stress on family life, . . . should have triumphed in a familiar and domestic genre."[34] However, the domestic tradition, which began with Fanny Burney, ended with Jane Austen. After the death of Jane Austen in 1817 and before the arrival on the scene of Charlotte Bronte in the eighteen forties, domestic fiction was produced but it was of little significance. In the second and third decades of the nineteenth century, domestic novel suffered a setback. The terror novel, however, continued to flourish, albeit in a modified form, and women were prominent among those who wrote this kind of fiction. The changing tastes of the novel-reading public were influenced by the changing social conditions in England during the first few decades of the Victorian era (1830-80). The Reform Act of 1832 helped the middle classes to prosper enormously in commerce and industry. Many were lured by fashionable society and were temperamentally prepared to read and enjoy stories depicting sophisticated life. The fate of the domestic novel, *Deerbrook*, written by Harriet Martineau, a Jane Austen admirer, illustrates how the middle-class domestic novel had at that time fallen on evil days. The publisher declined to accept it on the ground that it dealt with ordinary middle-class life, which was out of tune with the prevailing social milieu. In her *Autobiography*, Harriet laments, "youths and maidens in those days looked for lords and ladies in every page of a new novel."[35] In the eighteen thirties, sea-stories and detective fiction gained popularity. Historical novel declined and romanticism in the English novel almost came to an end. But by eighteen-forties, the fashions again changed.

'The novel-with-a-purpose' was slowly emerging. The novel's social range was widened. It reflected urgent preoccupations of the time. The most burning topics of the day in the eighteen-forties were the religious controversies and these were naturally reflected in most of the novels of the time. The fervent Evangelical writer, 'Charlotte Elizabeth's (Mrs. Tonna) *Helen* Fleetwood (1841). Paget's *Luke Sharp* (1845) and Gresley's *Colton Green: A Tale of the Black Country* (1846) all dealt with factory life, however, with an emphasis on the miners' need for religious teaching and church-building. These were called 'Church Novels' and in the forties, there was a mass of novels and tales bearing on controversial religious questions. The better-known religious stories of the time, while dealing with the everyday domestic life and social behaviour, discreetly propagated religious doctrines and beliefs. They never failed to underline the importance of family life, parents and children, brothers and sisters, in a secure and specified setting. Thus they paved the way for the rebirth of Domestic novel. "In the forties it [domestic fiction] was re-establishing itself in the novel, after a long exile, and to this, the religious novels notably contributed."[36]

Edward George Bulwer, first Lord Lytton (1803-73), was a mirror of his time. He was highly sensitive to the varying nuances of popular taste. Each succeeding literary fashion found its imprint in his work. While romance was the order of the day, he did excellently about it. Depending on the variations of literary tastes of the reading public, he produced novels in different styles, terror, sentimental and even historical. By about the middle of the century, the novels of domestic life were becoming fashionable. Arthur Compton-Rickett says, "during the mid-years of the century the novels of domestic life proved a serious rival to the romance in popularity."[37] Skilled literary opportunists like Bulwer Lytton promptly switched over to domestic fiction, completely abandoning all other types. Kathleen Tillotson says, "when . . . a prolific and popular minor novelist changes his groove, as Lytton did with *The Caxtons* in 1849, he testifies to the establishment of a major change in subject matter from extravagant romance to domesticity, from the extremes of high and low life to the middle class."[38]

After *The Caxtons*, he wrote *My Novel* in 1853 showing that public taste in domestic fiction remained unchanged even in the fifties. In the domestic novels of the time, the emphasis, however, was not on courtship and marriage as in the novels of Jane Austen's time, but on the relationship between parents and children. But after the eighteen fifties, public taste once again abandoned the quiet and uninspiring domestic fiction and seemed to switch its preference to the excitement of reading about the changing scenario in the areas, moral, religious, social, economic and political. Accordingly, conscious of a drift in the current taste after the sixties, Lytton discarded domestic fiction and continued to write fantastic romances till his death. His Utopian fantasy, *The Coming Race*, was published in 1871.

Towards the middle of the nineteenth century, novelists began to concern themselves intermittently with social problems. Elizabeth Gaskell's (1810-66) work appeared to be 'philanthropic' social propaganda. Her contribution to this field has been remarkable, specially because of her attempt to widen the scope of domestic fiction so as to include the major social problems of the day and to depict their repercussions on the home front. Her important theme was class-war, the clash between capital and labour. She embodied the social, industrial and economic conflicts of the day in her novels *Mary Barton* (1848), *North and South* (1855). She appeared to be trying to fulfil the twin objects of portraying the intricate emotional problems in the private lives of individuals and also presenting them against the background of the then prevailing complex social conditions. That is why David Skilton aptly says that *North and South* is successful "in combining the private and the social in one story by exploiting both the scope of the social novel and the method of minute analysis bequeathed by Jane Austen."[39] Thereafter, she abandoned the theme of social reform and wrote in *Cranford* (1853) about the life in a village in the midland: "This was a novel without a purpose, a delicate picture of the society of a small provincial town, which recalls Jane Austen and Miss Mitford, and at a greater distance Addison and Goldsmith."[40] The apparent absence of a specific purpose turned out to be a source of advantage to the literary world. It led to the composition of her most famous novel, one of the masterpieces among domestic novels in English. Mrs. Gaskell is half-humorous and half-fanciful in describing the elegant economy of the Cranfordians: "If we walked to or from a party, it was because the night was so fine, or the air so refreshing, not because sedanchairs were expensive."[41]

The only novel where she reminds us of Jane Austen is *Wives and Daughters*. The story depicts essentially the contrast between different kinds of parental relationships and different kinds of children. Didacticism or ulterior message is totally absent. Writing about this novel, W.A. Craik says that it is regarded "as nineteenth-century heir to the riches of Jane Austen. . . . *Wives and Daughters* resembles Jane Austen's novels in its materials, part of its form and some of its techniques."[42]

Arthur Pollard also offers the same comment: "If a rough comparison is permissible, *Wives and Daughters* shows Mrs. Gaskell operating somewhat in the manner of Jane Austen, whereas *Sylvia's Lovers* approximates rather to that of the Brontes."[43]

Charlotte Bronte (1816-55) elevated the tone of domestic novel by depicting strong passions, so far unknown in that realm. She was not interested in romances or historical novels which were popular at the time of her writing career. The tone of moderation and the subdued language had to give way to a turbulent world of tempestuous passions. There was a Byronic strain in her, though refined by her religious upbringing and moral discipline. S. Diana Neill says, "The contribution made by the Bronte sisters to English literature in the eighteen forties has a unique flavour—a strange pungent mingling of wild romance and domestic realism."[44] Saintsbury also expressed the same opinion when he wrote "she introduced a new cross and blend which was at once domestic and romantic." Usually her plots are exciting or even melodramatic. However, in *Shirley* (1849), the plot and setting are more homely, occasionally resembling Jane Austen's. Charlotte Bronte's theme is love. She deals with passion, but not the institution of family as such where the passion fulfils itself. In a letter to W.S. Williams, she accuses Jane Austen for her utter disregard of the passions: "the passions are perfectly unknown to her; she rejects even a speaking acquaintance with that stormy sisterhood."[46] The poetic quality of her work and her ability to suggest a lot with the help of minimum simplest words possible distinguish her from other writers. "It was a curious laugh—distinct, formal, mirthless. I stopped. The sound ceased, only for an instant. It began again, louder . . . though very distinct, it was very low."[47]

Emily Bronte (1818-48) begins with home, but soon transcends its limits and hovers on things unconnected. Her only novel, *Wuthering Heights* is a whirlwind arrested in words.

One usual complaint against domestic novels in general and the novels of Charlotte Bronte in particular is that these novels made love and marriage the main business of life. But that complaint is not valid in the case of Mrs. Gaskell. Bronte sisters apply their romanticism to everyday life whereas Mrs. Gaskell adopts the more realistic methods of Jane Austen, but with a difference. She lays greater stress than Jane Austen did on the emotional aspect of life. More than being a domestic novelist, Mrs. Gaskell may justifiably be regarded as the pioneer of the novel of character of which George Eliot is the first brilliant exponent.

George Eliot (1819-80) is deeply religious and she attaches much importance to moral values. Love and faith stabilize the home in her novels. Religion, politics, and social life dominate in her novels and home and family life occupy a back seat. All the same, she accords to 'home' its due importance as an effective medium for the exposition of social, moral and religious problems. She enlarges the scope of domestic novel so as to bring within its ambit social consideration affecting the private lives of individuals.

Charlotte M. Yonge (1823-1901), who comes after George Eliot, portrays "idealized family life in numerous novels."[48] She treats the complex theme of home admirably well. Besides domestic fiction, she has written historical novels, but all her novels, historical or domestic, are directly or indirectly didactic. "The family . . . had reached its apotheosis in the novel-writing of the Victorian era. The immense family chronicles of Charlotte Yonge . . . present this pattern of living at its most complete development."[49]

All the novels of Jane Austen veered round domesticity, pure and simple. But her successor in domestic fiction, not excluding Charlotte M. Yonge, who too depicted middle-class home-life added extra dimensions to their works by introducing moral, religious or romantic touches. In a way, they extended the scope of domestic novel by injecting broader social issues of the day. Charlotte M. Yonge, who was deeply religious, laid special emphasis on moral values. Baker observes: "In brief, she took domstic fiction as it had been shaped by Miss Edgeworth, Charlotte and Anne Bronte, and Mrs. Gaskell, and wrote it with a vigilant eye for moral values, and for the influence of religious convictions."[50]

All her novels are more or less about the effect of religion on middle-class families. The Oxford Movement which began in 1833 reached its height during the 1840s and was a disturbing force among English Churchmen. Miss Charlotte Yonge was influenced by this movement and was agitated by all sorts of mental and moral questioning.

In the eighteen fifties, after two historical stories for children, Yonge brought forth, by combining a series of her sketches, her first Domestic novel, *The Daisy Chain* or *Aspirations* (1856). It is an endeavour to identify the aspirations of youth in a family set up. It is a study of the young minds developing in a household and among circles where goodness has to be devoutly cultivated and lived, where girls must be lady-like besides being dutiful and unselfish and where life must be lived according to the Prayer Book.

The novel centres on the self-sacrifice of a dutiful, intelligent and high-principled girl, Ethel May. Miss Yonge believes in parental authority. Her novel, *The Heir of Redclyffe* (1853) illustrates her conviction that a child has to obey her parents even at the cost of sacrificing her happiness. In this aspect she differs from Susan Ferrier who thinks that bullying parents are to be blamed for friction. Gertrude in Susan Ferrier's *The Inheritance*, respects her mother but does not submit like a slave. She wrote *The Trial, More Links in the Daisy Chain* (1868) as a supplement to *The Daisy Chain*. After writing a few more novels which were not strictly domestic in nature, she came back to the theme in *The Pillars of the House* which she produced in 1875.

One such domestic novelist is Mrs. Craik, also known by her maiden name Dinah Maria Mulock (1826-87). She had a pretty long creative career in the second half of that century. She wrote several novels including *Ogilvies* (1849), *Olive* (1850), *A Life for a Life* (1859), *Mistress and Maid* (1862), *The Woman's Kingdom* (1868), all of which are now out of print. Her well-known novel, *John Halifax, Gentleman* (1856), however, is still in print. As a moralist, she can be compared with George Eliot. Her novels are prized more for the sentiments and wholesome ideals in them than for the picturization of domesticity.

Novels with moral questionings, public controversies and organized movements, politics, economics and science were being published after 1860s. However, as Baker points out: "Mrs. Oliphant, Miss Thackeray, as well as Miss Yonge, with a crowd of the more ephemeral, were to maintain an abundant supply of domestic fiction, showing the reactions of thoughts and feelings on conduct and character within that homely but vital sphere."[51]

In the writings of Wilkie Collins (1824-89), domesticity and romantic adventure are pleasantly blended. He was the first English novelist to deal with the detection of crime. He became popular with his hits, *The Dead Secret* (1857), *The Woman in White* (1860) and *The Moonstone* (1868). He gives minimum importance to characterization subordinating it to the mechanics of plot, mystery, suspense and surprising revelations.

Writing about the fictional trends of the late nineteenth century, Baker writes: "Kipling and Conrad . . . Henry James, Hardy, and Stevenson, were all competing at the circulating libraries when, for a season or two during the eighteen-nineties, they were dislodged from favour by a group of Scottish writers. . . . For the chronicling of the pathos and humour of domestic life in the Scottish lowlands was an established branch of fiction."[52] The progenitor of this brand of Scottish writers, George Macdonald (1824-1905) followed the tradition of Galt and Susan Ferrier. However, he kept apart the two themes, domesticity and romantic adventure. Though a vein of mysticism is found, his *David Elginbrad* (1863) and *Alec Forbes of Howglen* (1865) are essentially domestic in nature. Criticism of the Church is found in *Robert Falconer* (1868). *Malcolm* (1875), *The Marquis of Lossie* (1877) and *Thomas Wingfold, Curate* (1876), are highly romantic. *Sir Gibbie* (1879) and *Heather and Snow* (1893) are his most popular novels.

Margaret Oliphant (1828-97) also wrote domestic fiction but interspersed it with biographies and travel tales. She has a voluminous production of nearly ninety novels to her credit. Though all are not of the highest quality, at least some of them, as Merryn Williams says: "are only a little below the level of Jane Austen and George Eliot. . . . She had fresh and original things to say about self-sacrifice, the claims of a woman's family, work outside the home and the problems of marriage and parenthood. Her outlook is so much more sophisticated than that of her contemporaris that she often seems to belong to another age."[53] Her stories, as is common with domestic fiction, are relevant to all times. Commenting on this aspect, Baker says, "In truth, the novels of domestic life by her and her like belong to no particular era, even if incidents and social and religious embarrassments here and there such as could not have occurred at any other period give some of them a date."[54] She has sympathy for women and contempt for men's superiority. Her *Agnes* shows that women's suffering goes unrecognized in the society. To Agnes, the death of her child is a more painful blow than her husband's death implying the author's belief that husband and wife relationship is not as sacrosanct as it is generally made out to be. In *The Doctor's Family*, women are shown to be highly responsible, even shouldering other people's burdens. Lucilla in *Miss Marjoribanks* becomes an excellent administrator exemplifying Mrs. Oliphant's belief that given a chance, women can strive like men in the administrative field. *The Curate in Charges* shows that career is important for a girl. *The Ladies Lindores* studies the fate of a woman who submits to 'duty.' *Joyce* and *Kirsteen*, both recognize the achievements of the single women Joyce and Kirsteen who shun marriage but shine in their careers. They prove that the real achievement of a woman is not dependent on romance or marriage.

In spite of the contributions of novelists, both major and minor, Domestic novel went into total eclipse. Finding that the novel was an ideal means for propagating their ideas, some theorists and satirists, in the seventies and eighties of the last century, freely exploited it for their onslaughts on contemporary society.

Chief among the satirists was Samuel Butler (1835-1902) who wrote domestic fiction from a different perspective. All the novelists who wrote about family life had so far glorified it, highlighting its values and virtues. Butler was the one who subjected the family, one of the most cherished institutions of the Victorians, to a merciless scrutiny and exposed unsentimentally the hypocrisy, malice, deception, cruelty and gloom that pervaded the English upper middle-class households at that time. He himself had a horrible experience of family life. It filled him with sentiments of revulsion and a strong desire to escape. Since the stress in his novels is on the psychological aspect of family life, they came to be called psychological novels. His *The Way of All Flesh,* published posthumously, "is a bitter indictment of the Butler family in particular and of the hypocrisy and subtle sadism of the Victorian middle-class family in general."[55] It is a faithful portrayal of both the brighter and the darker sides of family life, steering clear of undue glorification or unjustified condemnation. In a way, Butler set the tone for the new trend in all the domestic novels to follow. Ivy Compton-Burnett, the twentieth century novelist, who was ruthless in exposing the Victorian hypocrisy and tyranny, was influenced by him.

The writers of the late nineteenth century were interested in the psychological, philosophical and more especially scientific ideas. Novelists like George Meredith accepted the theories of evolution and saw in them the glorious promise of a new spiritual dawn. Realism was given a go-by in spite of the immense popularity of realists like Dickens, Thackeray, George Eliot, Trollope and Reade and the last decade of the nineteenth century heralded a tidal wave of romanticism. Readers turned to R.L. Stevenson whose romances were more thrillingly adventurous than those of Scott. But the craze for romanticism was short-lived. It did not last longer than about fifteen years. About the same period, the English novel was lightly affected by the 'aesthetic movement' and the result was the novels of Walter Pater and Oscar Wilde.

By and large, the early twentieth century fiction was influenced by Darwin, Marx and Freud. The so-called higher values and aristocracy were declared to be false and even dangerous. In the first few decades, everything which seemed to provide a basis for established order was attacked—public schools, the church, the world of politics, sex relationships, and puritan restraints. Conrad, George Moore, Frederick William Rolfe, Rudyard Kipling, Somerset Maugham and H.G. Wells are the writers who occupied the post-Stevenson literary scene and made a prolific contribution of all fiction in general, without special emphasis on the domestic aspects. There was, at that time, a marked revival of interest in religion. Two distinct trends were noticeable in the fiction produced at that time. Two main tendencies influenced the subject matter and method of presentation in modern fiction. One was the revolt against reason, in the nineteen twenties, associated with D.H. Lawrence, and the other, the technique of Stream-of-Consciousness so deftly handled by Virginia Woolf, Dorothy Richardson and James Joyce.

It is already observed that a marked disinclination is obvious in the novelists in the post-Jane Austen period to choose to write on domestic life. An increasing tendency on their part to deal with bigger issues like religion, politics and science, besides romance or morals, is discernible. Women writers dominated the Victorian scene. However, they did not confine themselves to depicting only the home life. At the end of the nineteenth century, the handicaps of women like their limited range of experience and exclusion from higher education, began to diminish after the vast upheaval in social and intellectual conditions. Women entered universities and mingled with men in public affairs. Their increased social status gave the necessary impetus to some of the women novelists of the day not to confine themselves to fiction about home life.

It is against this background that the contribution of Ivy Compton-Burnett to Domestic novel in English is to be examined and evaluated.

NOTES

1. Adams Henry Hitch, *English Domestic or Homiletic Tragedy,* p. 1.
2. Karl Beckson and Arthur Ganz, *A Reader's Guide to Literary Terms* (London: Thames and Hudson, 1972), p. 53.
3. S. Diana Neill, *A Short History of the English Novel* (London: Jarrolds, 1954), p. 81.
4. Ernest A. Baker, *The History of the English Novel* (New York: Barnes and Noble, 1969), Vol. 5, p. 79.
5. Oliver Goldsmith. *The Vicar of Wakefield* (London: J.M. Dent, 1983), pp. 1-2.
6. Walter Allen, *The English Novel* (Gt. Britain: Penguin, 1970), p. 82.
7. Baker, p. 81.
8. Robert C. Rathburn and Martin Steinmann, Jr., ed., *From Jane Austen to Joseph Conrad* (Minneapolis: University of Minnesota Press, 1958), p. 21.
9. Neill, p. 85.
10. George Sampson. *The Concise Cambridge History of English Literature* (London: O.U.P., 1972), p. 426.
11. Fanny Burney, *Evelina* (London: O.U.P., 1982), Vol. 2, p. 194.
12. Burney, *Cecilia* (London: Annie Raine Ellis, 1882), Vol. 2, p. 42.
13. Sampson, p. 426.
14. Michael Stapleton. *The Cambridge Guide to English Literature* (Cambridge: C.U.P., 1983), p. 116-17.
15. Baker, p. 187.
16. *Ibid.*, p. 189.

17. Merryn Williams, *Women in the English Novel, 1800-1900* (London: The Macmillan Press, 1984), p. 64.
18. Baker, p. 13.
19. *Encyclopaedia Britannica* (Chicago: William Benton, 1968), Vol. 16, p. 678.
20. Arthur Compton-Ricket, *A History of English Literature* (New Delhi: Universal Book Stall, 1983), p. 260.
21. A.W. Ward and A.R. Waller, ed., *The Cambridge History of English Literature* (Cambridge: C.U.P., 1953), Vol. 12, p. 231.
22. R.W. Chapman, ed., *Jane Austen's Letters to her Sister Cassandra and Others* (London: O.U.P., 1952), p. 401.
23. Chapman, p. 469.
24. *Ibid*., pp. 452-53.
25. Jane Austen, *Pride and Prejudice* (London: J.M. Dent, 1978), p. 1.
26. Baker, p. 227.
27. Williams, pp. 69-70.
28. Ward and Waller, p. 247.
29. Ian Jack, "English Literature, 1815-1832," *Oxford History of English Literature*, ed. Kenneth Allott and Norman Davis (London: O.U.P., 1963), pp. 235-36.
30. Stapleton, p. 304.
31. Compton-Rickett, p. 261.
32. Clarence L. Barnhart, ed., *The New Century Handbook of English Literature,* p. 374.
33. Ibid., p. 552.
34. Ian Watt, *The Rise of the Novel* (London: Chatto and Windus, 1957), p. 300.
35. Harriet Martineau, '*Autobiography,*' qtd. in *Novels of the Eighteen-Forties*, Kathleen Tillotson (London: O.U.P., 1956), p. 84.
36. Tillotson, p. 135.
37. Compton-Rickett, p. 548.
38. Tillotson, p. 5.
39. David Skilton, *The English Novel* (Gt. Britain: David and Charles, 1977), p. 131.
40. Emile Legouis, *A Short History of English Literature* (Oxford: The Clarendon Press, 1953), p. 330.
41. Elizabeth Gaskell, *Cranford* (London: J.M. Dent, 1938), pp. 12-13.
42. W.A. Craik, *Elizabeth Gaskell and the English Provincial Novel* (London: Methuen, 1975), pp. 200-2.
43. Arthur Pollard, *Introduction to Sylvia's Lovers* (London: J.M. Dent, 1964), p. v.
44. Neill, p. 164.

45. George Saintsbury, *A Short History of English Literature* (London: Macmillan, 1953), p. 749.
46. T.J. Wise and J.A. Symington, ed., *The Brontes: Their Freindships, Lives and Correspondence* (Oxford, 1932), Vol. 3, p. 99.
47. Charlotte Bronte, *Jane Eyre* (Gt. Britain: Penguin, 1983), p. 138.
48. Allen, p. 199.
49. G.D.H. Cole, *Samuel Butler* (London: Longmans, 1952), p. 18.
50. Baker, Vol. 3, p. 103.
51. *Ibid.*, p. 111.
52. *Ibid.*, p. 157.
53. Merryn Williams, p. 159.
54. Baker, Vol. 10, p. 200.
55. Georgia Dunbar, "A Critical and Biographical Profile of Samuel Butler, *The Way of All Flesh*," p. 11

Ivy Compton-Burnett: Perspectives

The connotations of the term 'domestic' vary in the novels focussing attention on home life, depending partly on the point of emphasis, and partly on the degree to which extraneous factors influencing personal relationships are given importance by the novelist. It has never been absolute in its application, and has had, from time to time, to expand its rigid confines to accommodate matters outside the four walls whenever their repercussions are bound to be felt within. The twentieth century, and to a large extent even the closing decades of the earlier one, have witnessed 'home' stretching itself to hold more than it was used to in literary works. It is in this context that a study of the novels of Ivy Compton-Burnett gains added significance while examining her contribution to Domestic novel in England.

Robert Liddell considers her works as "pure," having kept political, religious and such other factors strictly outside their purview: "Miss Compton-Burnett has freed herself from all irrelevancies in order to write the pure novel."[1] He finds it a point in their favour, as the concentration does not get diffused from the purely 'domestic' aspects. This statement, correct at the first appraisal, is open to modifications as one finds that Ivy Compton-Burnett did not write conventional novels dealing with 'home-truths' in a simple, direct manner. Keeping the deceptively normal home-front as the frame-work, the novelist probed deeper, and succeeded in exploring the workings of the different minds involved, and came up with discoveries shocking in their naked reality. Frederick R. Karl sums it up: "Miss Compton-Burnett has of course taken the Victorian family novel and turned it inside out, revealing the dirt behind the romantic exterior. . . . She recognized that below normal social behavior lies a swamp of discontent, mixed motives, and deception."[2] Her attempt to turn the domestic novel "inside out" was with a specific purpose. Probing far beneath the veneer of respectability and sophistication, she found evil lurking there in several manifestations, silently eating at the very roots of happiness. Total lack of concern for others, a clearly unethical attitude, was the 'home-truth' she discovered.

She was more concerned with the structure and fabric of the family than with any individual member of the group. Anthony Powell describes the introspective aspect in her novels: "large gloomy moderately rich families in largish, though not immense, houses in the country, going as a matter of course to Oxford or Cambridge, interested in acquiring property or money, yet lacking almost all contact with an outer world, living in a state of almost hysterically inward-looking intensity."[3]

The 'inward-looking intensity' is what distinguishes Ivy Compton-Burnett's novels from the earlier works of Domestic fiction in England. An apparently calm, placid surface of a 'refined,' sophisticated British family of the Victorian age shows facts which are too stunning to be believed. David Daiches refers to her novels "in which the elegant surface of her plots as a variation of the modern theme of the inevitable disparity between social gesture and private reality," and adds that "the titles of her novels suggest the restricted domestic atmosphere within which the counter-pointing of horror and gentility is developed."[4] Walter Allen discovers an extra dimension to Compton-Burnett's choice of themes. He finds them not realistic in the ordinary sense but reflecting an altogether different form of reality. He explains: "She writes of what is possible rather than of what normally is; her characters commit the crimes that people more often dream of than commit. One could almost say that in her novels unconscious desires become conscious and are acted upon."[5] This dimension helps in the development of a new perspective from which her novels are to be examined and evaluated.

Almost all possible kinds of evils find places in her works, but all are worked out in the most subtle and covert manner possible. There are recurring cases of marital infidelity leading to a liberal distribution of illegitimate children; manipulation of wills for personal benefits and other forms of fraud abound in her world. Even murder, very skilfully manipulated, is not rare. It is from this perspective that an investigative survey of her novels is to be undertaken. The angle of vision from which Ivy Compton-Burnett scrutinizes the apparently complacent, unruffled Domestic front is strictly her own, having helped her enrich English domestic novel with a unique approach.

Most of her titles, like *Brothers and Sisters, Men and Wives, More Women than Men, A House and Its Head, Daughters and Sons, A Family and a Fortune, Parents and Children, Elders and Betters, Mother and Son* and *A Father and His Fate* illustrate the restricted domestic atmosphere she confines herself to. Her titles are so unique that any other bearing resemblance to these by any other author is popularly commented upon as being 'Ivyish.'

The scene of action in all her novels is the countryside in England of the late Victorian period, reflecting the life style in the declining upper middle class families during the last fifteen years or so of the nineteenth century. The solitary exception is *Pastors and Masters* which encompasses the closing stages of the first World War, around 1918 to be precise.

This setting has contributed to the significance of her novels from another point of view. Separated from her own age by about three or four decades, the setting has the ideal distance in time. Kathleen Tillotson refers to her as "the single survivor of a great tradition" which began with *Waverley*.[6] The 'distance' is neither too short nor too long, not strictly 'contemporary,' nor too far back into the past to remember relevant details. The novelist herself has said: "I do not feel that I have any real or organic knowledge of life later than about 1910. I should not write of later times with enough grasp or confidence. I think this is why many writers tend to write of the past, when an age is ended, you see it as it is."[7]

The world of her novels is recognizably similar to Ivy Compton-Burnett's own family background. Hers is a large and sequestered Victorian household which has very little contact with outsiders. The household is run in a rigid pattern. All this is faithfully reflected in her novels. By choosing that particular period, she aimed at depicting a world which was unshaken by modern warfare, a community settled in one place with ample scope and a stable background for the display of tyrannical passions which she wanted to portray. She remained a child during that period and so she could recreate it from her memory, however faint.

Usually the family spreads to three generations, one or two grand parents, parents and children. Occasionally, an aunt or an uncle of the children substitutes a grandparent. Besides the family members, nurses, governesses, tutors and servants also live in the ancestral houses. All remain preoccupied with their own domestic problems and have no time or inclination to look beyond the family. For Ivy Compton-Burnett what matters is the family as a whole and not the individual member as such.

The significant contrast of the life in a house as against the life at home is brought out more vividly in *Parents and Children*. Eleanor Sullivan is so unhappy in her house ruled by her mother-in-law that she cannot consider it her real home. She unsuccessfully persuades her husband, Fulbert, to set up a home of their own. Believing the false news about her husband's death, she agrees to marry the villainous Ridley, almost entirely because she is basically home-bound. Bernard Donne *(Elders and Betters)* desperately says: "I do not feel that this house will ever be a home to me." (*EB*, 17)

In *The Mighty and Their Fall*, Ninian faces opposition mainly from his daughter, Lavinia, to his marriage with Teresa. But he tells her firmly that Teresa will be welcomed into the family. "All will be done to make this house a home to her, and her own home." (*MF*, 151) Fabian and Guy (*The Present and the Past*), the children of Cassius by his first wife, discuss the arrival of their mother. The thirteen-year-old Fabian, whose mother left when he was four, is not happy with his stepmother in the household. He tells his brother:

> "I wish we could leave this house that has never been a home to us."
>
> "What is a real home like?"
>
> "It is something you do not know, and I can only just remember. My life was over when I was four." (*PP*, 48)

Though the servants in general play very little role in the development of main theme, there are instances of a few governesses proving their loyalty at crucial times. Miss Patmore in *Brothers and Sisters* is an important character in the novel, guarding a vital family secret. Violet Powell observes: "Miss Patmore is the fore-runner of a succession of companions, uneasily situated between the gentle-folk and their domestics, sometimes transformed from governesses and sometimes changing into them, but in most cases their only reward for suffering the exactions of their employers being the delight of a furtively satisfied curiosity."[8]

In *Elders and Betters,* the novelist gives some importance to the servants. "The scenes involving servants in *Elders and Betters* are clearly experimental, for they play little part in the action of the book, but in *Manservant and Maidservant*, Bullivant, the butler, has almost as important a part as his master, Horace Lamb."[9] Servants play prominent role in the affairs of home and for the first time, Ivy Compton-Burnett studies them in an elaborate way.

In Ivy Compton-Burnett's homes, the primary education of the children in the family usually takes place in the school room of the house itself. Even grown-ups are pinned to a school room. The nineteen-year-old Audrey's (*A Father and His Fate*) education is unduly extended and she receives education in the school room under the supervision of Miss Gibbon. Boys alone are sent to universities for higher education. Usually those who can afford it send their sons to Eton, by way of preparation for their entry into a university, Oxford or Cambridge. Mark and Clement (*A Family and a Fortune*), study at Eton.

Hamish, the unacknowledged son of Simon (*A Heritage and Its History*) has passed from Eton to Oxford. Jermyn (*Men and Wives*) goes to Cambridge. Daniel and Graham (*Parents and Children*) are Cambridge under-graduates. Walter (*A Heritage and Its History*) goes to Oxford. Those who cannot afford it, like Graham and Ralph (*A Heritage and Its History*), Chilton and Victor (*Daughters and Sons*), are coached privately and economically at home for their university entrance examination.

However, older people have no high opinion of education and consider the expenditure incurred in this regard as a sheer waste. Sir Jesse Sullivan (*Parents and Children*) is one such grandparent who thinks that he has not lost anything by the lack of good education. The sight of his grandsons reminds him to the money he has wasted on their education.

Usually girls are educated at home. History, Literature, Arithmetic, a little French and music are considered advisable for them. If they study Greek and Latin along with their brothers, at a certain age, may be at fifteen or so, they are forced to give up learning them. This allowing of daughters to share lessons with their brothers occurs only in households with liberal parents. Usually, at a certain age, tutors replace governesses for boys whereas girls continue to study under the governesses. In almost all the families, girls have no need to earn their living. So a girl preparing for an entrance examination to a college is something rare and strange. However, sending girls to boarding schools for secondary education is not uncommon. In *Pastors and Masters*, Mr. Bentley's children study in Mr. Merry's school. In *More Women than Men*, a girls' boarding school is the scene of action and several girls are shown studying there. In *Two Worlds and Their Ways*, the two Shelley children are sent to schools. In *The Last and the First* also, Amy is shown to be studying at school.

In so far as a school does not by itself constitute a thematic variation for the novelist, a school or a school room in Ivy Compton-Burnett's novels is nothing more than an extension of the house or a substitute for the house. "School, the milieu of three of Miss Compton-Burnett's . . . novels, is not much different from home. Its concern is presumably the training of the young, it occurs in a house some floors of which are class and common rooms, and its relations are scarcely more public than those of home."[10] In *More Women than Men* and *Two Worlds and Their Ways*, a school setting is used by the author instead of a home but with a similar structure of human relationships. Robert Liddell says, "She has chosen the school simply as an example, like the family, of a group of people living too closely together."[11] The personal, emotional and psychological problems confronted by the teachers are brought under focus rather than the actual process of teaching.

Josephine Napier heads the school as well as the home and thus provides the nexus between the two.

In a later novel, *Two Worlds and Their Ways*, Ivy Compton-Burnett again depicts the school atmosphere but with a difference. She does not confine herself to the school alone as in the case of *More Women than Men* but pays equal attention to both the school and the home. In *More Women than Men*, the school is no doubt the background, but the emphasis is on its managerial aspect. The educational process and the pupils exposed to it remain relatively obscure. Similar school-home correlations are elaborately discussed in *Two Worlds and Their Ways*. There are two schools, one for girls and another for boys. As in a family where the members try to outwit one another for supremacy, the students of these schools cheat fellow students and even their teachers. Occasions like parties, dinners, birthdays, Christmas, christening characterize the home-life. Similarly the school too has its own functions like the visiting day for parents, the school concert and so on.

School and home play a major role in her last novel, *The Last and the First*. As in *More Women than Men*, partnership problems of a school are dwelt upon. As in *Two Worlds and Their Ways*, children's psychology is focussed upon. Children trained under governesses in the school room of a house, find it difficult to adjust well in the school.

It is found that both the home and the school have their own drawbacks as the centres of education. Like some of the incompetent governesses, Miss Petticoat (*Two Worlds and Their Ways*), Miss Gibbon (*A Father and His Fate*) and Miss Hallam (*Darkness and Day*), some of the school teachers like Mrs. Chattaway (*More Women than Men*) and Mrs. Merry (*Pastors and Masters*) are unqualified and inefficient. Some teachers like Juliet (*Two Worlds and Their Ways*) are not proud of their profession and therefore they lack application. However, there are some like Lesbia in the same novel who work with involvement and dedication.

A judicious consideration of all these factors appears to have influenced the author to develop a predilection for the home as the proper place for children's education and upbringing. "The author sees clearly both the merits and the defects of home, and appears to be in favour of home in *Two Worlds and Their Ways* as a means of ensuring a genial atmosphere for the growth of affection; in which latent possibilities . . . find favourable climate for their growth."[12] These self-contained families evince little or no interest in social conditions outside the family. Only a few friends and neighbours can penetrate into their closed world.

Society is generally neglected or ignored in her novels because "one achieves something, or is destroyed, not because of the world but because of the family; . . . The family is all; it dominates, circumvents, encloses, frustrates, and provides one with mates."[13] "They are avid to assist at the simmering dramas to be observed at the big house."[14] The neighbours are peripheral to the central action. In *Daughters and Sons*, for the first time, two neighbouring families take part in the main plot.

Compton-Burnett's characters are particular of preserving their social image, and therefore follow the norms relevant to their individual status: "Her [Compton-Burnett's] characters care deeply about the proper conduct of the tea-table, about precedence, about domestic hierarchy."[15] Taking of breakfast and meals by the family is a formal procedure. They are important activities for them calling for the strict observance of certain manners. In fact eleven out of her twenty novels begin with the breakfast scene. Usually this is preceded by prayers. Startling revelations are made at the dining table whether it is a routine family gathering or a formal one where guests are present. Strange and sad things happen at the table. Sabine Ponsonby (*Daughters and Sons*) breathes her last at the dining table. Dining halls in her novels bear witness to the most crucial developments. Plots develop, characters are revealed and conflicts brew during breakfast or dinner around the dining table. John Preston points this out: "The dinner-table is one of the most obvious and telling ways in which society refines a simple biological need into a ceremony."[16] In the words of Violet Powell, breakfast did have a special role in Ivy Compton-Burnett's novels. One of her gifts was "her literary ability to approach the day's first meal from an ever-fresh angle."[17]

Dinners for neighbours are infrequent, but when they are arranged, they are grand and formal. But this ceremonious extravaganza is in sharp contrast to everyday economy. With the visitors around, the normal running of the household is disrupted.

Her characters take little or no interest in sports. Going for walks is a part of their daily routine. In *Manservant and Maidservant*, such a walk assumes vital importance. The children conspire the death of Horace during one such walk.

The family insists on good manners and decent behaviour both at home and in society. "Nothing goes deeper than manners, . . . They are involved with the whole of life. It is they that give rise to it, and come to depend on it. We shall all remember it." (*LF*, 16)

Career interests appear to have been limited in the world of Ivy Compton-Burnett. Medicine, church and law are the three fields in which men evince interest. There are occasional references to business as in the case of Sir Jesse in *Parents and Children* who has retired from business in South America. There are others without any gainful avocation. Those who own land are preoccupied with the task of caring for it, trying to arrest the decline in its value. A few, like the two elder sons of Benjamin Donne (*Elders and Betters*), are in government service in an undisclosed capacity. Teaching is another profession which attracts even women. Besides teaching at school, women are employed in the affluent households as governesses and men as tutors. This is not treated as a very coveted profession commanding high status in society.

Writing as a career is taken up by a few characters like John Ponsonby (*Daughters and Sons*) and Hereward Egerton (*A God and His Gifts*). Compton-Burnett's people are not interested in politics. Newspapers are rarely mentioned. Only Sabine Ponsonby (*Daughters and Sons*), governesses, Miss Lacy (*Elders and Betters*) and Miss Mitford (*Parents and Children*), are referred to as reading newspapers. Doctors are held in respect by the society and they are found to be dedicated to their profession. Clergymen, usually treated with respect and goodwill by novelists like Goldsmith and Jane Austen get a rough deal at the hands of Compton-Burnett. "Solicitors are treated by Compton-Burnett somewhat better than clergymen, but not so well as doctors."[18]

None of Ivy Compton-Burnett's characters is in the service of the crown. Country gentlemen never come down to the level of yeomanry. No one joins the army or the navy. No one is seen taking up music and painting as a profession, eventhough music is taught at schools.

The novelist herself explains why she had not evinced deeper interest in the professional careers of her characters. In an interview with Margaret Jourdain, Ivy Compton-Burnett explains that the professions and occupations are merely indicated in passing as she is more concerned with their personal lives and "following them into their professional world would lead to the alternations between two spheres."[19]

Ivy Compton-Burnett's attitude to Christianity was rather indifferent. During the first half of the nineteenth century, Evangelical Christianity had loosened its grip on the nation. Darwin's *Origin of Species* (1859) ushered in the creed of skepticism. By the 1880s, many intellectuals, including clergymen, turned agnostics, but, at the same time, probity in everyday life continued unsullied.

Ivy Compton-Burnett is not religious and has neither faith nor interest in it. She tells Elizabeth Taylor, the novelist, Christianity has yielded no good results as its foundations are laid in fostering guilt in people.[20] In spite of having been born in a religious family and having received religious instruction, she developed no special liking for it even though she did not disbelieve it. The advancement of science influenced her understanding and very soon, she was mature enough to reject it.

Cicely Greig observes: "about religion . . . Ivy would say that she disliked the usual prayers and church services as a child, and gave it all up as soon as she became her own mistress."[21] Ivy Compton-Burnett herself tells Kay Dick, "But I never liked the religion. I never liked it."[22]

Several of her characters, especially children, appear to have been influenced by the modern thought at the instance of the governesses. They grow up mistrusting religion. Thus seven-year-old Megan and eight-year-old Henry, children of Cassius Clare (*The Present and the Past*), ignore the significance of religion while discussing the subject of the origin of man. (*PP*, 13) Even the rectors who preach, like Bellamy (*Men and Wives*) and Dr. Chaucer (*A House and Its Head*), do not appear to be very sincere in their faith. Oscar Jekyll (*A House and Its Head*) is sceptic and considers a believer to be a stupid man. (*HH*, 20) In *Pastors and Masters*, God's personality is dissected and Emily makes a daring statement that "He is one of the best-drawn characters in fiction." (*PM*, 32) This observation practically sums up the novelist's attitude to religion, and explains the stand she has taken regarding normal concepts of sin and morality. All the same, external symbols of religion are being followed more as a matter of routine, though not backed up by conviction. Elizabeth Sprigge points out: "with her ruthless honesty Ivy despised the disguise of social observance as divine ones."[23] Angus Wilson observes: "Nevertheless the Christian ruins are the backcloth of her family dramas—establishment, orders of society, feeble ends of Christian ethics."[24] On the whole, it may be said that Compton-Burnett's people are sceptic and have abandoned their faith.

All through her works, home forms the focal point of interest. However, this is not the case in *Pastors and Masters* which becomes the first of the series, as the novelist wishes to disown her first novel, *Dolores*. "*Pastors and Masters* is mainly a study of society as the author's subsequent novels are known to be a study of home,"[25] says one critic. However, in this novel, along with Mr. Merry's school, Henry Bentley's home is neatly painted foreshadowing Compton-Burnett's interest in the study of home in her later novels. From her next novel *Brothers and Sisters* onwards, she gives the society a go-by and studies domestic themes almost exclusively and unswervingly. In this novel, she introduces the first domestic companion, Miss Patmore and studies the problem of how incestuous relationships wreck a home. Tyranny, which is mild in the previous novel, emerges as a major domestic problem threatening its peace. This continues as a major theme in the novels to follow. In *Men and Wives* also, the novelist continues to focus her attention on home. Here she deals with the problem of the divergence of wishes between the parents and children affecting domestic peace. Servants of the house appear for the first time in this novel and are given individual treatment and identity. After these two novels of family life, Ivy Compton-Burnett shifts attention to school life in *More Women than Men*. The scene is laid in a big boarding school for girls. School life with teachers and students is more elaborately shown than in *Pastors and Masters*. However, gradually the background is narrowed down to the head-mistress, Josephine Napier's home. In her next novel, *A House and Its Head*, she returns to her favourite milieu, home. Here Duncan's home is the centre of action. *Daughters and Sons*, her next novel, introduces Ponsonby's house as the centre of attention. Home continues to engage her attention from this novel onwards. She enriches home here by extending its sphere and including new interests. The eleven-year-old Muriel, the forerunner of the wonderful and devastating children of her later novels, makes her presence for the first time. Governesses play an important role. In *A House and Its Head,* only a glimpse of the school room is given. The families focussed in the next two novels are those of the Gavestons in *A Family and a Fortune* and of the Sullivans in *Parents and Children*. Children play increasingly significant role in these novels. In "*A Family and a Fortune* and *Parents and Children*, children attain equal, often superior, status in Miss Compton-Burnett's casts."[26]

In her next novel, *Elders and Betters*, the households of the Donnes and the Calderons engage her attention. At this stage, Ivy Compton-Burnett "is moving towards a hermetically sealed society"[27] and has started introducing very few neighbours and even then, only when they are absolutely necessary for the development of the plot. Children continue to steal the show. Though she has started taking notice of the household servants, the scenes involving them are unmistakably experimental as they play little part in its action.

In *Manservant and Maidservant*, the Lambs' house with ill-provided children is the centre of attention. Here, for the first time, the novelist makes an elaborate study of the world downstairs. Constance Lewis observes: "Although an occasional butler or nursemaid or governess has had a role in the novels before *Manservant and Maidservant*, this is the first of Dame Ivy's works in which a group of servants has shared center stage with the major family; indeed, by the end of the novel, they almost have the stage to themselves."[28] Its title *Manservant and Maidservant* and the title given to it in the USA, *Bullivant and the Lambs*, both indicate the importance given to the servant class. For the first time, the servants are presented as being individualistic. In an earlier novel, *Daughters and Sons*, all the maids in the Ponsonby household have been called Gertrude just to save the trouble of addressing them by their individual names and until *Manservant and Maidservant*, the level of individuality is not conferred on them. The lives of the servants and of the masters are knitted together, and the novelist, from this novel onwards, uses the servants to highlight, though indirectly, the absurdity or emptiness of the masters.

At this stage, Ivy Compton-Burnett further expands her essential truths about home and stresses the element of humour is now changed to the servants' hall. Education of children by tutors and governesses in the school room of the household or in the school is presented in a comic way in the novels, *Pastors and Masters, A House and Its Head* and *Manservant and Maidservant*. Even in *More Women than Men*, where the scene of action itself is a boarding school, the author is more concerned with the intricate problems common in a family like jealousy, incestuous love of an aunt for her nephew leading to a murder, homosexuality and so on rather than with education itself. But in *Elders and Betters*, education is given a serious thought and it reaches its pinnacle in *Two Worlds and Their Ways*. Here she takes up the important problem as to whether the home or the school is the right place for education. A remarkable improvement in the treatment of servants is that they are drawn into the family itself. The butler of the house turns out to be the master's illegitimate son. Unlike in earlier novels where she was interested in maintaining a close texture, now by bringing masters and servants into the same domestic arena, she has explored different levels of activities of home and thus made a considerable progress in its study. From *Daughters and Sons* onwards, Ivy Compton-Burnett has started exploring other parts within the house like nursery, school room and servants' hall and also started connecting the home with other issues of life outside. She lets life "gradually stretch around from a central point within home to reach up to its surroundings, by acknowledging the impact of some newly introduced ideas and opinions on life."[29]

In her next novel, *Darkness and Day*, she resists the temptation of extending her scope further. A problem taken up in an earlier novel, *Brothers and Sisters*, is taken up again with a difference for examination. From *Pastors and Masters* to *Manservant and Maidservant*, domestic oppression of children by their parents and of servants by their masters gains seriousness interfering with the peace and happiness of the members of family as a whole. However, in the novels from *Daughters and Sons* to *Two Worlds and Their Ways*, there is no incest or adultery barring that of Sir Jesse Sullivan in *Parents and Children.* From *Darkness and Day* onwards, extra-marital relations are quite common. Incest also figures in three novels. However, tyranny, though present, is mild and it gradually fades away. In the novels from *Daughters and Sons* to *Two*

Worlds and Their Ways, unhappy married life is depicted but it is not caused by infidelity. In the two novels, *Two Worlds and Their Ways* and *Darkness and Day*, tyranny is conspicuously absent.

In the next novel, *The Present and the Past*, as in many other novels, a home is concentrated upon. The two levels of love, conjugal and filial, are presented. How a divorced wife comes back to see her children and disturbs domestic peace is depicted. Servants and children continue to be in the forefront. *Mother and Son* presents an adulterous, loveless couple, though not actually separated, nevertheless leading separate lives under the same roof. In addition, tyranny, reintroduced in *The Present and the Past*, is made to figure in this novel on an intensified scale. Besides the Humes' house, attention is focussed on the house of Emma Greatheart. In *The Present and the Past*, the three-decker arrangement of the house is clearly marked. But home is not symbolically depicted as a three-storeyed building from *Mother and Son* onwards.

In the earlier novels like *Daughters and Sons* and *Elders and Betters*, greed for money and power is the focal point. *A Family and a Fortune, Parents and Children, Manservant and Maidservant* and *Two Worlds and Their Ways* are concerned with unhappy domestic life. However, this unhappiness has nothing to do with conjugal disloyalty.

In the later novels, *Darkness and Day, The Present and the Past, Mother and Son* and *A Father and His Fate*, Ivy Compton-Burnett continues to deal with tyranny, adultery and conjugal disloyalty which shatter domestic happiness. In *A Father and His Fate*, the home is extended to include outsiders, Malcolm and Verena, who play important roles in the development of the theme.

From *Darkness and Day* onwards, Ivy Compton-Burnett pinpoints the essence of the institution of family and traces the source of its strength. *Darkness and Day, The Present and the Past, Mother and Son* and *A Father and His Fate* are merely exploratory. They lead to the finding that the bonds between husband and wife and parents and children are inviolable. Thus the novelist continues to search for and find answers to several problems besetting domestic life. To the problem of a mother's overpossessive love that destroys the peace of the home, as in the case of Humes (*Mother and Son*), the solution is offered in *A Father and His Fate*.

Strict confinement to home and its problems continues in the next novel, *A Heritage and Its History*. Here she deals with incest and points out how it affects the principles of inheritance and wrecks marital happiness and domestic peace. In a much earlier novel, *A House and Its Head*, the same problem of incestuous adultery and inheritance is dealt with by the author. Foul means are used to restore inheritance. The wife of the disinherited arranges to do away with the little heir. In *Darkness and Day*, mistaken incest is adverted to but the author seems to evade the real issue to ensure a happy ending. In *A Heritage and Its History*, Ivy Compton-Burnett fails to find a satisfactory solution. However, Simon Challoner's confession of incest solves the problem of further incest. In the next novel, *The Mighty and Their Fall*, she describes how a supposed widower's infatuation for a young girl disturbs domestic harmony. Lust for power continues to be one of the recurring problems. In *A God and His Gifts*, incestuous adultery and marital happiness constitute the theme. Here though Hereward is a writer, reference to him is confined to the aspect of his domestic life.

The two novels, *The Mighty and Their Fall* and *A God and His Gifts*, illustrate how, given the will, rapprochement is possible between seemingly irreconcilable persons in the family. Lavinia and Ninian, and Ada and Hereward mutually adjust themselves very well showing that problems in home life are to be solved within the home itself. The author seems to drive home the essential truth that subsisting mutual affection in a family is the sine qua non for sustained happiness at home.

In her last novel, *The Last and the First*, she comes back to the familiar, recurrent problem, tyranny but with a difference that other familiar problems like adultery are not brought in simultaneously. She devises a satisfactory solution to the problem by making Hermia use her power wisely and discreetly. Servants continue to hold supremacy. The butler recalls Bullivant of *Manservant and Maidservant*. As in the earlier novels, there are two households, dissimilar in dignity and status. In the earlier novels, amalgamation of the two households has been attempted, but here, the two are successfully brought closer together.

In all the novels, family unhappiness is the curse of every home. This is in conformity with the belief that the Victorian period was synonymous with unhappy families. "The Victorian period was the classical age of the unhappy family: parental tyrannies, suppressed hatreds, sacrificial lives, unvoiced griefs, crimes concealed by respectability."[30] Robert Liddell also makes the same observation: "the nineteenth century in England . . . was the great age of unhappy families."[31]

Ivy Compton-Burnett explored the inexhaustible potential of the basic theme and analyzed the psychological factors behind such truths. Disintegration in a family starts with the straining of the emotional and psychological relationships between the members of a family.

The dictatorial and high-handed attitude of elders towards children is another major factor causing friction in a family. Domestic conflict arises due to the divergence of views and inclinations between parents and children. Ruthless oppression of that kind by the elders ruins the homes of the Staces (*Brothers and Sisters*), the Haslams (*Men and Wives*), the Edgeworths (*A House and Its Head*), the Sullivans (*Parents and Children*), Ponsonbys (*Daughters and Sons*), Gavestons (*A Family and a Fortune*), Calderons (*Elders and Betters*), Lambs (*Manservant and Maidservant*), Humes (*Mother and Son*), Clares (*The Present and the Past*), Mowbrays (*A Father and His Fate*), Challoners (*A Heritage and Its History*), Middletons (*The Mighty and their Fall*), Egertons (*A God and His Gifts*) and Heriots (*The Last and the First*).

By depicting these unpleasant aspects of domestic life, it is not Ivy Compton-Burnett's intention, as R.N. Sarkar points out, "to trace the gradual decay of the Victorian home, but to explore the unhappy facts so as to bring out the very essence of home life."[32]

One remarkable feature noticeable in Ivy Compton-Burnett's novels is that her 'homes' are inexorably drawn into the vortex of collapse through internal strife and then, as by some contrivance, she rescues them, if not all, at least in the majority of cases. This is as it should be, for it cannot certainly be her purpose to sound the death knell of the family life in her chosen stratum of society in the late Victorian England.

In almost all the novels, home, appearing to be on the verge of collapse, survives by its inherent strength for adaptability and thus a possible tragic conclusion is avoided. All the 'homes' of Ivy Compton-Burnett are found to be stabilized by exposure to stress. In *Brothers and Sisters*, the Stace children leave the place of disgrace and scandal in the hope of starting a new life. Further incest is prevented by the timely revelation of their parents' incest. In *Men and Wives*, Harriet's death relieves the house of the tyranny. The children come round and accept the course recommended by their mother. In *More Women than Men*, Gabriel along with his father makes a separate home away from Josephine's tyranny. The Edgeworth's home in *A House and Its Head* is saved from ruin by the marriage of Duncan to the good-natured Cassandra. Death of Sabine and marriage of Hetta save the home of Ponsonbys (*Daughters and Sons*) from collapse. John Ponsonby's marriage to Edith Hallam brings peace to the family. In *A Family and a Fortune*, the reconciliation between the brothers, Edgar and Dudley, and the loss of Matty's power helps resurrect the Gaveston home. In *Parents and Children*, Fulbert returns home to save Eleanor from bigamy and the children become happy with the restoration of both the parents.

In *Elders and Betters*, Anna's marriage and her intention of setting up a separate home relieves the homes, both of the Donnes and of the

Calderons from tyranny and unhappiness. Horace's reformation helps to free the Lambs' home (*Manservant and Maidservant*) of tyranny and Charlotte's decision not to leave the home helps to stabilize it. Happy reconciliation is found in *Darkness and Day*, where the problem of incest troubling the family is found to be a misapprehension. The husband's pre-marital affair or the wife's illegitimacy troubles them no longer. The Clares' home (*The Present and the Past*) is saved by the death of the tyrant father and the removal from the neighbourhood of his divorced wife with her children. Miranda's (*Mother and Son*) death makes the members of the family breathe freely. The adultery of both the husband and the wife does not interfere with the stability of the home. Verena's exit and Ellen's return stabilize the Mowbray's home in *A Father and His Fate*. Miles Mowbray has to bow his head in the end to the greater forces of family unity. Simon's (*A Heritage and Its History*) timely confession of his incest avoids further incest. He regains his lost inheritance and peace is restored in the Challoners' home. In the Middleton home (*The Mighty and Their Fall*), affection between father and daughter is restored and peace and happiness return to their family. Understanding and adjustment of Ada saves the home of the Egertons in *A God and His Gifts*. Timely financial help prevents the Heriot family in *The Last and the First* from falling. Removal of Eliza from power brings back peace.

Even death does not shatter the lives of people. No survivor grieves for the deceased. Immediately after the death of wife or husband, they contemplate second or even third marriage. Life is not too difficult even for Gabriel (*More Women than Men*) who has lost his wife, very soon after his marriage. The only exception seems to be Sophia (*Brothers and Sisters*) who grieves a good deal and makes the lives of her children miserable. Home appears to be an abiding shelter for the members even in the face of a threat to its peace. Christopher Gillie sums up: "a family can proceed equably until it undergoes stress, and the balance of this one is upset, and then restored, by its encounter with multiple stresses."[33]

If insults, outrages, incest, adultery, murders and so on which abound in Ivy Compton-Burnett's 'homes' do really happen in life, "the result would inevitably be a fine quarrel and the dissolution of all ties. But here the family remains together."[34] Frederick R. Karl comments on this feature: "some spark of vestigial feeling usually keeps the family together. Perhaps it is not feeling that finally unifies, but the law of the jungle."[35]

If, however, some venture to leave the home for good, it becomes inevitable for them to be back soon. Those women who marry and set up families are an exception to this phenomenon. Hetta (*Daughters and Sons*) leaves home wanting to teach a lesson to the neglecting family. Disappointment in love makes Dudley (*A Family and a Fortune*) leave the house whereas the desire to escape torture of a step-mother prompts Hermia to leave home. However, all these stage a return after a while, unable to bear the rigours of living outside the home. "In the home, they remain semi-developed, immature, clinging, and protected, but atleast alive; outside, where the wicked world awaits them with an entirely different set of values, they can hope for no solace whatsoever."[36] Rabindranath Sarkar expresses more or less the same view when he points out: "They know that the home can be a nest of evils, yet there is nothing to replace it, for the roots of their life lie deep down in it."[37] Even after the most shocking revelations of incest, adultery and illegitimacy, home is kept intact and life is somehow continued. "The family's . . . potency as a force that can still hold the allegiance of its members is perhaps the most fundamental feature of Miss Compton-Burnett's work."[38]

NOTES

1. Robert Liddell, *A Treatise on the Novel* (London: Jonathan Cape, 1965), p. 148.
2. Frederick R. Karl, "The Intimate World of Ivy Compton-Burnett," *A Reader's Guide to the Contemporary English Novel* (London: Thomas and Hudson, 1972), p. 203.
3. Anthony Powell, "Three Obituaries," *The Art of I. Compton- Burnett*, ed. Charles Burkhart (London: Victor Gollancz, 1972), p. 188.
4. David Daiches, *A Critical History of English Literature* (London: Secker and Warburg, 1969), Vol. 4, p. 170.
5. Walter Allen, *Tradition and Dream* (London: Phoenix, 1964), p. 188.
6. Kathleen Tillotson, *Novels of the Eighteen Forties* (Oxford: O.U.P., 1956), p. 94.
7. Ivy Compton-Burnett qtd. in *Orion*, ed. R. Lehmann (1945), p. 255.
8. Violet Powell, *A Compton-Burnett Compendium* (London: Heinemann, 1973), p. 17.
9. Bernard McCabe, "Ivy Compton-Burnett, An English Eccentric," *Critique*, 3:2 (1960), p. 59.
10. Lotus Snow, "Good is Bad Condensed: Ivy Compton-Burnett's

View of Human Nature," *Western Humanities Review*, 10:3 (1956), p. 272.

11. Liddell, p. 148.
12. Rabindra Nath Sarkar, *Ivy Compton-Burnett: A Trend in English Fiction* (Calcutta: Firma KLM, 1979), p. 37.
13. Karl, p. 208.
14. Powell, p. 19.
15. John Preston, "A Heritage and Its History," *The Art of I, Compton-Burnett,* ed. Charles Burkhart, p. 72.
16. Preston, p. 73.
17. Powell, p. 77.
18. *Ibid.*, p. 20.
19. Margaret Jourdain, "I. Compton-Burnett and M. Jourdain: A Conversation,' *The Art of I. Compton-Burnett*, p. 23.
20. Elizabeth Taylor, qtd. Hilary Spurling in *Secrets of a Woman's Heart* (London: Penguin, 1984), p. 76.
21. Cicely Greig, *Ivy Compton-Burnett: A Memoir* (London: Garnstone Press, 1972), p. 16.
22. Kay Dick, *Ivy and Stevie* (London: Allison and Busby, 1983), p. 24.
23. Elizabeth Sprigge, *The Life of Ivy Compton-Burnett* (London: Victor Gollancz, 1973), p. 40.
24. Angus Wilson, *The Novels of Ivy Compton-Burnett,* p. 131.
25. Sarkar, p. 1.
26. McCabe, p. 59.
27. *Loc. cit.*
28. Constance Lewis, "*Manservant and Maidservant*: A Pivotal Novel," *Twentieth Century Literature,* 25.2 (1979), p. 228.
29. Sarkar, p. 41.
30. Mario Praz, *The Novels of Ivy Compton-Burnett*, p. 125.
31. Robert Liddell, *The Novels of I. Compton-Burnett* (London: Victor Gollancz, 1955), pp. 19-20.
32. Sarkar, p. 146.
33. Christopher Gillie, *Movements in English Literature 1900-1940* (London: C.U.P., 1975), p. 109.
34. "Analysis by Dialogue," Rev. of *Daughters and Sons, The Times Literary Supplement*, 10 Apr. 1937, p. 273.
35. Karl, p. 201.
36. *Ibid.,* p. 218.
37. Sarkar, p. 147.
38. "Family feeling," Rev. of *A Father and His Fate, The Times Literary Supplement,* 16 Aug. 1957 p. 493.

Domestic Tyranny

Thematic analysis of a domestic novel must necessarily highlight the delineation of character and the author's handling of personal relationships with home as the focal point. It is appropriate that domestic fiction should include negative aspects of the family as well as the usual positive values such as love, filial affection and patriotism. Idealized or glorified virtues had become far from real, and the undesirable tendencies in human character began demanding attention. Convinced of the imperative need for a change of approach to fictional characters, Ivy Compton-Burnett takes up the challenge and concentrates on human weaknesses, manifesting themselves in several forms, the most dominant being lust for power or tyranny.

Domestic dictator was a common figure in the Victorian Age. It might have been rare, perhaps, in Jane Austen's days as the social conditions differed from those of the Victorian Age. In Jane Austen's days, parents were mainly concerned with the marriages of their daughters. Perhaps it became necessary for the self-centred Victorian parents to devise some methods of disciplining their children. This might have led some of them to grab power and to function as tyrants in the family.

The law did not provide a list of parental rights and responsibilities towards children. A father was usually unchallenged as no one was prepared to challenge his rights. Even courts recognized father's rights, however with very few limitations like criminal law punishing the more serious forms of ill-treatment and courts declining to enforce a father's claim to possession if he was highly unfit. The law changed gradually giving more and more recognition to mothers' rights over children. Finally, in 1925, the courts were expressly told to ignore the question of whether the father's rights were technically superior to those of the mother or vice versa and that their rights to act as, and appoint, guardians were also made equal.[1]

Conflict is found between the social expectations attached to a role and the self-interested individual who fills it. The word parent implies provision and protection, sanctioning authority and discipline. At the surface level, social order prevails.

Ivy Compton-Burnett's characters are true to 'Self': "Self—there is no escaping the interpretation—is the motivation for every human actions, and self is greedy for all lures of the world, the flesh, and the devil that will exalt it."[2]

In this sense, her characters are 'true' to themselves, in the sense that they satisfy their own basic cravings, the most conspicuous being those of the greed for power, money and lust. These are manifestations of the will to dominate, directly or indirectly. The relentless striving for assertion of oneself is the predominant theme in almost all her novels. V. Ramakrishna Rao explains: "It is this psychic component that is mainly responsible for man's lust for power, *libido dominant*, which is all-pervasive in these novels. . . . Their sole interest is self; their ambition to rule; their purpose to survive; and if their means are fair or foul they never care. . . . They illustrate Shakespeare's 'Sin of self-love possesseth all mine eye.'"[3]

Miriam Allott points out that the strong basic theme is the source of strength to her novels in the technical sense: "Her sense of hidden forms of violence and treachery beneath the superficial amenities of social intercourse gives her work its shapeliness and energy."[4] Both the warp and the woof are but different manifestations of self-interest, strengthening the structure of the novel.

Explaining the meaning of the expression 'true to oneself' in the context of Ivy Compton-Burnett's novels, Lotus Snow explains: "But which is the deeper meaning for Miss Compton-Burnett? The concept of truth to self as submission to the precepts of religion or ethics, or as obedience to the dictates of one's own nature? The answer—and it is basic to Miss Compton-Burnett's art—rests not with the sense of the word *true*, but with the sense of the word symbol *self*."[5] Mario Praz also explains the role of self in her novels: "the dominant theme is the lust for power. In every family there are tyrants, victims, and witnesses; secret calvaries, unspoken hatred, struggles to bend the will of another who, according to the ethos of the time, owed a tribute of submission, struggles to obtain favours in a will."[6]

G.S. Fraser observes regarding Ivy Compton-Burnett's novels: "either the father or mother is usually a tyrant, and the parent who is not a tyrant is usually a weakling or a fool."[7] Even the unmarried aunts, owing to their age and position in the family, and with active support from the parents, try to exercise power over children.

The cases of domestic tyranny in Ivy's novels look highly exaggerated and unconvincing, especially when examined in terms of modern realism. The novelist has a reasonable justification for the extra dark colouring she has given to ordinary characters: "Real life seems to have no plots. And I think a plot desirable and almost necessary, I have this extra grudge against life. But I do think there are signs that strange things happen, though they do not emerge. I believe it would go ill with many of us, if we were faced by a strong temptation, and I suspect that with some of us it does go ill."[8]

It was but logical that she should have developed "the signs that strange things happen" into extra-ordinary events tearing across calm and unruffled domestic atmosphere. Tyranny develops such a sharp edge that one wonders whether her works could be considered realistic. Walter Allen states categorically that Ivy Compton-Burnett is not a realistic novelist: "In her novels, the strange things emerge—from the tyranny of family life, and they would be very strange indeed if Miss Compton-Burnett were a realistic novelist, which she is not."[9] The critic endows this aspect with a psychological dimension and explains the incidence of violence from this perspective: "in her novels the factor of violence is extremely high: wills are forged or suppressed, incest is not uncommon, murder takes its course, power exercises itself, emotional blackmail is constant; all this despite the surface decorum of her work."[10]

Dolores, Ivy Compton-Burnett's first novel, is totally devoid of any form of tyranny. Therefore, the evolution of the domestic tyrant can be traced from Reverend Henry Bentley of *Pastors and Masters*, her second novel. He is an early sketch of the parental bully of the subsequent novels. His bullying complaints at his family's lateness for breakfast remind the readers of Duncan Edgeworth of *A House and Its Head.* Something of Sir Jesse Sullivan (*Parents and Children*) and Simon Challoner (*A Heritage and Its History*) is also found in him when he strongly believes that his sons' education will hardly make them fit to earn their bread.

He is a nagging and self-pitying dictator of a family tyrannizing over his dependent children. Besides Mr. Bentley, there is Mr. Merry, the headmaster of the school, who is a despot ruling the school children. He treats them with a mixture of abuse and servility. He is not only a bully but a hypocritical bore also. This type is later developed in the school mistress, Josephine Napier of *More Women than Men*.

"*Pastors and Masters* . . . is a study of exploiters and exploited, of tyrants and victims, in many guises."[11] Here only dictators of home and school are found. In the subsequent novels, only domestic tyrants are presented barring *More Women than Men* where the tyrant's province is a school. Though not fully developed, the character-type, domestic tyrant, is experimented in the novel, *Pastors and Masters*.

Full-fledged tyrants are present from her next novel, *Brothers and Sisters*, onwards. The novelist presents, in succession, powerful tyrants like Sophia Stace (*Brothers and Sisters*), Harriet Haslam (*Men and Wives*), Josephine Napier (*More Women than Men*), Duncan Edgeworth (*A House and Its Head*), Sabine Ponsonby and Hetta Ponsonby (*Daughters and Sons*). Matilda Seaton (*A Family and a Fortune*), Ann Donne (*Elders and Betters*) and Horace Lamb (*Manservant and Maidservant*). Except for an aged, worn-out tyrant in *Parents and Children*, from her third novel to the eleventh, this procession of bloody tyrants is seen. After the total disappearance of tyrants in the next two novels, *Two Worlds and Their Ways, Darkness and Day*, the mild or not-so-powerful tyrants, Aunt Sukey (*Elders and Betters*), Cassius Clare (*The Present and the Past*), Miles Mowbray (*A Father and His Fate*), Simon Challoner (*A Heritage and Its History*), Ninian Middleton (*The Mighty and Their Fall*) and Hereward Egerton (*A God and His Gifts*) emerge. The only exception in this group of mild tyrants is Miranda Hume (*Mother and Son*), who properly belongs to the earlier group of Sophia, Matty, Josephine and others. In the last novel, however, a powerful but benevolent tyrant, Hermia (*The Last and the First*), is present along with two other mild tyrants.

The tyrants' domineering grip on the family is depicted in one sentence by Sarkar thus: "In a Compton-Burnett family the tyrant head has displaced God and dictated rules to others forgetting that he has anything or anyone above him to owe allegiance to."[12]

One significant fact that emerges is that women tyrants outnumber men tyrants and among the powerful, bloody tyrants, who are around ten in number, only two are men. Pamela Hansford Johnson elaborates this point: "Most of her males are eaten by their women. Her villainesses commit crimes of power; her villains, for the most part, crimes of weakness, . . . The spider analogy might, indeed, be carried further; her men are like insects in the process of being devoured who, seeing that the female has omitted a leg, obligingly turns around and presents the remaining limb in order to make the meal easier."[13] For the sake of convenience, Ivy Compton-Burnett's tyrants may be divided into powerful ones and mild ones. Whether powerful or weak, her portrayal of these tyrants is a manifestation of her perfect comprehension of the psychology of despotism.

After the shadowy Bentley of *Pastors and Masters*, a full-grown tyrant is present in the next novel, *Brothers and Sisters*. Sophia Stace is a highly possessive, tyrannical mother. Some qualities are further developed in Miranda Hume of *Mother and Son*. Even Josephine Napier (*More Women than Men*) is possessive, but she is so towards her nephew with more lust than love.

Sophia is not a deliberate tyrant. Despotism in her case is the result of frustration. She becomes one of the author's monstrous domestic tyrants. Burkhart says, "In its tragic heroine, Sophia Stace, who is married to her brother, she created a tyrant whom no later hero or heroine surpasses in authority and interest."[14] After her father's death, she becomes the ruler of the house, managing the land, her husband and children. She plans all matters for her family and herself. Her will is the law in her house. Among female tyrants, she is particularly interesting because she derives no pleasure from her tyranny. She appears as a saint to her husband and differently to the children who know she is a harridan. The author sums up Sophia's character thus: "Sophia made life easy only for her husband. Sophia was a woman to whom one man was her life. For her children her love demanded more than it gave." (*BS*, 26) Some of her characteristics reappear in Harriet Haslam of *Men and Wives*, Hetta Ponsonby of *Daughters and Sons* and Matilda Seaton of *A Family and a Fortune*.

Like Sophia, Harriet Haslam (*Men and Wives*) is a devouring and tyrannical mother. She is selfish and obsessive and wants everyone to pay special attention to her. But she differs from Sophia in her aims and methods. She is a hypochondriac and always complains of insomnia. She lacks Sophia's vigour, self-importance, self-confidence and her manner of mixing love and command.

In her ways of bringing her children under her control, she uses power, perhaps more repulsively than Henry Bentley. She attempts suicide not out of genuine despair but just to threaten the family. The same device is used by other tyrants, Hetta Ponsonby in *Daughters and Sons* and by Cassius Clare in *The Present and the Past*. Unfortunately, the attempts by both are unsuccessful whereas Harriet's has drastic consequence too. When she comes back, she tries to regain her former hold on them, tries to rule them with her high idealism and nervous sickness. Repulsed by her behaviour and aware of her opposition to the girl of his choice for marriage, her son, Matthew, causes her death by mixing up some poisonous tablets with her sleeping tablets.

In trying to keep everyone under her grip, she is quite successful in having her husband, Sir Godfrey, fully under control even after her death. It is ironic that she is more successful only after her death. While alive, her children resist her attempts at planning for their future. But her death makes them follow her wishes. The agonized Mathew repents and confesses his guilt and is in turn rejected by Camilla for whose hand he committed matricide. Camilla has an abhorrence for a matricide. Thus Mathew and the other children are forced to adopt courses as their mother had desired. It appears as though she had to die to be all-powerful.

In *More Women than Men*, Josephine Napier's tyranny, as in the cases of Sophia and Harriet Haslam, stems from her frustration in life. But she stands out as a tyrant with criminal propensities.

The arena is shifted from home to a school as Josephine happens to be the headmistress of a large boarding school. While Mr. Merry of *Pastors and Masters* directs his tyranny on the pupils, Josephine's victims are the staff. Her methods are of a subtler type but the effects are stunningly cruel. "She has the ability of beguiling others into following her implicitly. She is ruthless, intensely possessive and, like men, she is physically strong and mentally tough." (*MWTM*, 176) She puts on a picture of goodness and usefulness to all and tempts others to appreciate her goodness. Only Miss Rosetti, one of the teachers of the school, sees her without illusion, as she has had several occasions to observe her in her true colours.

For instance, when Ruth is exposed to icy drought, Rosetti suddenly enters the room and sees her in Josephine's arms. Josephine says that Ruth was out of bed in a second and she could not lift her by herself. "'It was a strange thing to happen,' said Miss Rosetti, her glance going up and down Josephine's frame, as though measuring it against the task that had been beyond it." (*MWTM*, 159) At the wedding of her nephew, Gabriel, she appears in widow's robes. Gabriel says:

> "It is quite a long time, nearly six months, since uncle Simon died."
>
> "Five months, twenty-three days and nineteen hours," said Josephine, with her voice dying away and her eyes on space. (*MWTM*, 135)

This shows Josephine's hypocrisy. The fact is that she never loved her husband, and never bemoaned his death. Yet she wants to project the image of a devoted wife.

Josephine is very clever. To win over Rosetti, the only witness of her murderous impulse, she now readily offers her the partnership of the school which she refused earlier. Rosetti, realizing that this is a bribe to silence her, declines the offer.

Josephine is a rare specimen of a tyrant who does not change or admit defeat. Still, to the end, she is in complete control of herself and of her world. She continues to be the school proprietress, Gabriel's foster-mother and the bully of a group of women teachers who hate her and yet feign politeness. There is no reformation in her and she is 'demon triumphant.' This type of tyranny is further developed in the character of Anna Donne in *Elders and Betters*.

Duncan Edgeworth of *A House and Its Head* is the ruler of the family whose word is law. This insistence on absolute power brings violent nemesis but he has the ability to talk his way out of the most shameful predicaments such as his second wife's adultery and his daughter's involvement in an infanticide.

Robert Liddell comments on Duncan: "Like all the more developed tyrants he is not a mere monster of egoism: he has some of the qualities of his defects, notably probity and moral strength. He is not without generosity."[15] His little vices have become powerful and he is turned into a monster. He is the first tyrant to be treated like a God. This is developed later in *A God and His Gifts*, where Hereward behaves like a God according to one of his sons. The irony in the title of the novel referring to him as a God conveys the strong satirical touch making it clear that the novelist is exposing the immoral and tyrannical heads of families with their self-proclaimed godhead.

In the next five novels, starting from *Daughters and Sons*, we have real tyrants. Tyranny is more conspicuous in them than in their predecessors. In *Daughters and Sons*, there are two domestic tyrants instead of the customary one and these two happen to be women. One is Sabine Ponsonby, the eighty-four-year-old grandmother and the other is her daughter, Hetta Ponsonby, a forty-eight-year-old unmarried aunt of the children.

Sabine "seldom spoke anything but evil of any human being." (*DS*, 6) She rules harshly over the motherless grandchildren. But she is "frank about her despotism: she was born in an earlier and more honest age and is downright as a man."[16] Though outwardly harsh, there is an undercurrent of love in her for her grandchildren. Even they recognize her power.

Hetta Ponsonby is the deputy head of the house. She is like an assistant to her mother. Between them, Hetta is more cruel and more tyrannical. Like Josephine Napier of *More Women than Men*, she is very possessive. She is extremely devoted to her brother, John Ponsonby, a writer since his wife's death, "for eleven years he had lived under her control, finding his dependence and gratitude becoming constraint and doubt." (*DS*, 38-39)

Sabine represents the old form of maternal authority whereas Hetta stands for the new form.

> Hetta was the only person who did not fear Sabine, and Sabine alone was normally at ease with her daughter; but they were both the only people in much of what they did. . . . (Hetta) was an influence at once dubious and powerful, at once natural and sinister,

> an authority at once lower and higher than Sabine. (*DS*, 38)

Sabine does not hesitate to hurt people even if they are her guests. Burkhart fittingly remarks: "tyrannical grandmother, Sabine Ponsonby . . . attacks . . . with an aged virulence unmatched for elegance in the earlier tyrants."[17]

The terrible Matilda Seaton (*A Family and a Fortune*) is the most wicked of all domestic tyrants because of her insatiable lust for power. "Anna Donne is monstrous, and so is Josephine Napier; but Aunt Matty far surpasses them."[18] She has no moral or material gain from her exercise of power. This motiveless craze for power makes her the most cruel of Ivy Compton-Burnett's tyrants.

Hetta Ponsonby (*Daughters and Sons*) and Aunt Sukey (*Elders and Betters*) atleast contribute to the household expenses. Matty, on the other hand, is dependent on her comparatively richer sister's family for extra comforts. She is physically handicapped owing to an accidental fall from a horse and therefore walks with a stick: "but her energy seemed to accumulate, and to work itself out at the cost of some havoc within her." (*FF*, 37) She exploits this disability to gain advantages and "has known all her life how to use every occasion to gain ascendancy for herself over those about her."[19] She cannot tolerate if anyone is superior to her in any way. "It sometimes upsets her to hear that people have much more than she has." (*FF*, 40) Finding fault with others is a dominant trait in Matty. (*FF*, 110)

Anna Donne of *Elders and Betters* is a tyrant-criminal. She is comparable to Matty of *A Family and a Fortune* in point of deliberate cruelty. For both, power is a delightful game. But unlike Matty, Anna's tyranny has a strong motive. Her desire for power can be realized with her sweet tongue with which she can win over anyone, and achieve anything. This ruthless, calculated autocrat rules her father's household and everyone is submissive to her.

She is a work-minded tyrant: "Work first, drink afterwards," said Anna. (*EB*, 11) Between Anna and Sukey, Sukey is slightly better as she is capable of self-criticism. She recognizes her mean acts. Realizing that will-changing is an unjust act, she trusts Anna and requests her to destroy the newly-made will. Anna betrays her trust for reasons justified according to her own standards.

Horace Lamb (*Manservant and Maidservant*) is a mean tyrant as he combines miserliness with despotism. He is the most evil and brutal one as he takes advantage of parental authority offering his children neither affection nor sympathy but demanding obedience from them. His power is accidental and egotistical. He expects no personal gain by his overlordship of the family. He is so obsessed with thrift that his children are virtually made to starve. In his comfortless household, the children are under-fed, under-warmed, under-clothed and under- educated. Even his tutor's mother comments, "I expect we live in more comfort." (*MSMS*, 64) When his children complain of cold and implore for a bigger fire, Horace suggests a method that can keep them warm and yet would cost no money. "All up together! Heads up, hands at your sides, quick march!" said Horace, " . . . that is the way to be warm; that is the way to get the sluggish blood to flow. There is no need to pile up the fire and brood over it. There are quicker and better ways than that." (*MSMS*, 32) He drills all his children including the seven-year-old Avery till they are wise enough to admit that they are warm. Horace's restrictions on the subject of the fireplace economy drives his son Marcus into tears, the point to which Horace always carries an argument. His high water mark of victory is when his opponent weeps.

Even the apparent reformation of their father is not taken seriously by the children who can never trust him. Without warning him, Jasper and Marcus watch Horace as he walks ignorantly towards an unsafe bridge. But, luckily for him, he finds the bridge blocked by a warning notice and he returns safe to the house only to realize that his sons had watched him going to possible death. Later, the children admit that they did so with the fear that the bad old times might be returning with Horace's behaviour at the breakfast table. (*MSMS*, 184-85) To escape from his clutches, the children even wish death for him so that they could lead a new life with freedom. Robert Liddell comments: "He is the only male tyrant forced by events to a realization of what he has done and is unique in making a real attempt to reform—though it is self-centred and doomed to failure."[20] He treats even George, who plotted his death, with affection. Horace is lovable in spite of his draw-backs. Bullivant, the butler, speaks about the emptiness in the house and corresponding emptiness in his heart if Horace had died.

While Horace is the despot upstairs, this set up is neatly repeated downstairs by Bullivant. He, along with Mrs. Selden, rules over the servants, George and Miriam.

The oppressive mother in *Mother and Son*, Miranda Hume, is one of the deadliest tyrants of Ivy Compton-Burnett's creations. She can be likened to Sabine Ponsonby of *Daughters and Sons* and Josephine Napier of *More Women than Men*. But she is devoid of the savagery of Sabine and sexual passions of Josephine. Like Sophia of *Brothers and Sisters*, she is highly possessive of her son. But she lacks Sophia's love for her husband. Like all the tyrants, she too bullies the young.

She exhibits intense love and affection towards her son, Rosebery.

She says, "I can trust no one. No one but my son. Not my husband, not the children whom I took into my house as homeless babies." (*MS*, 42) Rosebery is brought up in such a way that he does not even dare tell his mother that he has outgrown his childish love for sugar: "Miss Wolsey. . . . I take sugar as a rule, because I have not had the heart to break it to my mother that I have lost my taste for it. (*MS*, 69)

Eliza Heriot (*The Last and the First*), cannot be classed with the powerful tyrants. At the same time, she is not so weak as to be grouped with the weak. As the second wife of Sir Robert Heriot, she rules the family. The novelist, for the first time, gives a vivid picture of her dominating role in the family when she sums up like this:

> The power in the family was vested in Eliza, . . . She wielded the power as she thought and meant, wisely and well, but had not escaped its influence. Autocratic by nature, she had become impossibly so, and had come to find criticism a duty, and even an outlet for energy that had no other. (*LF*, 17)

Though she is the financial dictator of the family enjoying power, she protests "Oh, I am not an autocrat . . . I am no tyrant." (*LF*, 29) But she believes that she was a 'general' in her previous life and behaves accordingly. Her son, Angus, tells her: "you might be a figure in history, corrupted by power. It is what you are, except that you are not in history." She retorts: "It is a pity I am not. It is where I ought to be." (*LF*, 87)

This resentful stepmother resembles the inconsolable widow, Eliza Mowbray (*A Father and His Fate*). Both are alike in looks as well as in character. (*FF*, 31) Both are jealous and competitive. Like Eliza Mowbray, her absolute power too is not without stiff resistance from her subjects and the most rebellious of them is Hermia, her step-daughter. She resents Eliza's power. They are not afraid of each other. It appears as though the aging tyrant is at war with a fledgling tyrant. As Charles Burkhart points out: "the distinctive theme, the significant variation of *The Last and the First*, is the overthrow of Eliza by a younger and stronger tyrant, her step-daughter Hermia."[21]

Eliza's daughter, Roberta, predicts, "Mater will soon be afraid of Hermia." (*LF*, 29) Finally, Eliza's meanness is exposed when her deceitful attempt to prevent Hermia's marriage becomes known and she is forced to acknowledge defeat. On the other hand, Hermia's nobility also helps her to capture the number one position in the house. Money brings her power and she uses that power wisely and discreetly.

Sir Jesse Sullivan (*Parents and Children*) who believes in his divine right to control his family refuses to moderate his attitude of domestic dictatorship. He is not very cruel, but indulges in the constant nagging of his two eldest grandchildren for the expenses incurred towards their education. He is an ineffectual, worn-out tyrant. He is no longer active and his wife, Reagan, takes his position and exercises her authority on Eleanor, the daughter-in-law and her children. It appears as though the real tyrant is Reagan and not Sir Jesse. But she is unable to interfere when Eleanor decides to marry Ridley. Ironically, Sir Jesse's position is not much shaken even when he is found to be maintaining his illegitimate children in the same village.

Cassius Clare (*The Present and the Past*), though not the central figure, is still the bullying head of the family. As Violet Powell observes: "Cassius may qualify for a niche in the Compton-Burnett pantheon of domestic tyrants, but it would be in a lowly position, suitable for one who lacks the single-minded egotistical drive to maintain an unquestioned rule. Cassius exacts love and fear in inadequate quantities."[22]

Aunt Sukey (*Elders and Betters*) is a weak tyrant in the household of Thomas Calderon. Like Aunt Matty (*A Family and a Fortune*), she is the sister of the mistress of the house and an invalid also. She has a weak heart and may die at any moment. Taking advantage of her own weak points, she rough-rides the entire household. Like Matty, she also has a very high opinion of her beauty and charm, and turns out to be a scourge to the family. She reigns from her sofa as if from a throne. "Her tendency to autocracy and self-esteem had been fostered and responded to the treatment . . . the life of her sister's house was not easier for her presence." (*EB*, 47) Unlike Matty, who depends on the family, Sukey is a source of financial help to the family. She believes that money is an instrument with which she can control the financially not-so-sound family.

Miles Mowbray of *A Father and His Fate* is the patriarch who, like Horace Lamb and Cassius Clare, bullies the members of his family. For him people are no more than pawns and he feels himself exonerated of all faults and blame. When he wrongly believes that his wife is dead in the shipwreck, he decides to marry Verena, his heir's fiancee. He goes on with his plan even after he comes to know that his wife is alive. Finally when it is discovered, he rationalizes his conduct strongly.

He stubbornly uses his financial hold over his daughters to crush their criticism of his proposed marriage with Verena. This diabolical misuse of power over his daughters, who have no alternative but to be dependent on him, deprives him of the sort of sympathy which Sir Godfrey Haslam of *Men and Wives* invokes.

Verena is the female tyrant in embryo. Her desire to marry Miles instead of Malcolm betrays her love of power. In her overbearing desire for immediate power, she finds it difficult to wait as Malcolm's wife and a guest in the house until death removes Miles. With her marriage to Malcolm and not to Miles, a great tyrant in the making is prevented and the house is happily rid of a future tyrant.

Eliza, the mother of Malcolm, holds her family in fear. Her sons give her only the feelings she forces from them. Like Aunt Matty of *A Family and a Fortune*, she likes to dominate every scene but her dominance is challenged and opposed. Though she thinks she is a goddess, she is reduced to be just an overpossessive mother.

Simon (*A Heritage and Its History*), is obsessed with money. His heart is set on his uncle Sir Edwin's estate. Simon, unfortunately, develops illicit relationship with Rhoda, his uncle's wife and she gives birth to a child. His uncle takes a subtle revenge for this deception. He accepts the child as his heir and disinherits Simon. Simon with his mother and brother has to find a new home and he solves this problem by marrying Fanny, Rhoda's sister. But his frustration over disinheritance persists and causes him to develop into a disagreeable parental bully, harassing his five children. The love of dominance in other tyrants springs from their selfish arrogance or egoism whereas in the case of Simon, it is the result of his frustration. Yet his constant nagging is not without opposition from his children.

Selina is the unquestionable ruler of the family in *The Mighty and Their Fall*. She is supported by another budding tyrant, her granddaughter, Lavinia. Her position in the family is demonstrated in the very opening of the novel when Lavinia dictates the order to Agnes, Hengist and Leah contesting for access to the cloakroom and sees that it is followed. The author describes her: "A suggestion of maturity was the result of her being also an autocrat, an intellectual, a widowed father's companion and a grandmother's support." (*MF*, 6) Between the two, the real tyrant is Selina who rules the family. She tells the children: "You will accept what I say, you will not differ from me or voice thoughts of your own. When I have spoken, I have spoken. And you must know it." (*MF*, 11)

Ninian, Selina's son, is also a tyrant but not a match to her. He, at the end, as the butler says, feels he is still mighty whereas in fact he is far from being so. With Ninian no longer mighty, Selina removed from the scene by death and Lavinia's change of fortunes—the Middleton household, it appears, is relieved from much of tyrannizing. So a powerful tyrant, tyrannizing and victimizing, is no longer the novelist's concern now.

Hereward Egerton, the writer-tyrant, is a God with his supernatural gifts. He is proud and confident and considers his defects as virtues. He bewitches every young woman he comes across and uses his power to maintain his amorous relationships. Even when they are exposed, he is not shaken. Self-condemnation is not one of his virtues. Invariably, they accept him with all his defects. This may be partly because they cannot imagine life without him, or, he being the bread-winner of the family, they are inevitably bound in servitude to him.

Jocasta Grimstone, "a highly sketched matriarchal type,"[23] in the words of Violet Powell, holds sway in the Grimstone family, the household besides the Heriots in *The Last and the First*. She is not powerful like Eliza Heriot. She is a lesser tyrant. Like Sabine Ponsonby (*Daughters and Sons*), she is an aged, worn-out tyrant. Her attacks are only intermittent. She says: There is nothing I don't know and see, (*LF*, 93) and also "you know what I have asked for, and you know I will have it." (*LF*, 71) She is plagued by disobedience and is unable to command the people around. Moreover, she is treated comically by her family as well as by the novelist.

The display of tyrants' authority usually begins at the breakfast table. Bentley is a self-centred man behaving like a tyrant and not a father:

> "I am sorry we are late, Father," Mr. Bentley did not look at her. . . . There was a suggestion about her of remembering their being late.
>
> "We shall have a windy walk to the college chapel," said Mr. Bentley.
>
> "What did you say, Father?" said Delia. Mr. Bentley did not answer.
>
> We shall have a windy walk to the chapel," he presently said, in a still lower voice.
>
> "What did you say, Father?" Mr. Bentley did not answer.
>
> "Would you like lunch at one or half-past, Father?" Mr. Bentley was silent.
>
> "Would you like lunch at one or half-past, Father?" Mr. Bentley was silent. (*PM*, 74-75)

He simply teases the children. Though not as malignant as Rev. Bentley of *Pastors and Masters*, Sophia Stace (*Brothers and Sisters*) has her own way of admonishing children for coming late to the breakfast table:

> Dinah, run up and call to the boys. It is tiresome of them not to be in time. I have taken the troublee to be down. . . . I can't go on having to call and implore my children to come and eat the breakfast that is ready for them. It is because it is all done for them

> without any trouble for themselves. It would do them good to have to get it. (*BS*, 26-27)

Duncan, Edgeworth of *A House and Its Head*, whose word is law, which everyone should obey, is particularly extravagant in his display of tyranny. His opinion is open and ruthless. His is the last word on everything. At the breakfast table, he observes that Grant has received a book as a gift from Ellen.

> "What is that book, Grant?" . . .
>
> "Did you remember that I refused to give it to you?" . . .
>
> Duncan took the book, and walking to the fire, placed it upon the flames. (*HH*, 12-13)

The breakfast table is generally the scene of power struggle. The seating at the dining table reflects the person's status in the family. The tyrants, being power-conscious, always sit at the head of the table. Sophia occupies a supreme, unchallenged position in her family: "Sophia sat in her father's seat at the head of his table . . . the seat was symbolic of Sophia's position." (*BS*, 25) Sabine Ponsonby (*Daughters and Sons*) always sits at the head of the table. She "had never relinquished the head of the board to her son. It was her natural place, as the opposite one was her daughter's. John sat at the side by his sister." (*DS*, 52)

The female companions like Miss Patmore (*Brothers and Sisters*) are the domestic victims of the moods of their employers. Yet they are unable to escape from a net woven by love and custom.

The impact of tyranny is mainly felt by the governesses. In *Daughters and Sons*, Sabine exerts herself more when governesses come late for breakfast. She treats Miss Bunyan, the governess, contemptuously. She further insults her by telling her that her company at dinner would be superfluous as her son and daughter are expected home. Sabine's insults hurled at her grandson's tutor have resulted in his leaving the house; and the author comments: "Feminine endurance is said to be higher than masculine, and no other explanation can be offered of Miss Bunyan's not having followed the tutor." (*DS*, 11)

The strange conviction common to the tyrants is that they make sacrifices every minute for their children. Mr. Bentley is no exception. "do not say a word to your father, who makes sacrifices all day, that you may have every advantage; and was trying to arrange something else, that you might have further pleasure. Go away then and do not speak." (*PM*, 88)

Horace Lamb is another such parent who believes that he has sacrificed his whole life to his family. He never misses an opportunity to remind them about his sacrifice.

Eliza Heriot pities herself that she has done much for the family: "What has my life been? Years of care and contrivance, of asking little for myself and accepting less, in order to . . . save the family home." (*LF*, 106)

Some of the tyrants are self-appreciative of their talents. Sophia (*Brothers and Sisters*) displays supreme self-confidence and a claim of superior sensitiveness to other people. Acknowledging her husband's appreciation, she asserts, "I sometimes find myself marvelling at the gulf between the average person and myself." (*BS*, 100)

Eliza Heriot, Miranda Hume and Sophia also are highly confident of themselves. Matty (*A Family and a Fortune*) had a grossly exaggerated notion of herself being beautiful and gifted. She had many chances to marry but did not, because "she had never met a man whom she saw as her equal, as her conception of herself was above any human standard. . . . Even her lameness she saw as giving a touch of tragic interest to an already remarkable impression." (*FF*, 38)

Aunt Sukey of *Elders and Betters* also has a very high opinion of her beauty and charm in spite of her deformity.

Tyrants like Sophia, Harriet, Matilda, Anna and Sukey have some deformity or the other and they want to take advantage of it. While the defects of the others are physical, Harriet suffers from weak nerves resulting in insomnia.

Reading others' letters secretly is another characteristic of the tyrants. For instance with a desire for dominance, Eleanor opens a letter written by her husband to Isabel, his favourite daughter. When Isabel questions, Eleanor justifies her action by saying that she has every right to do that. Lavinia (*The Mighty and Their Fall*) is ahead of all others as she conceals a letter to prevent a marriage out of jealousy. It is with professional skill and confidence that such characters go ahead prying into others' letters without any sense of guilt.

Tyrants are covetous: they are obsessed with desire for money. Anna Donne (*Elders and Betters*) suppresses and destroys the right will in order to get hold of Aunt Sukey's money. In the process, she even drives her aunt Jessica to suicide. Sabine Ponsonby (*Daughters and Sons*) bows to money and makes her son marry the governess, Edith Hallam, under the wrong impression that Edith is capable of earning money. Simon (*A Heritage and Its History*) becomes a despot only after his disappointment in inheritance. Horace in *Manservant and Maidservant* marries Charlotte only for her money and his aim in life is to save money. Ninian's (*The Mighty and Their Fall*) greed for money in explicit. He destroys the will of his brother made in favour of Lavinia and prevents her marriage only to enjoy her inheritance.

In every case, it is seen that tyrants exercise power because of their economic hold on others. Money and tyranny are found to be complementary to each other. Power generally results from the possession of money which is almost a synonym for power. R. Glynn Grylls rightly thinks that, "most important in its relation to power is money."[24] Burkhart too supports this reading: "Money means power."[25]

Most of them who tyrannize the weak are themselves mentally weak. Only they put on a garb of strength to cover their weaknesses. For instance, though Sabine Ponsonby (*Daughters and Sons*) maintains a tyrannous control over her large family, she is afraid of her daughter. On her advice, John is to propose to Edith Hallam, the governess, as she thinks she is the benefactress. Meanwhile she is supposed to prepare Hetta for this news. But finally, when John and Edith go to the room where Sabine and Hetta are together, "The mother had meant to prepare the daughter, but had not dared." (*DS*, 165)

Horace Lamb (*Manservant and Maidservant*) is afraid of his butler, Bullivant. "Horace merely feared him, except in his moods of nervous abandonment, when he feared nothing and nobody." (*MSMS*, 6)

Miranda Hume (*Mother and Son*), who terrorized the entire household, is very weak at heart. On learning that Francis, Adrian and Alice are not her nephews and niece as she believed them to be, but her husband's natural children, she dis of a heart attack.

Cassius Clare is very weak and emotionally insecure. As a consequence, he becomes depressed. He begins to be lured by the idea of suicide in the expectation of his survivors becoming remorseful on that account. His weakness of expecting too much sympathy from others brings his doom. In *The Last and the First*, Eliza Heriot is so weak-willed that at the end of each heated exchange of words with Hermia, she ends up in tears. Even Hetta Ponsonby (*Daughters and Sons*) is not very strong. She almost collapses under the emotional strain. She seems to stagger and look around for her seat and Chaucer, very wisely, comes to her rescue to claim her hand in marriage later. Harriet (*Men and Wives*) has weak nerves which she inherits from her ancestors. Like Cassius Clare (*The Present and the Past*), she attempts suicide when the house is full of people and a party is going on. Even the all-powerful, all-commanding, self-willed Sophia (*Brothers and Sisters*) becomes very insecure after her husband's death. Both aunt Sukey (*Elders and Betters*) and aunt Matty (*A Family and a Fortune*) are invalids. Sukey has a weak heart too and could die any moment.

Some of the tyrants are cruel and possess criminal instincts. They are responsible for crimes and even murders, directly or indirectly.

Matty is devoid of human feelings. She is a sadist. She speaks only to hurt people. She derives pleasure if people suffer from her words. "She broke off as she remembered that Blanche would not hear and suffer from her words." (*FF*, 170) Matty laughs at Miss Griffin:

> "What about scattering some coats and hats about the road, for people to pick up who have fared forth without them? It is really a funny story . . ." Matty bent her head and seemed to try to control her mirth. . . . No one joined in the laughter, and Matty wiped her eyes and continued it alone. (*FF*, 255-56)

With the timely rescue by Dudley, Miss Griffin is saved. Otherwise she would have been frozen to death.

Duncan Edgeworth's (*A House and Its Head*) first victim is his wife, Ellen. The victimization takes the form of ruthless economy in domestic matters, and lack of sympathy with her while her health steadily deteriorates. His insistence on absolute power over his family brings a nemesis both violent and subtle.

Hetta Ponsonby is cruel towards her brother's children and their governesses. She is particularly so towards Edith Hallam who competes for John's affections along with Hetta. She feigns suicide to teach them a lesson which is resented by John. He tells her that she has lost her place to Edith. Also Hetta is morally, if not legally, responsible for her mother's death.

Josephine Napier (*More Women than Men*) is the only tyrant who commits murder. She perpetrates a crime as a means of preserving her domination and power: "the ailing newly married wife of Gabriel by Josephine, his aunt, justly tempts us to label her as 'whole-hearted tyrant' and Miss Compton-Burnett's typical demon."[26]

Josephine is the sort of a woman who longs to have a man emotionally dependent on her. Because of her obsessive passion for Gabriel, she thinks murder of Ruth is the only way to regain him for herself. She, like all other tyrants, is a person of ferocious energy operating half-consciously with catastrophic consequences for the weaker and dependent members of the household.

While Josephine's crime stamps from her incestuous passion for her nephew, Anna Donne's (*Elders and Betters*) springs from her lust for money. No one is aware of Anna's criminal ruthlessness. Besides driving Jessica to suicide, as if to complete her cold-blooded villainy, she gets herself engaged to Terence, son of Jessica and plans for her marital happiness.

Anna reaps the benefits of her ill-deeds. Evil appears triumphant as it defeats goodness and innocence. Anna is victorious with her villainous hypocrisy. There is no just retribution for her crimes as she lives happily thereafter. "She is unalloyed wickedness, wickedness crowned with success, wickedness with sceptre of power, and wickedness with a triumphant grin."[27]

Tyrants themselves sometimes become victims to the machinations of others. Horace Lamb towards whom his children develop bitter animosity is an example. Though Horace has providential escape, Harriet Haslam (*Men and Wives*) succumbs to the vengeance of the oppressed.

Tragedy attends ruthless tyranny. It has drastic psychological impact on the minds of the victims. Hatred of children towards their tyrannical parents is what one perceives in almost all the novels. Under the dictatorial and harshly oppressive control, the victims become silently vindictive. They want to grab the first opportunity to get out of the house, out of their cruel clutches. Strained relationship between the tyrant and the victim is vividly noticed. Little Avery's hatred for his father is explicit:

> "Is father gone now?" said Avery. "I don't want him to come here. He is always in all the places. I don't want him to come where I sleep. I don't like to think he might look at me in the night." (*MSMS*, 55)

Children's pricking of the wax-effigy of their father is a sad symptom of how innocence gets warped and distorted under tyranny, resulting in unnatural reactions.

It is not totally correct to say that these tyrants are unchallenged. The weak are submissive but at some point, they rise to rebel. Generally two groups are seen in these families: parents or adults and children. Children always try to rebel against the dictatorial attitude of their parents or some other close relative.

In *Daughters and Sons*, when Sabine and Hetta torture Muriel, a girl of eleven-and-a-half-year's age, under the pretext of discipline, Clare, the eldest of the girls, boldly says thus:

> "Leave her alone, Aunt Hetta," said Clare. "What good does it do to torment her?"
>
> "Are you the mistress of the house?"
>
> "Yes, I am, when you and Grandma fail in the part. I come

> next Muriel, you can go to bed, and you need not say good night."
>
> Muriel threw her sister a look of relieved acceptance of the account she gave of herself, and disappeared. (*DS*, 142)

Hetta goes away from the house to teach her family a lesson, to make them realize her value in the house. But, on the contrary, they get so adjusted to her absence that when she returns it is she who learns a lesson that she has lost her hold on the family and particularly on her brother, whom she wishes to have under her sway. John Ponsonby says,

> We shall learn nothing. It is you who will learn. You will learn that you cannot resort to evil to work your way, to achieve any petty purpose. You cannot return after conscious wickedness, and be received as if nothing had happened, as if we were under some compulsion to bow to your despotic will, as if you were justified in any extreme to force us under it. . . .
>
> You will not be welcomed back as if everything depended on you. Things depend on you no longer. You have taught us that your service to us is not worth the price we have paid. (*DS*, 232)

Even the young people begin to deal with their aunt on easier terms. Servants also recognize Edith's authority.

In *A Family and a Fortune*, as Violet Powell observes: "Tyranny has only one practitioner, and only one victim."[28] They are Matty and her paid companion, Miss Griffin. Matty's attempt to tyrannize her sister's family utterly fails. Even Miss Griffin rebels when she realizes that even after being with her for thirty years, Matty feels nothing for her. So for the first time, to Matty's coldness there is an answering coldness in Miss Griffin.

But there are a few exceptions. Some people are on the side of autocrat, maybe for some reasons like weakness, cowardice or hope of personal profit. Harriet Haslam is fawned upon by her lawyer, Dominic Spong, who always placed himself on the side of power. Sabine and Hetta are toadied by their clergyman, Dr. Chaucer. Alfred, the tutor, also gains the advantage of their favour, particularly Sabine, with his devotion. Most of the neighbours love and respect Duncan. Because of their moral cowardice, these people are blind or pretend to be blind to the evil of the tyrants.

Though these tyrants are wicked and malicious, there are some who are good with positive qualities. The tyrant monsters like Sophia, Josephine and Matilda Seaton (aunt Matty) are intelligent.

Matty is generous to Maria Sloane, her friend, though she has uncontrollable malice and bitterness for others, particularly, Miss Griffin. She selflessly serves the family in Dudley's illness and shows symptoms of goodness and kindness in her. She is, sometimes, very sensitive, sympathetic and full of understanding. Dudley appreciates Matty when he says, "I think you have got me over my first moment better than anyone." (*FF*, 209)

The ruthless Hetta Ponsonby also sometimes tries to live for others. She is a little reformed towards the end. After her engagement to Doctor Chaucer, she is a little softened towards the members of her family.

Duncan is considered to be God by his family members. His love for power ellipses his good nature. Cassandra, the good-natured governess, readily agrees to marry him only for his noble nature. She knows that his tyranny does not have negative results. Devoid of rancour, he tends to forgive all for their lapses. He forgives Grant who commits incest with Duncan's wife and more than that adopts the son born into the family.

Horace Lamb is also capable of reformation and becomes a loving and sympathetic father and model husband. He wins back, to some extent, his wife and his children.

Regarding Harriet, Violet Powell says: "The irrational state of Harriet's mind and the pain she inflicts on her family is conveyed with such power that her good qualities are obscured. It is at times difficult to believe that Sir Percy Hardisty, a simple kind man, and Rachel his shrewd and intelligeent wife could feel such affection and respect for Harriet as Compton-Burnett would wish her readers to imagine."[29] Harriet is capable of criticizing her own behaviour. Robert Liddell notices that Harriet "is the only female tyrant who ever doubts her own righteousness."[30] She is "a love tyrant," and as Elizabeth Sprigge says, her "loving tyranny brings about her own death at the hands of her eldest son."[31]

Like Harriet, another tyrant who keeps her family's interest in mind and works for it even if it means to be ruthless in her dealings is Sophia. Unscrupulous egotists like Sabine Ponsonby or Josephine Napier have their own positive aspects which do not go unacknowledged even by their victims.

Victims are strangely disillusioned when they are suddenly released from the clutches of a tyrant. When the tyrant dies, all feel sad. When Sabine Ponsonby dies, the pesecuted family members feel dismayed.

When Horace is lying critically ill, everyone of the household, without exception, needs the nagging despot, Horace, to guide them. They think that "the trial, the bondage, the safety of their lives would be gone. They would be free, unprotected, dependent on themselves. The helpless lives they had defended, would be their own responsibility, their own burden." (*MSMS*, 227) The butler, Bullivant, loves his master so much that along with Mortimer, he raises a protective wall around him to save him from the worst effects that arise due to his mishandling of his children.

The novelist does not seem to consider her tyrants as detestable monsters. She expresses her opinion: "They don't seem to me such monsters as they do to other people. I think . . . that a good many of us, if subjected to a strong and sudden temptation, without any risk of being found out, would yield to it."[32] She urged Robert Liddell to stress the goodness of her characters and particularly that of her tyrants.[33]

In an interview with John Bowen, Ivy Compton-Burnett says, "I think there was a tendency for parents to misuse power. . . . Nothing's more corrupting than power."[34] Roughly after two years, speaking to Michael Millgate, Ivy Compton-Burnett says that tyranny does not corrupt people:

> I don't think it corrupts people. I think their dislike of it, if anything, would send them the other way. . . . I've seen people who were tyrannized over as children being careful not to be tyrants themselves, and people who were indulged too much as children rather tyrannical in their own families. It may be the natural reaction working.[35]

It tends to contradict the novelist's opinion expressed to John Bowen earlier. She seems to think that the persons who grab power or are given power, may be corrupted by that very power and they tend to misuse it. But the others who are victimized, do not want to retaliate by becoming tyrants. So power corrupts only those who are invested with it and not those victimized by it.

However, it cannot be categorically said that tyranny does not breed tyranny. Traces of tyranny in seed form are visible in some children like Chilton (*Daughters and Sons*), Nevin (*Patents and Children*), Lavinia (*The Mighty and Their Fall*), Verena (*A Father and His Fate*), and Justine (*A Family and a Fortune*). It can also be argued that victims, when they gain power in due course of time, may not like to persecute and wield power over others. One may hope that the formidable parental tyranny will not recur and persist. What is certain is that tyranny distorts and warps innocence and leads to unnatural reactions. Certainly victims are corroded by the misuse of power. So it has to be agreed that power is corrupting and that her characters suffer a kind of moral corruption. Even if it is natural, still tyrannizing is repugnant and must be condemned.

Barring cruel and selfish tyrants, possessive tyrants like Sophia, Harriet, Sabine, Miranda and Eliza Heriot are oppressive only because of their love for their families. The nagging Bentley (*Pastors and Masters*) does not consider himself a tyrant and thinks that what all he does is only for their good.

> And now, because I try to keep a wise and firm hand over people for their own good, and to prevent them from sinking down, down, down, for their own sakes—whose, if not for theirs, I should like to know?—to be given as much to bear as if I were a tyrant and a monument of selfishness, instead of. . . . (*PM*, 84-85)

Eliza Heriot thinks that her tyranny is for the benefit of all "I am a tyrant, because I order the house for the good of us all." (*LF*, 32) Eleanor and Harriet are highly ambitious regarding their children and they nag them only out of fear that their hopes may not be realized.

Though Ivy Compton-Burnett sympathizes with her tyrants and endows them with some touches of goodness or fineness, readers cannot be blind to their darker side and do not therefore completely exonerate them. Still it is astonishing to see that "the tyrants are never punished; they are feted."[36] Readers may desire for just retribution to fall on the unjust. But no tyrant is punished for his or her misdeeds. Josephine suffers no legal retribution for her killing of Ruth. Matty is not punished for her ruthless act of driving away Miss Griffin. The callous Anna drives Jessica to suicide, marries her son and enjoys her money. Nothing distasteful comes her way by way of punishment.

This is so because Ivy Compton-Burnett does not believe that evil is punished in this world. She says, "I don't think guilty people meet punishment in life."[37] In an interview with her friemd, M. Jourdain, she says that misbehaviour may meet with little retribution, sometimes it will not even be recognized: "*The New Statesman* wanted wickedness to be punished, but my point is that it is not punished, and that is why it is natural to be guilty of it. When it is likely to be punished, most of us avoid it."[38]

One of the rare cases of punishment being meted out to the guilty is that of Lady Haslam who is killed by her son Mathew who in turn, commits greater sin than his mother did. His own punishment begins with losing the very object with which he committed matricide.

Verena (*A Father and His Fate*), who is wicked suffers and does not escape punishment. Ridley (*Parents and Children*) also cannot achieve his intention of marrying Eleanor. This kind of atonement for evil-doing is rare to find.

It is observed in almost all her novels that though tyranny casts its gloomy shadows on the home, it is not triumphant at the end. The tyrants who have reigned supreme like Sophia, Harriet, Sabine, aunt Sukey, Miranda and Cassius even before their death and Hetta before her marriage, have certainly become weak and ineffective losing much control over the children. Other tyrant-monarchs like Josephine, Matty, Horace, Duncan, Miles, Simon, Hereward and Eliza Heriot, though continue to have grip over the family, have certainly lost effective control over the families and are not as powerful in the end as in the beginning. The unbearable torments of power are no more to be experienced.

Power and tyranny appear to form a vicious circle in Ivy Compton-Burnett's novels. Power gives rise to tyranny; the tyrant looks for more of power. A vague pattern emerges out of her portrayal of these evil aspects, the last novel of hers, *The Last and the First*, striking a proper balance between the two. Power is both used and abused; a perfect balance is struck between self-defence and self-sacrifice. Hermia represents this balance which the novelist arrived at towards the close of her creative career. Power is safe in her hands as she is endowed with intelligence and generosity. Money to her is a source of benign influence over the others, and meant to use wisely. Hermia practises it and guides the family's destiny in the proper direction.

Ivy Compton-Burnett had shown the misuse of tyrannical power in her earlier novels, always detrimental to family interests. Hermia is the great discovery, acting as the novelist's spokesman, proving that power and wealth need not corrupt if handled with maturity and wisdom.

Ivy Compton-Burnett's analysis of tyranny as the most dominant human impulse is highly original and powerful. She has presented this repugnant aspect of human character with unique moral courage resisting the normal temptation to idealize one's favourite heroes and heroines. The novelist's handling of personal relationships within the confines of the family is again unlike that of any predecessor or contemporary. Normal and abnormal relationships including several forms of perversions are introduced in her works with masterly confidence characteristic of Ivy Compton-Burnett.

NOTES

1. Brenda M. Hoggett, "Parents and Children," *Social Work and Law* (London: Sweet and Maxwell, 1977), p. 6.

2. Lotus Snow, "Good is Bad Condensed," *Western Humanities Review,* 10 (1955), p. 275.
3. V. Ramakrishna Rao, *Ivy Compton-Burnett: A Critical Study* (Waltair: Andhra University, 1974), p. xx.
4. Miriam Allott, "The Ethics of the Novel," *The Novelists on the Novel* (London: Routledge and Kegan Paul, 1959), p. 180.
5. Snow, p. 271.
6. Mario Praz, "The Novels of Ivy Compton-Burnett," ed. Charles Burkhart, *The Art of I. Compton-Burnett* (London: Victor Gollancz, 1972), p. 125.
7. G.S. Fraser, *The Modern Writer and His World* (Penguin, 1967), p. 151.
8. "I Compton-Burnett and M. Jourdain: A Conversation," *The Art,* p. 28.
9. Walter Allen, *Tradition and Dream* (London: Phoenix, 1964), p. 188.
10. Allen, p. 189.
11. Stanley B. Greenfield, "*Pastors and Masters:* The Spoils of Genius," *Criticism,* 2:1 (1960), pp. 68-69.
12. Rabindra Nath Sarkar, *Ivy Compton-Burnett: A Trend in English Fiction* (Calcutta: Firma KLM, 1979), p. 152.
13. Pamela Hansford Johnson, *I. Compton-Burnett* (London: Longmans, 1951), p. 23.
14. Charles Burkhart, "I. Compton-Burnett: The Shape of Career," *The Art,* p. 162.
15. Robert Liddell, *The Novels of I. Compton-Burnett* (London: Victor Gollancz, 1955), p. 26.
16. *Ibid.,* pp. 26-27.
17. Burkhart, *I. Compton,* p. 165.
18. Johnson, p. 14
19. Christopher Gillie, *Movements in English Literature 1900-1940* (London: C.U.P. 1975), p. 110.
20. Liddell, p. 26.
21. Charles Burkhart, "A Critical Epilogue," in I. Compton-Burnett, *The Last and the First* (London: Victor Gollancz), p. 153.
22. Violet Powell, *A Compton-Burnett Compendium* (London: Heinemann, 1973), p. 162.
23. *Ibid.,* p. 231.
24. R. Glynn Grylls, *I. Compton-Burnett* (London: Longman, 1971), p. 9.
25. Burkhart, *A Critical,* p. 153.
26. Johnson, p. 29.

27. J. Bhagyalakshmi, *Ivy Compton-Burnett and Her Art* (Delhi: Mittal, 1986), p. 79.
28. Powell, *A Compton,* p. 77.
29. *Ibid.,* p. 26.
30. Liddell, p. 28.
31. Elizabeth Sprigge, *The Life of Ivy Compton-Burnett* (London: Victor Gollancz, 1973), p. 82.
32. Michael Millgate, "Interview with Miss Compton-Burnett," *Review of English Literature,* 3:4 (1962), p. 106.
33. Robert Liddell, qtd. in Hilary Spurling, *Secrets of a Woman's Heart* (London: Penguin, 1984), p. 154.
34. John Bowen, "An Interview with Ivy Compton-Burnett," *Twentieth Century Literature,* 25:2 (1979), p. 169.
35. Millgate, *Review,* p. 110.
36. "An Extra Grudge against Life," Rev. of *A God and His Gifts, Time,* 83 (1964), p. 100.
37. Millgate, *Review,* p. 108.
38. Burkhart, *The Art,* p. 30.

Personal Relationships: I

Referring to women writers and their difference from men writers, Edward Sackville-West observes: "Gifted with rapidity, the female intelligence is far less given to pedantry and sententiousness. Its characteristic weapons are the adroit phrase, the cunning sentence, the startling yet homely image, the eye which pierces to the heart of a complex personal relationship, and a refreshing freedom from those political obsessions which nag and distort the visions of men."[1] Ivy's contribution in this respect is unparalleled. She has written domestic novels which are quite unlike those of her predecessors in the field on this specific point. She concentrates on the ugly, exposing the lowest in a human heart. It is with a surgeon's dexterity and a psychologists's precision that she delves deep into the heart of ordinary men and women and lays her finger correctly on the weakness with tragic potential almost matching the classical Greek themes. An analysis of the nature of the relationships she handles will substantiate the unique method she has adopted.

Domestic fiction must necessarily handle the exploration of personal relationship within the confines of the family, in a realm exclusively meant for the manifestations of varying degrees of affection, love and intimacy leading to intense and complex emotional attachments. Ironically true is the fact that a family harbours within the framework, though not always very conspicuously, negative passions such as jealousy, greed, hatred, selfishness and indifference.

Describing the atmosphere in her novels, almost invariably suffocating the same way, Pamela Hansford Johnson refers to her characters as 'captives' in the world of the novelist's creation: "the atmosphere of her monstrous world is indeed wonderful and terrifying. The light is opaque, the air enervating. The predominant colours, were we told about them, would be the dark, blood-brown of mahogany, the Crimson of damask, the tallow-cream of faces shut away from the day or nipped with cold, and the blacks, sienas, purples, drabs, and sad-greens of clothing high to the neck and low to the ankles. It is almost a subterranean world, with the figures of men and women and captive servants and children feeling their cautious way through the semi-darkness."[2] In such an atmosphere where figures have to "feel their way" in the opaque lighting, the characters' relations among themselves are bound to be far from what is considered natural and normal. In fact, a detailed thematic analysis of her novels would reveal that though there is very little that is highly abnormal or unnatural, the same is the case with the simple, direct and ordinary.

Ivy Compton-Burnett's 'homes' are very exclusive in the sense that they exclude several normal aspects of family life, both in inter-personal relationships and in their social relationships. Even the characters are strictly limited in several ways. In the negative sense, the exclusion of such factors makes her novels "pure" as Robert Liddell terms them, thus facilitating the novelist to turn inwards and look into the minds of the characters within their highly circumscribed fields of action.

Her characters, men and women alike, never appear to have ambitions of any sort, either professional or of any nature other than the desire for more and more of money. The doctors, lawyers and writers she has introduced such as Christian Stace, Doctor Spong, Hereward Egerton and John Ponsonby are never seen to be thinking of their respective careers at all, or to be desirous of achieving professional excellence. The professions happen to be mentioned; very little else is added to testify to the degree of the characters' commitment to the fields of their choice. Quest in standards is never there; the quest is only for money. The men and women appear to have no specific purpose at all in their lives—no goal, no target except clinging on to their families with the maximum money and the power that goes with it. Existence seems to be the sole motto—the more the money, the merrier. The end is sure to justify the means of getting it.

Against such a background, considering the fact that Ivy Compton-Burnett has "turned the Victorian novel inside out," the relationships within the family as analyzed by her forms the major perspective to her novels. All the same, this proposition is not simple as almost every relationship has a touch of something rare about it. Ivy Compton-Burnett's character have no friends outside their family circles. There is so little in terms of social contact that the concept of 'family' shrinks to the smallest and the most limited area offering itself to the novelist for minute scrutiny.

A review in the *Times Literary Supplement* compliments Ivy Compton-Burnett for not having committed an omission which earlier novelists have been guilty of, that of having "ignored and tangled roots of life." The reviewer defines home as "that small community shut in together from infancy into domestic turbulence, domestic adventure, domestic feuds, alliances, jests, affections, jealousies, resentments, devotions, hostilities, unkindness, despairs—that intimidating trinity of parents and children on which life is built."[3]

"This intimidating trinity" appears repeatedly in the novels in minor variations. The inter-relationships are almost always similar. Genuine affection and attachment are rare. The tyrants apart, the other characters portrayed by the novelist are rather colourless. There is no feeling which is intense or conspicuous; life is dull and monotonous, punctuated only by the selfish actions aimed at selfish attainments of different sorts. Pamela H. Johnson describes this atmosphere: "Apart from the Monsters, Miss Compton-Burnett's people are neither good nor bad; they are horribly human—that is, they exemplify the real horror of human frailty, which men and women shrink from when they perceive it in themselves."[4]

"The real horror of human frailty" manifests itself in varying degrees in the novelist's characters. An attempt to analyze the personal relationships will prove that they can be classified broadly into what may be termed 'normal,' and the abounding cases of relationships verging on or actually straying into the abnormal or the perverted.

Even the first category including a study of the normal day-to-day life in Ivy Compton-Burnett's novels will testify to the novelist's interest in looking at the negative side of domestic life. Domestic novel in English has unquestionably been enriched by the moral courage with which she has portrayed the unconventional and the unpleasant, instead of glorifying the virtues in hackneyed expressions.

The husband-wife relationship apart, the other relations deserve a thorough analysis. Marital relations as well as several kinds of abnormal or perverted relations with sexual overtones deserve a separate study. The most basic among relationships is that between parents and children. Even here, Ivy shows her characteristic tendency to be different from others, though she begins with cases which are apparently normal.

Jenni Calder, in her study "Women and Marriage in Victorian Fiction," explains the general attitude towards children during the period under survey:

> Indulgence, it was emphasized, could lead to a loss of respect by children of their parents: you should teach your children that they must always obey you; that your word must never be questioned; your commands never neglected. . . . Break their wills betimes. Begin this work before they can run alone, before they can speak plain, perhaps before they can speak at all. Whatever pains it

> costs, break the will if you would not damn the child. . . . Let a child from a year-old be taught to fear the rod and to cry softly; from that age make him do as he is bid, if you whip him ten times running to effect it. . . . Break his will now, and his soul shall live, and he will probably bless you to all eternity.[5]

It is this breaking of the child's will that one always confronts with in Ivy Compton-Burnett's novels in different contexts, and in different forms; but the principle is the same.

Generation gap is an expression that connotes a wide gulf between the young and the old in respect of aspirations, expectations, values, standards, ideologies and dreams. Conflict between the generations is assumed to be usual, but not inevitable. However, in Ivy Compton-Burnett's families, it is unmistakably present, though in varying degrees.

The young are conscious of their generational differences. Justine (*A Family and a Fortune*) tells thus: "It sounds as if you suffer from a lack of companionship. We can't skip a generation and become your contemporaries." (*FF*, 29)

A sea-change in the system of education brought about by the Education Act of 1870 was followed by the Balfour's Education Act of 1902, which heralded the dawn of a new era. The progressive outlook in the religious ideas and beliefs during the reigns of Queen Victoria and of Edward VII ushered in a spiritual revolution leading to radical changes in English life. Below the static, methodical surface, there came to be a conflict between two philosophies of life, the old, ritualistic order and the new, emerging order. The development of a democratic outlook and a craving for greater rights and privileges among the people inspired them to depart from the old order. The new order originated from the materialistic, pragmatic ideas which have played a major role in the composition of the modern world. The foundation of belief in the established order and ideas was clearly shaken. In 1830, Lyell's *Principles of Geology* had undermined the authority of the Bible. In 1859, Charles Darwin's *Origin of Species* gave strong, new evidence for skepticism. Along with this, the theories of the naturalists and biologists such as Wallace, Huxley and Galton were equally staggering as they found in evolution "the key of the universe, asserting that protoplasm was the basis of all life, and explaining the origin of all diversity, from a shell-fish to Shakespeare by accidental natural selection."[6] In the 1860s, the battle between orthodox theology and aggressive, scientific materialism began and forces hostile to the established order in things religious and secular were let loose. The ordinary man who believed in Christ and yet found it difficult not to believe in science was in a dilemma. He pined for a radical, drastic and overall change in the whole gamut of values—social, moral, ethical and economic.

When Grant Edgeworth receives a scientific work as a Christmas gift, maybe a treatise on evolution in the year 1885, his uncle, Duncan, contemptuously throws it on the fire, considering it to be repugnant to the faith of the day.

The shift from authority to individuality and from faith to reason is reflected in almost all Ivy Compton-Burnett's families, but more markedly in Rev. Bentley's (*Pastors and Masters*) children, Harry and John, both at school and at home.

Non-parental domination, that of aunts and of grandparents, finds a place in six novels. But uncles are never portrayed as tyrants. The only novel which is conspicuously bereft of any such domination is *Two Worlds and Their Ways*. *The Mighty and Their Fall* stands out as an exception where more than one, other than parents, display tyrannical behaviour—Selina, the grandmother, her son Ninian and also her granddaughter, Lavinia. In all the other ten of her last novels, such domination by persons other than parents is not to be found. In the first ten of her novels, women dominate the homes whether it be as mothers or aunts or grand-mothers. In the last ten novels, mostly men play role.

In the first category, there are the old-fashioned, dominating, oppressive, egotistic and intolerant parents. Bentley (*Pastors and Masters*), Andrew (*Brothers and Sisters*), Duncan (*A House and Its Head*), Horace (*Manservant and Maidservant*), Cassius (*The Present and the Past*), Miles (*A Father and His Fate*), Simon (*A Heritage and Its History*), Ninian (*The Mighty and Their Fall*) and Hereward (*A God and His Gifts*) are fathers of that kind. Sophia (*Brothers and Sisters*), Harriet (*Men and Women*), Miranda (*Mother and Son*), and Eliza Heriot (*The Last and the First*) are mothers in that line. Sir Jesse Sullivan (*Parents and Children*) is the only grandfather whereas Sabine Ponsonby (*Daughters and Sons*), Regan (*Parents and Children*) and Selina Middleton (*The Mighty and Their Fall*) are grandmothers known for their harsh treatment of their grandchildren. Among the fathers, Horace Lamb is singled out for his inhuman, miserly treatment of his children. Bentley (*Pastors and Masters*) charges his children for insubordination, negligence of duty and ingratitude. The children, in their turn, dislike him for his nagging despotism. Andrew's (*Brothers and Sisters*) insistence on complying with his order prohibiting marriage between Sophia and Christian without explaining the reasons therefore is responsible for the whole tragedy. The other tyrant fathers—Duncan, Cassius, Miles, Simon, Ninian, Hereward—treat the children harshly. Cassius is emotionally distanced from his children, particularly the two sons by his divorced wife, as they feel that their father does not love them.

The scene in *Elders and Betters* where the delightful couple of children Julius and Dora Calderon practise their own private religion is revealing in several ways. It helps in an understanding of children's mind against the background where they have been almost ignored by the elders, especially after the death of their mother and aunt. More important is the fact that it reveals the children's understanding of what adulthood means:

> O great and good and powerful god, Chung, grant that our life may not remain clouded, as it is at this present. . . . For although we would have freedom, if it be thy will, yet would we be worthy of being our mother's children. And if there is danger of our inheriting the weaknesses of our mother and aunt, thy late handmaids, guard us from them, O god, and grant that we may live to a ripe old age. For it would not be worth while to suffer the trials of childhood, if they were not lead to fullness of days. And we pray thee to comfort our father and our brother and sister; and if they are in less need of comfort than beseems them, pardon them, O god, and lead them to know the elevation of true grief. (*EB*, 191)

Their reference to "the trials of childhood" is moving in its sincerity and directness. Then understanding of the adults' problems also is quite revealing, in spite of the touches of precocity which can be discerned in their prayer. Every child in Ivy Compton-Burnett's novels has to experience the 'trials.'

The conflicts between parents and children assume greater proportions in the houses of Ninian, Simon, Miles and Hereward, not merely because of tyranny but also due to other factors like attempted bigamy of Miles, the second marriage of Duncan, and, in the case of Ninian, his second marriage and his determined pursuit after his daughter's inherited fortune. Simon's attempt to prevent his daughter's marriage and Hereward's affairs with his sons' fiancees contribute to the friction in no small measure. Duncan stands out among them as the one who is consistent in his affection for his children. He is so kind towards his daughter, Sibyl, that he pardons all her misdeeds including the plot engineered by her for the murder of the infant-heir in the family. With all that, there has been estrangement between himself and his children because of his authorization approach and ideological incompatibility.

In contrast to this all-tyrannical mothers—Sophia (*Brothers and Sisters*), Harriet (*Men and Wives*), Miranda (*Mother and Son*), and Eliza Hariot (*The Last and the First*)—and even grandmothers—Selina (*The*

Mighty and Their Fall) and Sabine (*Daughters and Sons*)—have, despite their dominating disposition, bountiful love and affection for their children and grandchildren. Even the stepmother, Eliza Heriot, far from being a heartless woman, stoops to reconcile with her step-daughter, Hermia.

In spite of all the love bestowed by these tyrant mothers, parting of ways between them and their children becomes inevitable. The mothers' expectation of their children and the children's resistance to oblige leads to friction in their relationships.

Harriet Haslam (*Men and Wives*) strongly disapproves of her doctor son, Mathew, taking to research instead of practising in deference to his wish. Even her other son, Jermyn, wishes to write creatively rather than to choose useful academic career. She disapproves of her daughter, Griselda, taking a warm interest in the Reverend Gervase Bellamy, and not in a man of her choice. Harriet's attempt to exercise tyrannical control over her children and her frenzied opposition to their desires is the root cause of conflict between them. They find their mother's demands too ambitious. It irritates them when they are commanded to meekly submit to the whims and fancies of their elders thus denying themselves any say in shaping their own lives.

Sophia (*Brothers and Sisters*) gets more and more estranged from her children by continually teasing them for not fulfilling to her satisfaction the very excessive demands she makes on them as regards their behaviour. On the day of her husband's funeral, at the dining table, she tells her children that she would limit her meal to just a glass of wine and then carries on a nagging dialogue thus:

> I don't know whether you all like sitting there, having your dinner, with your mother eating nothing? On this day of all days! I don't know if you have thought of it. . . . I don't think I should be left without a little pressing today, sitting here, as I am with my life emptied. (*BS*, 158)

Life becomes intolerable for the children like Justine (*A Family and a Fortune*) and Lavinia (*The Mighty and Their Fall*) whose widower fathers, tyrants or otherwise, remarry and bring hostile stepmothers into the house. Usually the new wife hates anything that reminds her of the husband's first marriage. Hermia (*The Last and the First*), daughter of Sir Robert Heriot through his marriage is condemned to a neglected upbringing. She is forbidden to make any reference to her early childhood without inviting her stepmother's wrath. Thirteen-year-old Fabian Clare in *The Present and the Past* is sad and depressed as his childhood is overshadowed by his father's second marriage.

The parents try to nip literary instincts in the children in the bud. In *A God and His Gifts*, Hereward Egerton does not like the idea of his son becoming a writer like him fearing that he might overtake him. Harriet Haslam is dead against her son, Jermyn's desire to write creatively rather than to seek an academic career of usefulness. France's (*Daughters and Sons*) creative work appears to be rubbish to her grandmother, Sabine. However, as it is not an expensive hobby, she does not want to interfere. "We will leave her . . . as it costs us nothing. . . . We will leave her to waste her time in her own way." (*DS*, 48) The children are naturally frustrated because their dreams do not come true and their ambitions are not realized. They are discouraged and humiliated in every way. The Stace children (*Brothers and Sisters*) are slaves to their mother, Sophia, who demands their attention. Children generally do have freedom of thought, but are denied freedom of expression. This restriction tends to hamper their mental growth.

Because of the enforcement of strict discipline in the children in the house, they cannot mix with the children of other families. In *Darkness and Day*, Rose and Viola give the impression of strangeness and aloofness. Viola tells later: "The children said we were different from them." (*DD*, 79) In the presence of guests, children remain shy and nervous. Muriel Ponsonby (*Daughters and Sons*) remains dumb or giggles excessively. Hilary Spurling says: "outbursts of nervous laughter, sharply checked in the presence of adults and exploding in hysterical reaction behind their backs, come again and again in I. Compton-Burnett's accounts of children subjected to emotional pressure beyond their bearing. It was a form of release."[7]

These possessive mother-tyrants treat their children as their tools totally suppressing their individuality. In contrast, however, no father-tyrant depicted by Ivy Compton-Burnett is so possessive of his children. The mother does not accept that a child has his own ideas and if ever a child tends to be independent, she feels hurt and accuses the child of being ungrateful. Parental possessiveness almost certainly disrupts parent-child relationships. As independence, one of the basic needs of childhood, is denied, friction develops and the child feels let down and inhibited. Still he fails to muster necessary courage to openly rebel to gain the independence he badly needs as in the case of Rosebery (*Mother and Son*), Robin, Dinah and Andrew (*Brothers and Sisters*). When placed in a similar helpless situation, Matthew, among the children of Harriet (*Men and Women*), goes to the extent of secretly planning and succeeding in murdering his mother.

Some parents think that it is their solemn duty to pass on what they consider as the cultural heritage of their family to their children. In doing so, they impose their will on their unreceptive children instead of seeking to influence them by subtler and more affectionate methods. The children treat this as an affront and feel justified in expressing open resentment.

A clear-cut split occurs in some families, like the Lambs (*Manservant and Maidservant*) where the hostility between the father and the children assumes such dangerous proportions that the children stoop to plot their father's death. In the Egerton home, (*A God and His Gifts*), Hereward's sons hate their father for his seduction of daughter-in-law. Here a serious and real conflict of interest rather than mutual misunderstanding is found. Merton, Hereward's son, says: "This is the last time that I speak of him as my father, to him as another man. Henceforth to the end of our lives there will be silence between us." (*GG*, 118)

Among the non-tyrant parents, two categories are found, those who are indifferent albeit affectionate and those who are affectionate and loving. They are so deeply engrossed in their own affairs that they are unable to show concern for their children. They are both indifferent and negligent about them. They do not take steps to protect the children against the insults and torture from other tyrannical elders in the house.

John Ponsonby (*Daughters and Sons*), father of motherless children, is deeply involved in his literary career as a novelist and so he completely ignores his responsibility for the children. He is helped by his sister, Hetta, who keeps them at a safe distance from their father. They reel under his mother, Sabine and sister, Hetta. But he never attempts to protect them from their wrath and fury. It is only after his marriage with Edith Hallam that he understands the situation and endeavours to do something for his wife and children. However, he is more concerned about his wife than his children. The moment Hetta is made ineffective and powerless, the children are automatically relieved of oppression. He is obsessively jealous of the literary excellence of his daughter, France. Though impressed by her novel, he demurs acknowledging its merits fearing that the already dwindling sales of his works might decline further by the advent of a fresh, young writer from the same family. Though he has no great affection, he gives his children freedom. But his aloofness is not because of his faith in their maturity, but because of utter lack of interest in their affairs.

Christian (*Brothers and Sisters*) can be cited as another indifferent father as regards his children. His "health overstrained by his medical work, has never turned his mind to consider the burden that his wife lays on their children."[8] He has neither love nor hatred for his children.

Eleanor Sullivan's (*Parents and Children*) children consider their mother to be lacking in maternal instincts. Burkhart says: "Eleanor's maternity is less positive. In fact, her lack of gift for the role is commented on by her children, constantly in her presence and unfailingly when she has left a room."[9] She hates living with her tyrannical parents-in-law and a new home with Ridley promises the freedom and happiness she yearns for. So she is prepared to leave all her nine children, about whom she has been indifferent, and go to Ridley with the intention of marrying him.

Edmund and Bridget (*Darkness and Day*) have no patience or time to spare for the children as they are deeply preoccupied with their own problems. Children receive more affection from the servants than from their parents.

Edgar (*A Family and a Fortune*) too lacks affection for his children.

> Edgar did not love his children, though he believed or rather assumed that he did, and meted out kindness and interest in fair measure. . . . Justine believed that she was her father's darling, and Edgar, viewing the belief with an outsider's eye, welcomed it, feeling that it ought to be a true one, and made intermittent effort to give it support. (*FF*, 75)

He is tolerant to Justine's attentions in her own self-conceived role as his darling daughter. Though Dudley, his brother, accuses him of his indifference towards his children, "you do not care for your children," (*FF*, 236) he is a shade better in his relationship with his children when compared to others totally neglecting them.

Ada (*A God and His Gifts*), like Edmund and Bridget, is always immersed in her own problems. She suffers from her husband's negligence and incestuous adultery. But, on the whole, she displays a little concern for her children and is not totally indifferent. Godfrey Haslam (*Men and Wives*) appears to be loving his daughter, Griselda, though not his sons. He is indifferent to their problems, but does not neglect them altogether. Julius (*Mother and Son*) is indifferent to Rosebery, his son, maybe due to the fact that his wife deliberately keeps him at a distance from him. All the same, he is affectionate towards his illegitimate children.

Benjamin Donne (*Elders and Betters*) does not love his children at all. He has no concern for anyone other than his sisters. He is quite indifferent to their needs and problems.

Some fathers appear to be lacking in or afraid of showing love towards the children of their first wives like Robert Heriot (*The Last *and the First*) and Sir Roderick (*Two Worlds and Their Ways*). The children feel neglected and friction develops between them. When there is no love, these children decline to show respect to discriminating parental authority. Though these negligent parents are not dominating and oppressive, no amicable or cordial relationship subsists between them and their children. Their cold indifference is reciprocated by the children in the same manner. Anna Donne (*Elders and Betters*), after the shock of Sukey's death, shows some concern for her father, asks him to rest as a precautionary measure against any threat to his life. Benjamin is gratified to learn that his child does not desire his death and shows concern for him. However, going by her nature, Anna might even have expedited such an event, namely her father's death, if only it had suited her purpose and its detection was unlikely. However, all daughters are not wanting in affection towards their parents. France (*Daughters and Sons*), the novelist-daughter, wants to help her novelist-father, John Ponsonby, when his popularity is waning. When he is in need of money, she sends two thousand pounds of prize money for her novel, in two instalments, as from one of his admirers. In order not to hurt his feelings, she prefers to remain anonymous.

Affectionate and generous parents constitute the other category. Far from dominating, they readily accept their responsibilities and never do anything that leads to a conflict. Their love for their children is spontaneous and unconditional.

The ideal mother is found in Charlotte Lamb (*Manservant and Maidservant*). She is understanding and considerate and not restrictive. However, hers is not blind love as she can make her children distinguish between the right and the wrong. She is always willing to make any sacrifice and to do what all she can for the sake of her children. Her decision to leave the house with her husband's cousin, Mortimer Lamb, taking her children along with her is to insulate them from the miserly despotism of their father, Horace. But the moment Horace appears reformed, she stays back since her sole concern is the welfare of her children and not sharing her life with Mortimer. She provides a striking contrast to the selfish Eleanor Sullivan (*Parents and Children*) whose main concern is to marry Ridley and be happy, ignoring the plight of her supposed-to-be fatherless nine children in the house ruled by the dominating grandparents.

Blanche (*A Family and a Fortune*) provides an example of a loving mother. Like Charlotte, she is not able to protect her children as she herself is placed in a helpless position by her husband. She loves all her children. But her love for Mark and Aubrey is more than for Clement. An exemplary relationship subsists between her and her only daughter,

Justine.

Just like Blanche, Ellen (*A House and Its Head*) is another neglected wife. She is loving and sacrificing, but is not protective as she has herself no means and strength. Though she loves both her daughters, she shows an edge in favour of Nance, her elder daughter.

Jessica (*Elders and Betters*) is an ideal example of selfless and sacrificial mother. In spite of the popular belief in the superstition that the last of the thirteen to sit down at a party dinner would die, Jessica volunteers to do that very thing and thus demonstrates her innate good nature. When the monstrous Anna Donne tells her that her children hate her, the credulous and innocent Jessica commits suicide. She loves all her children uniformly though she seems to have a special liking for her eldest son, Terence.

Julia and Fanny (*A Heritage and Its History*), Flavia and Catharine (*The Present and the Past*) may also be included in this category as they are sympathetic, undemanding and kind towards their children. Fulbert (*Parents and Children*) loves his nine children, but is partially inclined towards his daughter, Isabel. Maria and Roderick Shelley (*Two Worlds and Their Ways*) are the doting parents of their children, Clemence and Sefton. Maria's excessive maternal love, her passion that her children should be highly successful and excel all others, make things miserable for the children. Jonathan Swift (*More Women than Men*) loves his son Gabriel. He does not want his son to be ruined like him and so begs Bacon to leave him alone and not to make him a homosexual.

Children reciprocate parents' feelings and affection. Charlotte's children look upon her as their saviour and protector. Justine shows great love and care for her mother, Blanche. Nance shows consideration and understanding for her mother. However, Sibyl, her sister, fawns on her father as he is powerful and despises her mother for her meek submission to his callousness. The Shelley children are aware of their parents' love and hopes and they try to make them happy by hook or crook.

A sort of synthesis between the old and the new is discernible here. The parents are enlightened. They accept the right of the young to be free. But they are not unmindful of their needs. They are still friendly and loving and willing to make sacrifices for them. The children, in their turn, respond with a sense of gratefulness and love. This is a constructive approach that the novels present concerning the institution of family.

Children too can be classified into three categories. There are those, though a few in number, who fawn on their parents to achieve their ends and also to escape from tyrannical oppression. There are others who are meek and docile. They allow their dreams to be shattered unceremoniously under the subjugation of the parents who are unsympathetic to them. Rosebery (*Mother and Son*) takes generous lumps of sugar in his tea just because he does not have a heart to hurt his mother who wants him to take that much of sugar. Sophia's children criticize her and refer to her by name as Sophia in her absence. Almost all the children conspire and talk freely at the backs of their parents. They develop a negative attitude and it results in constant friction. But that never develops into open rebellion.

There are yet others who adopt an attitude of complete defiance and open revolt against those who are out to mercilessly trample upon their aspirations. They develop critical outlook, thanks to the influence of the new age. They display wit and intelligence. They do not hesitate to freely and openly criticize anything that is not to their liking. Though they are exploited and oppressed, though they are powerless and vulnerable, they do not meekly submit to tyranny hands down. The most oppressed child of all the Compton-Burnett families, Tamasin, son of Horace (*Manservant and Maidservant*), is assertive. "Let us keep our early privileges," he says. "No new ones seem to arise for us." (*MSMS*, 81) They do not tolerate suppression of individuality and exploitation. Isabel (*Parents and Children*), Hermia (*The Last and the First*), Clare (*Daughters and Sons*), Merton (*A God and His Gifts*) and Marcus (*Manservant and Maidservant*) are but a few examples of the kind.

However, children do not always seek revenge for the oppressive constraints imposed on them. "The trials of childhood naturally foster, at first by instinct, later from hard experience, the growth of reticence and caution."[10]

The Lamb children in *Manservant and Maidservant* drive pins into an effigy of their father to torture him and finally throw it into the fire. Their secret wish for their father's death is revealed by their not warning him when he is walking towards the bridge under repair. They repent later for what they have done. They are not criminals, but the emotional stress and strain they are forced to undergo in the name of strict discipline coupled with merciless miserliness is responsible for their callous behaviour. For them, even a stale cake is a luxury. Hiding beneath sofas or in doorways, like Rose in *Darkness and Day,* children become aware of everything that takes place in the house. Their comments upon their parents are based on their understanding of exactly what is happening around them.

When children rebel, they do so unitedly. When Thomas (*Elders and Betters*) comes to enquire into a fight between Dora and Julius, they promptly and firmly deny of any such thing though it is clear that Julius is bitten and scratched whereas his sister's hair is torn. Older children like Clare (*Daughters and Sons*) and Isabel (*Parents and Children*) protect their younger sisters and brothers from the tyranny of their elders. In spite of their general unhappiness due to oppression, in their own world, in their own innocence, in their own way, they try to be happy and cheerful.

Apart from parent-child relationships, emotional cross relationships between other elders and youngsters of the family provide interesting study. One such, which does not concern children directly, is the mother-in-law—daughter-in-law relationship.

Regan (*Parents and Children*) is one such mother-in-law who loves all the thirteen in the family—her husband, deceased son and daughter, surviving son, Fulbert, and his nine children—to the exclusion of Eleanor, the daughter-in-law. The reason offered is that she is not her blood relation. Though there is no love lost between them, Regan's attitude towards Eleanor is not one of hostility. She respects her and is even grateful to her for enriching the family with children. Summing up the relationship between the two women, Ivy Compton-Burnett says: "The two women lived in a formal accord, which had never come to dependence; and while each saw the other as a fellow and an equal, neither would have grieved at other's death." (*PC*, 14)

Amiability and cordiality mark the relationship between Julia and her daughter-in-law, Fanny, and Rhoda and her daughter-in-law, Marcia (*A Heritage and Its History*), Julia has to shift to her daughter-in-law's house as her son, Simon, is disinherited and is asked to set up a separate house. There they both get on smoothly. Rhoda too lives harmoniously with Marcia.

Joanna (*A God and His Gifts*) is affectionate towards her daughter-in-law, Ada, and the latter reciprocates her affection and even praises her for her impartiality. "Taking no sides, understanding everyone, condemning no one. Just there to help by being the whole of yourself." (*GG*, 47) Ada treats her own daughter-in-law, Hetty, with consideration and understanding.

Julia, Rhoda, Joanna and Ada are, by their nature, good and not of the demanding type. But Selina Lovat (*Darkness and Day*), Regan (*Parents and Children*), Eliza (*A Father and His Fate*), Sabine (*Daughters and Sons*) are proven tyrants in harassing the children. One would have expected them not to be different towards their daughters-in-law. But there is no evidence of a single instance of ill-treatment of daughter-in-law.

Contrary to what one would have expected from her nature, Selina Lovat is very kind and considerate towards the daughter-in-law, Bridget.

As a gesture of good-will and with a view of avoiding further complications, she casts into fire the photograph of Bridget's mother. In spite of her initial opposition to her son's marriage with Verena, once she becomes the daughter-in-law, Eliza refrains from hating or ill-treating her.

Sabina Ponsonby is all gratitude for her daughter-in-law, Edith Hallam, as she thinks mistakenly that she is the anonymous benefactor of the family financially. But the moment she comes to know the truth, she dies of shock. It is anybody's guess how she would have treated Edith after this revelation.

Generally mothers-in-law are said to display an attitude of suspicion, intolerance, narrow-mindedness, prejudice, hostility and even callousness towards their daughters-in-law. Contrary to this, in Ivy Compton-Burnett families, this kind of disharmony is conspicuous by its absence.

The relationship between stepmothers and their stepchildren is generally strained. The conversation between Sir Robert Hariot and his daughter by his first marriage, Hermia (*The Last and the First*), illustrates how they are resentful of each other.

> Sir Robert: No one would choose to have step-children.
> Hermia: And who would choose to have a stepmother? There was no choice for either of us there. (*LF*, 22-23)

The step-children who have a vivid recollection of their own mother will be fiercely hostile towards their new mother. They cannot forgive and reconcile with the usurpation and always bitterly resent even their stepmother's presence in the family. The eldest daughter, who feels dethroned and supplanted from the much-coveted role of the mistress of the family, will have special reasons to despise the stepmother. In the *Mighty and Their Fall*, Lavinia conceals a letter of acceptance from Teresa Chilton to marry her widowed father, with a view to preventing their marriage.

In *Two Worlds and Their Ways*, Maria, the second wife of Roderick Shelley, has no affection for her stepson, Oliver. His very existence is not relished by her. He is a constant reminder to her that her own son is blocked from the rights of succession. If she pretends to be a little generous towards him, it is only to cultivate her husband who seems to appreciate this particular trait in her.

There is marked hostility between Eliza Heriot and her stepchildren, Hermia and Madeleine. Eliza is constantly plagued by Hermia's rebellious behaviour. Complete rupture in their relationship surfaces with Hermia leaving the house after buying a partnership in a school. However, Hermia inheriting a fortune alters the situation. Her generosity in saving the family from financial ruin restores Eliza's affection for her.

Flavia is really a good stepmother for Fabian and Guy (*The Present and the Past*). She tries to be impartial between her own children and the step-children and the latter readily acknowledge this fact: "she has been the same to all of us." (*PP*, 107) The eleven-year-old Guy is particularly attached to Flavia and if he decides to go with Catharine, his real mother, it is with a heavy heart because he cannot bear the separation from his brother, Fabian, who prefers his real mother to stepmother. All the same, Fabian has no grievance against Flavia. He is unable to accept her as his mother, for he has not forgotten his own mother who left them when he was four years of age.

A sympathetic and loving stepmother is found in Edith Hallam for Ponsonby children (*Daughters and Sons*) and in Cassandra Jekyll (*A House and Its Head*) for the Edgeworths. Teresa Chilton (*The Mighty and Their Fall*), Maria Sloane (*A Family and a Fortune*) and Alison (*A House and Its Head*) do not come into limelight and therefore it is not possible to study their precise attitudes towards their step-children. Nevertheless, there are no instances to indicate that they are antagonistic or dominating.

It cannot therefore be said categorically that the relationship between stepmothers and step-children should always be strained. It can always be other way about.

How the aunts and their nephews or nieces react with each other is another important aspect of the family relationships between the elders and the youngsters.

Hetta (*Daughters and Sons*) has no love for her brother, John Ponsonby's motherless children. More so, she tries to keep the children at a distance from their father. Her hostile and tyrannical attitude is resented by the children. The sense of relief and happiness that the children exhibit even at the prospect of Hetta marrying and leaving the home for good shows the depth of their contempt for her. Similarly, the Gaveston children (*A Family and a Fortune*) hate their aunt, Matty, for her lack of love for them and for her attempts to dominate them. Justine, in particular, is outspoken in her accusations and revulsion. Sukey (*Elders and Betters*) is another aunt who is devoid of affection for her nephews and nieces. Yet she demands attention from them. She feigns affection to Anna Donne, her brother's daughter, with an ulterior motive and Anna also reciprocates but with a motive of her own. Finally it was Anna who succeeds in her deception.

Zillah (*A God and His Gifts*) is indifferent to her brother,

Hereward's children. Like Hetta, she is attached to her brother. But unlike her, she is not hostile to her nephews. At the same time, she does not show love and concern for them.

Jessica Calderon (*Elders and Betters*) stands out unique in the whole gallery of aunts in being affectionate and considerate. She continues to love Anna even after her treachery in taking away Sukey's money, which should otherwise have come to her, comes to be known.

Aunt Maria (*A House and Its Head*), the invalid sister of Duncan, is shadowy as she does not make her physical presence in the novel. What is learnt about her is through the conversation of others. She favours Sybil and leaves all her fortune to her. Sybil shows gratitude to her while Nance is indifferent.

Thus the relationship between aunts and their nephews and nieces is not always amiable. Intolerance, narrow-mindedness, prejudice, antagonism and callousness are reflected in the attitude of aunts towards the children.

When compared to aunts, uncles maintain warmer and more friendly relationship with their nephews and nieces.

Dudley (*A Family and a Fortune*) is kind and understanding. He loves his nephews and niece so much that he pledges almost his entire inherited fortune, £ 2000 a year, in allowances to them. They in turn love their uncle so much that when they come to know about his critical condition in a farm-house, they anxiously rush in there thus proving their love and affection for him. Like Dudley, Mortimer Lamb (*Manservant and Maidservant*) is a sacrificial and affectionate uncle for the Lamb children. He is so understanding of their problems and difficulties that he does not object to Charlotte's proposal to take her children along with them, when she accompanies him, leaving her husband. When Horace is reformed and Charlotte drops her plan of deserting her husband, Mortimer understandingly does not bother her about their original plan. He shares with the mother her concern and affection for the children. Gaunt (*Darkness and Day*) is also found to be good and affectionate.

Ranson (*The Mighty and Their Fall*), who makes his brief appearance in the story, is the rich uncle of the Middleton children. With his huge fortune, he sets up a house in the neighbourhood and gives refuge to Lavinia, who is under a cloud in her home. Thereafter, he makes her heiress to his fortune thereby making her independent. However, he does not extend his affection for the other children. Another uncle, Hugo, like Ranson, loves only Lavinia. When it is revealed later that he is not her own uncle, he proposes to marry Lavinia. Lavinia's grandmother, Selina, through her will, leaves Hugo a sum of money which will give him the independence he has never had and also an injunction to abstain from marrying Lavinia. He accepts Selina's condition. He seems to care more for his comfort than for Lavinia.

Two uncles in two generations are found in *A Heritage and Its History*. Sir Edwin Challoner, uncle to Simon and Walter, has amiable disposition and cordial relationship with his two nephews. But when Simon has an incestuous affair with his wife, Rhoda, resulting in the birth of a boy, the relationship gets strained and Sir Edwin seeks revenge by owning the child and disinheriting Simon. Walter, on the other hand, is consistently good to his nephews and niece. No uncle appears to be temperamentally hostile or antagonistic towards the nephews and nieces except perhaps, Benjamin Donne (*Elders and Betters*) who, though not callous, is certainly unfeeling and indifferent towards Terence, Tullia, Julius and Dora.

Another interesting relationship in the family is between grandparents and their grandchildren. Of all the elders in the family, grandparents, more particularly grandmothers are found to be sympathetic, understanding and affectionate towards the grandchildren.

Regan Sullivan (*Parents and Children*) loves all her nine grandchildren. The children are closer to their grandmother than to their mother Eleanor Sullivan. When Eleanor ignores the pleas of his son, Gawin, of having seen his supposedly dead father, it is only Regan who listens to him patiently and trusts him.

Selina Middleton (*The Mighty and Their Fall*), though a tyrant like Regan, loves her grandchildren. She enforces discipline only for the good of the children. Lavinia suppresses, out of jealousy, a letter written by Teresa to her father and Teresa thinks that she has been rejected. Expecting the grandmother, who is seriously ill, to die, Lavinia tries to show that Selina has committed this mean action. Though she suspects that it is Lavinia's stratagem, Selina allows matters to rest there. Her grandmotherly affection is far too stronger than her desire for self-vindication. That is why when Selina dies, her grandchildren call her 'the loving and beloved grandmother.'

Sabine Ponsonby (*Daughters and Sons*) is another grandmother who loves her motherless grandchildren. Herself a tyrant, she often lapses into leniency. Selina Lovat (*Darkness and Day*) and Julia (*A Heritage and Its History*) are also portrayed as loving grandmothers. Julia supports Naomi, her granddaughter, and pleads with his son to allow Naomi marry the man of her choice. Joanna (*A God and His Gifts*) is shown playing with her grandchildren. But when they grow up, Joanna's love for them gradually recedes, but it does not yield place to hatred or even indifference.

As between grandfathers and grandmothers, the latter appear to be more indulgent towards their grandchildren. Sir Jesse Sullivan (*Parents and Children*), Sir Michael (*A God and His Gifts*), Oliver (*A Family and a Fortune*), Mr. Clare (*The Present and the Past*), Mr. Firebrace (*Two Worlds and Their Ways*) have never been found to be particularly generous and kind towards the grandchildren.

Most of the parents do not have favourites among their children. Bentley (*Pastors and Masters*), Sophia and Christian (*Brothers and Sisters*), John Ponsonby (*Daughters and Sons*), Roderick and Maria (*Two Worlds and Their Ways*), Edmund and Bridget (*Darkness and Day*), Horace and Charlotte (*Manservant and Maidservant*), Cassius, Flavia and Catharine (*The Present and the Past*), Simon and Fanny (*A Heritage and Its History*), Miles (*A Father and His Fate*), Hereward (*A God and His Gifts*) and Eliza Heriot (*The Last and the First*) are parents who, irrespective of how they treat them, treat all the children alike, without any discrimination or predilection.

There is surprisingly not a single instance of enduring love and affection as between a father and a son.

Under the influence of Freud (1963) and Parsons (1968) certain characteristics are commonly assumed in family life like the powerful father, warm and close mother, adventurous son and the compliant daughter. Under the same assumption, it is usually believed that fathers have more influence on the ideology of their children than mothers and that daughters are more susceptible to parental influence than sons. However, in Compton-Burnett's families, there are exceptions like Sophia (*Brothers and Sisters*), Harriet (*Men and Women*), Miranda (*Mother and Son*), Eliza Heriot (*The Last and the First*) who are more powerful than the fathers. Even the non-tyrant mothers like Charlotte (*Manservant and Maidservant*), Blanche (*A Family and a Fortune*), Ellen (*A House and Its Head*), Jessica (*Elders and Betters*), and Maria Shelley (*Two Worlds and Their ways*) are quite influential without being authoritative. Similarly, sons and daughters are treated alike and the sex of the child is never a relevant variable for parental influence.

The divergence in the values held by parents as distinct from their children is a constant source of friction. Parental behaviour is often conditioned by their lineage and social status. Their authoritative approach provokes resentment in the children and the gap in their relationship goes on widening. By their impulsive eagerness to show up their unique identity and independence, the children tend to exaggerate the difference between themselves and their parents. The parents who are nostalgic about their own childhood values feel embittered when they find their children undermining such values with a sense of abandon. But it is not unlikely that when these children grow into a more stable developmental stage, their values and attitudes move closer to those of their parents.

Parent-child relationships are of an exceptionally enduring nature. The differences between them are but a transient phenomenon. Whether or not family members see eye to eye with each other, the basic ties remain undisturbed and they continue to live under the same roof. The youth rebel against many things which are inconsistent with their dreams and aspirations. But they do nothing to shake the very foundations of the unchallengeable superiority and supremacy of the older generation. They learn to put up with opposition, suppression, neglect and imposition. They are not merely torelant towards their parental attitudes and interests but, by and large, they veer round to show positive regard for them. Thus starting from other children of Sophia (*Brothers and Sisters*) to Hereward (*A God and His Gifts*), all love their parents despite weaknesses. The seemingly total breakdown of relationships does never materialize. Invariably, in all cases, there comes about a finale of enduring reconciliation between the parents and their children.

Pamela Hansford Johnson finds Ivy Compton-Burnett's portrayal of children as one of her greatest achievements: "Her children have the awful truth of angels, the awful crystalline gaze that stares eagle-like at the sun; it is their truth that protects them, an Armour delicate as eggshell and perdurable as quartz. They are always the conquerors, and this conception of them illustrates Miss Compton-Burnett's single optimistic streak, her belief in a sole aspect only of the triumph of light. They are terrible starers, these children of hers, by their deadly wisdom demolishing their elders into the dust of shame and foolishness."[11] The statement is in keeping with the Victorian attitudes towards children which were really conflicting. "Here, there is the attitude that all children were limbs of the devil, and only by breaking their will could they be saved. On the other hand, children were also seen as original innocents, and the mythology of childhood as it developed in the Victorian period reflects thus. In fact, what was usually demonstrated in the average middle-class family was a mixture of these two attitudes."[12]

The deadly angelic wisdom displayed by most of the children in Ivy Compton-Burnett's world is reminiscent of the portraits of children drawn by certain other masters of fiction. Jane Austen has never attempted to concentrate on the introduction of children in her novels; her purpose was different. The focal point in her world was the universal quest she noticed all around—that of eligible matrimonial alliances. Fanny Burney and Elizabeth Gaskell studied the pictures of domestic life, displaying special concern over the fate of women characters against the shifting values in the milieu which served as the background. Goldsmith's masterpiece *The Vicar of Wakefield* did not present young children; the theme demanded characters of a different nature. Dickens and Thackeray did deal with different aspects of family life, paying great attention to the delineation of children's character, sketching love among siblings in all its warmth and richness. This is made all the more sharp and conspicuous against the tyrannical attitude of the parents in general, especially in the novels of Dickens and Thackeray.

Dickens found authoritarianism as a great evil in society, and in biting satire expressed in his novels he attacks "not so much the patriarchal pyramid as the irresponsible exploitation of this system."[13] The sheer severity of Victorian parents, aggravated with a degree of sadism is illustrated by Dickens in a number of his novels. The character Murdstone in *David Copperfield* illustrates this principle, and turns out to be "savage in his absolutism." Dickens presented genuine affection between parents and children and brothers and sisters showing their love for one another, love which is calm, self-denying and enduring. Dicken's children had personalities and wills of their own. A very conspicuous feature of his novels is that the parentless children portrayed by him have strong wills and are able to cope with any situation. David Copperfield is a fine example.

Thackeray presents the failure on the part of the parents to understand their children or to recognize the need to accept their independent identity. When they show excessive care or concern, it proves to be destructive in effect because of the lack of proper understanding. *The Newcomes* illustrates this disaster in the clash between Colonel Newcome and his son Clive. In *Vanity Fair*, Mr. Osborne and his son are portrayed in a similar way.

Jenni Calder explains how paternalism which was at the roots of Victorian concept of family came to be challenged by novelists: "criticism of paternalism challenged not only the structure of the family but the structure of society also . . . it was never fully realized or explored as such until Samuel Butler wrote *The Way of All Flesh* in the last years of the century. But the germ was there in the writing of the Brontes, in the analysis of George Eliot, in the cutting exposures of Meredith."[14]

The Bronte sisters portrayed children being smothered under the tyranny of the elders, but trying their best to break themselves free from the yoke. But the emphasis has been on girls who had to bear the brunt with double force, due to the sheer fact that they happen to be girls. Little Jane in Charlotte Brontte's masterpiece, *Jane Eyre* revolts against oppression, and does not hesitate to express what she calls 'truth' to her aunt. She reminds her that she is longing for love and kindness, and makes it clear that the treatment meted out to her by Mrs. Reed cannot be justified. She expresses herself frankly in an impassioned outburst:

> I tried of the routine of eight years in one afternoon. I desired liberty; for liberty I gasped; for liberty I uttered a prayer; it seemed scattered on the wind then faintly blowing. I abandoned it and framed a humbler supplication; for change, stimulus; that petition, too, seemed swept off into vague space: "Then," I cried, half desperate, "grant me at least a new servitude!"[15]

It is the novelist who reverts to 'new servitude' as the best of the bad bargain in girl can hope to have in such a society. Emily Bronte's *Wuthering Heights* is the story of Catherine whose sufferings reach the level of frenzy when her personality is being submerged by the will of the domestic tyrant. Emily Bronte longed for the world far away from the oppressing atmosphere she experienced all around:

> The world within I doubly prize;
> Thy world, where guile, and hate, and doubt,
> And cold suspicion never rise;
> Where thou, and I, and Liberty,
> Have undisputed sovereignty.[16]

George Meredith's *The Ordeal of Richard Feverel*, autobiographical to a certain extent "may be viewed as a tragedy, or as a lyrical love-tale with a mournful ending, or as a satire on doctrinaire education."[17] It is the satirical aspect that is relevant to the present context, the novel dealing with the disastrous results of the highly original 'systems' of education forced on Richard Feverel by his father Sir Austin Feverel. The failure of his experiment affects the father. As Ernest Baker points out, "He might have called his first regular novel 'The Ordeal of Sir Austin Feverel,' for it is Richard's overwise father that is really on trial . . . who would in later days have been psycho-analyst, with his opinionated scheme based on the most advanced principles of eugenics; he, not Richard, is to blame for the disasters."[18] The novel is a study of the repercussions of a father's experiments with a new system of education tyrannically imposed on the son, ending in failure, both the father and the son suffering in the bargain.

Samuel Butler's *The Way of All Flesh*, candidly autobiographical, is a caustic satire on parental tyranny. The novel is not strictly confined to a study of individuals and their relationship. In spite of clear references to the social and political developments such as the Evangelical movement and the Church of England, and the emergence and the final fall of Napoleon at Waterloo, the emphasis placed on the domestic aspects is never missed. In fact, it stands out against such a background, making it a domestic novel in the complete, comprehensive sense taking the background also into reckoning. It is satirical in essence, the targets being parental authority and clerical discipline. The tyranny exercised by father on son is traced through several generations of the Pontifex family. George Pontifex, the domineering father, bullies his son Theobald into taking orders, and tricks him into marrying Christina. Theobald, in his turn, tyrannizes his son Ernest whose childhood becomes miserable. He too is forced to join the church against his will. Disastrous consequences follow. But Ernest Pontifex does not ill-treat his children. He treats them with genuine affection.

> Mr. Pontifex may have been a little sterner with his children than some of his neighbours, but not much. He thrashed his boys two or three times a week and some weeks a good deal oftener but in those days fathers were always thrashing their boys.[19]

'Breaking the Will' of the children was the principle expected to be followed to enable them learn habits of obedience and discipline. It is this attitude which is being satirized by Butler. The novelist does not spare the women-mothers to be specific—who are totally ineffective in their roles as mothers because they fail to safeguard the children's interests and to protect them against the fathers' oppression. Women are concerned only about their roles as wives, seldom realizing the obligations and responsibilities of motherhood.

> Christina Pontifex is devoted to her husband. She is a good wife rather than a good mother. "She would have chopped Ernest or anyone else into little pieces of mincemeat to gratify the slightest wish of her husband."[20]

Family is a jungle of mutual antagonism and dislike. Family life horrified him and filled him with sentiments of repulsion and desire to escape. Despite enmity and animosity, despite all his abuse and quarrelling, Butler never broke right away from his own people, even though the bruised sense of grievance never left him. Ivy Compton-Burnett resembles Butler who considers it a child's duty to revolt against parental dictation, but not to break away totally unless it is absolutely inevitable.

NOTES

1. Edward Sackville West, "Ladies whose bright pens," ed. Charles Burkhart, *The Art of I. Compton-Burnett* (London: Victor Gollancz, 1972), p. 103.
2. Pamela Hansford Johnson, *I. Compton-Burnett* (London: Longman, 1951).
3. "The Unhappy Family Game," *The Times Literary Supplement*, 22 March 1947, p. 126.
4. Johnson, p. 17.
5. Jenni Calder, *Women and Marriage in Victorian Fiction* (London: Thames and Hudson, 1976), p. 86.
6. Sir James Butler, *The History of England, 1815-1939* (Oxford: O.U.P., 1960), p. 151.
7. Hilary Spurling, *Ivy When Young* (London: Allison and Busby, 1983), p. 118.
8. Violet Powell, *A Compton-Burnett Compendium* (London: Heinemann, 1973), p. 13.
9. Elizabeth Bowen, "Parents and Children," *The Art*, p. 54.
10. Spurling, p. 63.
11. Johnson, pp. 8-9.
12. Calder, p. 86.
13. *Ibid.*, p. 84.
14. *Ibid.*, p. 14.
15. Charlotte Bronte, *Jane Eyre* (London: MacDonald, 1955), pp. 90-91.
16. Qtd. Ernest A. Baker, *The History of the English Novel* (New York: Barnes and Noble, 1968), Vol. 8, p. 320.
17. *Ibid.*, p. 320.
18. *Ibid.*, p. 319.
19. Samuel Butler, *The Way of All Flesh* (New York: Dodd, Mead, 1957), p. 21.
20. *Ibid.*, pp. 375-76.

Personal Relationships: II

The relationship at the very core of a family is the one between husband and wife. The touchstone of the success of a domestic novelist, therefore, is the manner in which marital relationship is portrayed in all its complexity during the different stages such as love, pre-marital wooing, marriage, sex and domestic contentment. This aspect must be analyzed from two perspectives, one concerning the individual partners and the other treating the couple as an individual unit of civilized human society. Domestic novels centre round themes of personal relationships with varying degrees of intimacy, the portrayal of marriages and the allied aspects having undergone gradual changes depending on contemporary social conditions. Jenni Calder explains the importance of this subject during the Victorian era: "We live in a time when the role of women in society is the subject of impassioned debate, and the question of marriage, the family, sexual behaviour, the relation between freedom and constraint in society, recur in moral, sociological, political and literary discussion. A study of marriage and the family in Victorian fiction is therefore of particular interest to our generation, which is far from being the first to be concerned with such matters."[1]

In the novels of Fanny Burney and of Jane Austen, as in the case of several other contemporary novelists, marriage happens to be the only goal for well-bred young women mainly because it appears to be the only safe shelter for them from the parental tyranny in many cases and pressures from society in certain others. They had no viable alternative between one kind of constraint in the parental home and the total possession by a husband after marriage. Even in the Gothic novels such as Ann Radcliffe's *The Mysteries of Udolpho* (1974), the heroine who gets involved in adventures uncharacteristic of her breeding and social norms, finally finds fulfilment in a marriage to "a young man who could have stepped out of the pages of Fanny Burney."[2] Several Gothic heroines seem to follow the path of Camilla in this respect. Jane Austen had considered this question at length and tried to present themes where a moral sense could be conveyed through characters, especially the women. The most conspicuous fact behind such portrayals of marriages is the insecurity of women who had to have an anchor, both financial and moral, for they had no financial independence in any manner. With no right of inheritance, and no adequate educational qualifications for proper employment, women had to look for security, and could find it only in a proper marriage. If the marriage turned out to be disastrous, they had to bear the brunt of it.

"In the Victorian novel it is virtually impossible to get away from the concept of marriage as a financial transaction. The idea of money is there even when the cash is absent."[3] Thackeray was one of the first to reject the concept of marriage as the beginning of "living happily ever after" and to concentrate on exposing flawed marriages as in *Barry London, Vanity Fair* and *The Newcomes*. Though he believed that marriage is a union which can be worked out to yield happiness and has presented simple scenes of domestic bliss with parents and children, he found that in most cases it was a failure. As Jenni Calder observes: "His scene is much wider than that of Jane Austen, and the implications of marriage cannot be so self-contained. . . . Thackeray's husbands and wives tend to learn to hate their spouses as the disguises donned in order to effect the capture are let off. At best mutual tolerance is achieved."[4] Both submissive women like Amelia and Rachel Castlewood and rebellious ones like Becky Sharp are destructive in different ways.

Charlotte Bronte tried to present marriage as companionship and mutual assistance. Even though the depiction of violent passion and unconventional approach to life and love make her quite different from Jane Austen, she resembles Ivy Compton-Burnett in choosing conventional themes and handling them in an entirely novel way. She realized that women were considered inferior to men and therefore created poor, plain and parentless heroines who manage to win their way into the hearts and households of rich, eligible men. For instance, *Jane Eyre* portrays Jane rich in passionate love and independent in her views though she comes from a highly strained background. In this sense, she sounded a note of social revolt against the picture of the ideal woman as delicate, beautiful and helplessly dependent. She re-created the Cinderella type heroine, anticipating the modern emancipated woman.

In Elizabeth Gaskell's novels, the concept of a family widens into the portrait of the community. In her world, each unit is an integral part of the society which cannot be ignored in any family discussion. Community's ills have repercussions in every household, and the individual drama develops out of this elementary factor. The novelist attempted to show marriage as something more than a mere escape. Introducing the topic from a woman's perspective, Elizabeth Gaskell presented women who would learn and develop through experience.

Cranford, Mary Barton and *Wives and Daughters* testify to this. Marriage is not the only source of a sense of fulfilment; the success of a marriage would depend on the enlightenment of the woman and the sincere love which should enable the couple to work it out through mutual love and understanding.

Regarding Dickens, certain direct statements he made about marriage and the concept of home remain very significant.

> Let them cherish the faith that in home, and all the English virtues which the love of home engenders, lies the only true source of domestic felicity; let them believe that round the household gods, contentment and tranquillity cluster in their gentlest and most graceful forms; and that may weary hunters of happiness through the noisy world have learnt this truth too late, and found a cheerful spirit and a quiet mind only at home at last.[5]

It is ironic that he proved this principle more by exceptions than by positive cases. He concentrated more on unhappy unions where the partners felt entrapped than on cases of fulfilment or domestic felicity. Badly organized unhappy marriages abound in his works. He realized that he was trying to attack the institution of marriage as an instrument of society. Society was driving individuals to wrong marriages. Wrong marriages, in turn, affected the atmosphere of a healthy society.

George Eliot considered marriage to be at the very core of social continuity, and like Elizabeth Gaskell, she viewed family life as a unit of the society. Marriage was, therefore, more than a case of individual fulfilment. George Eliot portrayed family life in all its complexities, including feuds, frustrations and rivalries. In her novels, "she questions the naturalness of human relations within the most intimate unit of living. This is a very physical passage, 'bone and muscle,' 'heartstrings,' 'wrinkles,' and the 'modelling hand,' as if to remind us that living with people is a physical reality, not just a question of the various members of a family taking their proper places in a hierarchy. Parents and children, brothers and sisters, husbands and wives, live together, simultaneously linked and separate, aware of natural ties and resentful of them, submitting their individuality and protecting it."[6]

It is this paradox in marriage that novelists of the age attempted to handle. George Eliot herself testified to it through the heroines in novels like *Middlemarch* and *Felix Holt*. Maggie, Dorothea and Gwendolen experienced this conflict and became heroines and victims at the same time in the clash between status demanded by society and dynamism they represented as individuals.

Ivy Compton-Burnett is extremely original in her domestic sketches because of the perspective with which she chose to analyze situations and to delineate characters. In this attempt, she discovers the fact by "turning the Victorian novel inside out" that the murky undercurrents are shocking in their raw realities. The majority of the personal relationships she has presented between husbands and wives, fathers and daughters, brothers and sisters or among other relations, are on the borderline between the normal and the abnormal, the dividing line being very thin. What is beyond the natural or normal needs separate analysis.

Marriage does not appear to be the cherished goal for Ivy Compton-Burnett's characters. The institution of marriage is not sacrosanct, it becomes a contract for convenience, mutual or individual. Ada Merton (*A God and His Gifts*) accepts Hereward's proposal for practical reasons.

An instance of marriage as a means of escape from a deep sense of loss and depression can be found in *Mother and Son*. Rosebery contemplates marriage to escape from the unbearable sense of vacuum left by the death of his mother to whom he has been abnormally attached, further aggravated by the revelation that Julius is not his father as he had believed till that moment. Julius, in his turn, plans to marry Emma Greathart for the sake of companionship which will help him forget the unpleasant life he has had with his wife, Miranda. *A Heritage and Its History* presents Sir Edwin who is driven to the necessity of marrying Rhoda who, he hopes, will relieve him of the agony caused by his brother, Hamish. *Daughters and Sons* introduces marriages based chiefly on momentary considerations. Clare agrees to marry Alfred Marcon only on hearing about the provision in Sabine Ponsonby's will. When the truth that he is only an executor is revealed, she falls back on the commitment and chooses Sir Rowland Seymour. Dinah and Andrew in *Brothers and Sisters* and Eleanor Sullivan in *Parents and Children* think of a marriage only as an outlet from their present households. Sabine arranges for the marriage between her son John and Edith only out of the mistaken belief that she is the donor of the windfall wealth.

Mercenary motive underlines Horace's marriage with Charlotte in *Manservant and Maidservant*. The irony inherent in the situation is obvious:

> Horace had married her for her money, hoping to serve his impoverished estate, and she had married him for love, hoping to fulfil herself. The love had gone and the money remained, so that the advantage lay with Horace, if he could have taken so hopeful a

view of life. (*MSMS*, 11)

For Simon Challoner (*A Heritage and Its History*), marriage solves the problem of finding a new home. Mortimer Lamb (*Manservant and Maidservant*), who has an affair with Horace's wife, is asked by Horace to leave the house or to marry if he wants to remain in the neighbourhood. Mortimer prefers to marry Magdalen as that would enable him to remain in the neighbourhood, though in a little damp house. Longing for power and position makes Verena (*A Father and His Fate*) cancel her engagement to Malcolm, the heir to Miles Mowbray, when she learns that Miles' wife had died in a shipwreck. The further developments prove the total absence of moral considerations on the part of the characters as distinct from material ones.

Hester (*Mother and Son*) rejects Rosebery's proposal as she seeks immediate position and power as mistress to Julius. However, she fails to persuade Julius to marry her.

Anna Donne (*Elders and Betters*) is a calculating woman with a penchant for her own home and family and she haunts Calderons' house with an eye on winning the hand of their son, Terence, and ultimately succeeds in her design. She wins both money and the husband through dubious methods.

Miss Burke in *Mother and Son* accepts Rosebery mistaking him to be Julius' son and continues her affection to him, the prime motive being security. She breaks her engagement when she learns about Rosebery's parentage and about his rejection earlier by Hester.

Seized by sudden fancy for Hugo Middleton (*The Mighty and Their Fall*), the brother of Ninian Middleton, to whom she is betrothed, Teresa decides to cancel her engagement to Ninian. When she fails to persuade Hugo, she goes back to Ninian seeking his hand again.

Marriages are contracted on the spur of the moment without the foundation of love, attraction or respect. Proposals and acceptances are based on spontaneous decisions without proper planning and thinking. Sometimes, they are suddenly announced in the presence of all concerned. Hereward proposes to Ada in the presence of his sister and her father and aunt. Ada's father is so surprised that he asks: "why, I did not know that proposals took place in public like this." (*GG*, 33)

Regarding Hetta's marriage in *Daughters and Sons*, which is the result of a sudden decision, Pamela Hansford Johnson points out: "Miss Compton-Burnett's habit of marrying off her characters in the most arbitrary fashion, apparently on a moment's impulse, comes out sharply in this book when Hetta, having reached a supreme height of hastiness, receives an admiring offer of marriage from the toadlike family friend,

Chaucer."[7]

Doctor Chaucer in *Daughters and Sons* is in the habit of proposing to each and every lady he comes across. After being rejected by the two governesses in Hetta Ponsonby's house, Edith Hallam and Miss Blake, he proposes to Hetta herself and is luckily accepted by her. When Hetta makes the startling revelation regarding the benefactor in the presence of guests and the resulting shock kills Sabine, Chaucer proposes to her with the new-found courage that in betraying family secrets Hetta has come down to his level. Hetta very casually accepts him.

Sometimes, sympathy forms the ground for change of heart. In *A Family and a Fortune*, Maria Sloane engaged to Dudley Gaveston takes pity for Dudley's brother Edgar, when he loses his wife. She cancels her engagement and gets quickly engaged to Edgar.

Apart from considerations of security, money, status or passion which usually prompt marriages, they sometimes marry just for a change, but certainly never for love. While most of the men treat marriage as a mere convention, women see it as a way out of their troubles or in the case of some, for gratification of their passions.

When women do not shun spinsterhood and when they do not crave for marriage as a goal to reach or as a means to attain fulfilment in life, the natural inference is that they have a definite unsullied status in contemporary society and that they are not looked down upon.

With the loss of countless bachelors during the First World War, spinsterhood has become an accepted condition in the society. Though Ivy Compton-Burnett's novels are timed in the last decade of the nineteenth century, it has to be said that she has reflected and presented contemporary condition in this regard.

Spinsterhood is not a disgrace. Spinsters are not decried or ridiculed in the society. Only a few married women, on occasions, may have looked down upon them. No novel of Ivy Compton-Burnett is without single women. They are prolific and prominent. Some of the single women are envious of married women and sometimes, married women are proud that, "someone has wanted to spend his life with them. That is surely a cause of pride." (*MS*, 88)

For a few, spinsterhood may be the result of disappointed hopes as in the case of Emma, the eldest daughter of Sir Ransom (*Darkness and Day*). But for her sister, Anne, it is out of choice. In *Mother and Son*, Hester Wolsey, Emma Greathart and Miss Burke have to remain as spinsters as they are not satisfied with the offers they received. There are also others who deliberately eschew the idea of marriage. In *Men and Wives*, Rachel's step-daughter refuses to marry the man she loves only to pursue the vocation of poetry writing.

Spinsterhood is portrayed with vigour and understanding, especially in her earlier novels. Family life is shown to be full of tensions and responsibilities whereas spinsterhood is associated with pleasures. Spinsters in *Pastors and Masters* and *More Women than Men* are shown to be happily engaged in their work. In *Men and Wives*, the seventy-two-year-old Rachel Hardistic admits freely that her single years were the happiest period of her life.

> "I see how civilized it is to be a spinster," said Rachel. "I shouldn't think savage countries have spinsters. I never know why marriage goes on in civilized countries, goes on openly. Think what would happen if it were really looked at, or regarded as impossible to look at." (*MN*, 103)

Margaret Jourdain, Ivy Compton-Burnett's companion, had settled for spinsterhood out of choice. But Compton-Burnett wants us to believe that her single-blessednness has been forced on her by the war. She quite often says that she belongs to a generation of women many of whom have to live without marriage. She tells Kay Dick, "the men were dead, you see, and the women didn't marry so much because there was no one for them to marry."[8]

It it commonly observed that widowers, very soon after their bereavement, develop an irresistible longing for fresh partners. No one remains single, living in his dead wife's memories. Only Sir Godfrey (*Men and Wives*) and Julius (*Mother and Son*) are forced to remain so—Sir Godfrey because of the will of his wife, Lady Haslam, and Julius, because no one is willing to marry him.

Soon after a mistress dies, people start enquiring as to whom the master is going to marry. In *Mother and Son*, when the news of Miranda's death is conveyed to the children, Adrian enquires publically if Julius could marry Wolsey.

In *Two Worlds and Their Ways*, Sir Roderick, bereaved of his wife, very soon marries Maria whereas Mr. Firebrace hastens to find a mistress and even bestows his dead wife's jewellery on the mother of his illegitimate son.

Duncan (*A House and Its Head*) marries Alison soon after the death of his wife, Ellen. After Alison's elopement with Almeric, he quickly invites Cassandra, his children's governess, into his life.

Thomas Calderon (*Elders and Betters*), immediately after his wife Jessica's death, announces his engagement to young Florence, even though the marriage does not take place. Ninian Middleton, the widower with grown-up children (*The Mighty and Their Fall*), marries

Teresa Chilton. Sefton (*Two Worlds and Their Ways*) says, "The first wife has to die before a man can have a second." (*TWTW*, 141)

It need not be so always. Cassius Clare (*The Present and the Past*) divorces his first wife, Catharine, and marries Flavia. But there is Ridley (*Parents and Children*) who attempts bigamy with a supposed widow. Miles Mowbray (*A Father and His Fate*) knows fully well that his wife is not dead in the shipwreck as is supposed to be. Still, he is all set to marry Verena and quickly proceed to live with her.

However, bigamy is prevented in both the cases. Eleanor is prevented from unknowingly becoming a bigamist by the timely arrival of her husband. Similarly Miles' wife is brought back at the right moment to prevent his marriage with Verena.

Children consider second marriage degrading and disgraceful. They always oppose their parents contemplating marriage as soon as the spouse dies. Being very young and economically dependent, they could rage only among themselves like the spinster daughters of Miles (*A Father and His Fate*). Their dislike is based on hatred for stepmother coupled with the painful awareness of the fact that their loving mother is so rapidly and easily forgotten and replaced. In *Two Worlds and Their Ways*, Sefton's school-mates ridicule him for his father's second marriage. Though Sefton explains to them that his father married only after his first wife's death, they are not convinced. They tease him by insisting that his mother, being a second wife, must be a concubine. Sefton weeps out of shame. Tullia (*Elders and Betters*), Justine (*A Family and a Fortune*), Lavinia (*The Mighty and Their Fall*) oppose their father's remarriages.

In *Parents and Children*, when Eleanor tells her children about her impending marriage with Ridley, the children ask her some probing questions which indicate that they are unhappy about it. (*PC*, 226) When Aubrey in *A Family and a Fortune* learns about his father's engagement to Maria Sloane, he innocently questions: "Are men allowed to marry some one else as soon as they like after their wives are dead?" (*FF*, 204) Replacement is unimaginable. Even filling the vacant space of mother is not likeable. They do not like their fathers marrying again, even long after the death of their mothers. (*FHF*, 105) Miles' daughter asks him to think well before he takes any further step in the case of Verena. "Father . . . we beg you to pause and consider before you go any further." (*FHF*, 201)

Adolescent or youthful love is not commonly portrayed by Compton-Burnett. Most of the characters marry in their middle ages and their marriages are not usually the result of love. If they remain as spinsters or bachelors, it is not due to disappointment in love. Love is insignificant. It is not the basis for marriage. Courtship, proposal and marriage happen in a mechanical and casual way.

Referring to Ivy Compton-Burnett's attitude to ordinary concept of love, Pamela Hansford Johnson observes: "Like Jane Austen, she cannot portray ordinary sensual love. Her married couples seem like brothers and sisters; it is impossible to imagine even endearments passing between them, let alone imagine them in any sexual contact."[9]

Spontaneous love or emotional attachment are conspicuous by their absence in the novels of Ivy Compton-Burnett. Ruth and Gabriel, Hereward and Rosa, and Naomi and Hamish fall in love with each other. But they are not portrayed as lovers sharing moments of ecstatic joy. Several of these novels are truly passionate in theme, but any mention of passionate appeal is deliberately avoided as though it is an anathema to write about.

Agony of unfulfilled love poses a serious, irreparable damage to conjugal bliss. Compton-Burnett tells Kay Dick, "Love often changes a character's whole way of morality."[10] Hereward's disloyalty to Ada (*A God and His Gifts*), his wife, and his several extra-marital affairs, including incest are based on his disappointment in love with Rosa. He becomes unrestrained. He tells this to Rosa herself, "If I had married you, Rosa, these things would not have happened." (*GG*, 151) So the cause of his sexual delinquencies is traced back to Rosa's rejection of his offer.

As love is absent, most of the characters are guided by passion which is unrestrained. Grant (*A House and Its Head*) has a very weak heart which falls for each woman he comes across. He had been caught making public advances to a maidservant. He is an opportunist seducer. His crudest sexual gratification includes seduction of his uncle's eldest daughter. When she rejects him, he proposes to Nance's sister, Sybil, and is accepted by her.

Doctor Chaucer (*Daughters and Sons*) has a sort of amorous weakness for every governess in the Ponsonby House. After being rejected by them at a dinner, he suddenly proposes to the tyrant of that house, Hetty, and is accepted by her.

Ivy Compton-Burnett does not depict much of premarriage wooing and courting as her main concern is to probe deep into the several problems of marital relationships. If at all depicted, it is only to show that even women do not have moral standards and engaged women tilt their lovers and switch over to others, often much older than them. Camilla (*Men and Wives*), the coquette, divorces Ernest Bellamy and is engaged to Doctor Dufferin. Very soon Matthew replaces Doctor Dufferin as Camilla's fiance. After breaking her engagement with Matthew, she manages to get Godfrey, Matthew's father, to propose to her. Her rejection of Matthew may be natural abhorrence of a husband who has committed matricide. When Godfrey is prevented from marrying Camilla by the terms and conditions in his wife's will, Camilla gets herself engaged to the widowed Dominic Spong. Even after her marriage, she is one who keeps her matrimonial options open should there be a richer and more desirable person becoming available to her.

Maria Sloane (*A Family and a Fortune*) very easily transfers her affections from Dudley to his brother Edgar, Clare (*Daughters and Sons*), engaged to Alfred, discards when she learns that he does not inherit any money, and instead accepts Seymour.

Alison (*A House and Its Head*) marries Duncan, commits adultery with his nephew Grant and finally elopes with Almeric. Dulcia is one who sacrifices her sexual urges by referring to old scandals in public.

Verena (*A Father and His Fate*) gets herself engaged to Malcolm. But for power, she transfers her affections conveniently to his uncle, Miles. When Miles' wife returns, she marries Malcolm, but finally deserts him and goes away.

Love and sex are not distinct. Love is transitory, amoral and sexual. It is never portrayed as overwhelming the will and passion. In all her novels, sex is not portrayed directly and openly. It is treated indirectly by showing the circumstances leading to it and the results flowing from it.

Disastrous consequences like disinheritance, infanticide, matricide and separation of lovers follow from a moment's indiscretion. It is the root-cause of adultery and also incest.

In Ivy Compton-Burnett's novels, almost all kinds of sexual aberrations and perversions in all variation can be found portrayed, directly or indirectly. Almost every relationship appears to have a touch of the abnormal, being on the borderline between the normal and the prohibited. In some cases, the perversion is real; in certain other cases, it is just implied or suggested, existing only in the minds. It varies only in degrees; the sin is committed in the mind. Among such variations as incest and homosexuality, incest is the most common aberration found in her novels. Incest is defined as "any prohibited sexual relations between persons of the same culturally or legally defined kinship group . . . i.e., between brothers and sisters or between parents and children."[11] A more elaborate definition gives further details:

> Incest is any prohibited sexual association between persons who are members of the same culturally or legally defined kinship group. Every society undertakes to channel the expression of the sex drive through rules as to whom one must or ought to marry, at the same time discouraging of forbidding certain matings and mar-

> riages. Incest prohibitions are found in all cultures, primitive and civilized.[12]

In this sense, the shades of the abnormal can be very often traced in ordinary relationships if closely analyzed.

Incestuous love is found among brothers and sisters, though it is only a manifestation of intense love and affection which draw them together. *Brothers and Sisters* has such a prohibited relationship as the basic theme, even though the husband and wife never knew of their real relationship. *A God and His Gifts, Darkness and Day, More Women than Men* and *Daughters and Sons* have this theme presented in all its intensity. Almost all her novels glorify the brother-sister relationship to a degree which verges on the unnatural. For instance, Zillah, the sister of Hereward Egerton, the god in *A God and His Gifts* engenders such love for being in her brother's heart that he asks:

> "Zillah, we are brother and sister. If we were not, what could we be?"
>
> "Nothing that was nearer. It stands first among the relations. There is nothing before it, nothing to follow it. It reaches from the beginning to the end." (*GG*, 62)

The repeated use of 'it' gives the relation an identity of its own. It assumes a character of a concrete reality which has existed since the days of Adam and Eve. Benjamin in *Elders and Betters* explains the relationship almost in the same terms:

> The relation of brother and sister goes back to the first days. It has its roots in the beginning. There may be stronger feeling, but never the same understanding. It is not your time to know it. (*EB*, 84)

But in this case it is genuine affection between siblings that exists between Benjamin and his sisters, though the language verges on the perverted.

Even the conversation among very young children in *Parents and Children* centres round the same view:

> "You can't marry your sister," said Gavin.
> "He can marry who he wants to. And he will marry Hatton." . . .
> "Why can't brothers and sisters marry?" said Gavin.
> "Because they have to start a family," said this sister.

> "If they married people in the same one, there would never be any new ones. But they can live together."
>
> "Do they have any children then?"
>
> "I don't think they do so often. But they can adopt some." (*PC*, 39)

Coming from children, this conversation is bringing animals and human beings closer together.

Brothers and Sisters with its basic theme of incest, is closely reminiscent of Greek drama. Oedipus and Jocasta come alive in different roles as brother and sister, get married unaware of the truth which is revealed about twenty years and three children later. In spite of Compton-Burnett's casual dismissal of the suggestion that her works show clear influences of Greek drama, the points of similarity are quite obvious. But what stands out even more conspicuously is the fact that there are significant points of difference in execution.

The character of Christian Stace loses colour compared to his Greek counterpart not only because of the general lack of sharpness or brightness in his character, but because of a major deviation in the development of the story sequence. Christian dies instantaneously on the discovery of the fatal truth; the novelist, consciously or otherwise, loses a great opportunity. Or, on the other hand, it could even be a deliberate evasion of a responsibility and she could be diffident. Portraying the reaction of Christian to the situation, to the circle of readers who are bound to recall Oedipus would have been a real challenge to any artist. But the opportunity was let go. The scene with the most intense tragic appeal in *Oedipus the King* is the scene of the discovery of truth ending with the appearance of the king with blood streaming down his eyes—a martyr on the altar of 'truth.' The rest of his life is a prolonged period of expiation.

Even in the case of Sophia, the tragic appeal the character should have had is almost completely eclipsed in Ivy Compton-Burnett's handling. Jocasta kills herself, but her agony pulsates in the very act which is executed in the flash of a moment; it is clear she is punishing herself. Sophia who continues to reason out within herself in an attempt at justification does not display any such sense of consuming sin or guilt. She appears to draw the same pleasure or even more of it in nagging her grown-up children into a kind of uneasy submission, demanding their sympathy and attention too much for their comfort. The comic touches the novelist has given to Sophia's character after the revelation of truth has diluted the tragic intensity even further, making the novel totally pale and bloodless regarding the theme of incest, discovery and reaction.

The two characters who are elevated to the level of tragic dignity in this novel are Andrew and Dinah Stace, the children of the unnatural couple. Robin takes life a little more easily and therefore the burden is not so heavy on him. Andrew and Dinah are victims of the fact that the sins of the parents generally visit the children. Deprived of a chance for normal marriages and normal family lives as brother and sister should have, they have to plan for a future which is bound to be unique in the sense of doom and the curse it carries. But with supreme dignity in the face of such a fate, and with tranquillity which can arise only in the case of a truly great tragic character, the sister declares to the brother:

> "You and I will be wedded to each other, Andrew," said Dinah.
>
> "That sounds dubiously in accordance with family traditions. But Robin will marry, and you and I will give our lives to keeping the family secret for his sake. Robin is the most like Sophia, and has the right to survive." (*BS*, 270)

This passage, it is quite obvious, does not imply a real marriage; they have to be together for the rest of their lives, proper normal marriages having been ruled out. There is no question of incest in the literal sense; she means that they are committed to each other's company, being bound together by a quirk of fate. Acceptance is the only way out. It is reconciliation to a situation which demands the greatest strength of mind. They have it. Robin can manage to be 'normal' in spite of the abnormal background. The novelist dismisses him.

This scene is reminiscent of the masterpiece *Mourning Becomes Electra* in which Eugene O'Neill has handled another theme from classical Greek tragedy, the story of Orestes. The Oresteia trilogy in all its complexities has been re-created against the twentieth century background, keeping himself faithful to the original story. Lavinia, the modern counterpart of Electra loses everybody; she is all alone with the overwhelming sense of guilt. Expiation for the sin should not be through a quick disposal of herself by suicide. She could live on, all alone, in the years to come with no companion other than the awareness of her situation. This is the most severe punishment meted out to any criminal by her own self; mourning really becomes her, with black colour all around. In Ivy Compton-Burnett's novel, Dinah and Andrew are enveloped in gloom, the blackness being only metaphorical.

Mary McCarthy finds the theme of incest in *Brothers and Sisters* rather too over-worked to have had the tragic effect. She explains how the introduction of incest, both real and possible, has given a comic twist to the story: "Take *Brothers and Sisters*, which is assumed to be about the 'curse of incest,' since the principal couple Sophia Stace and her husband, are revealed to be brother and sister—half brother and sister. There are six pairs of brothers and sisters in the novel, one of which is married. And what is interesting to the author is not the sin but its mathematical permutations . . . what the children of these new unions would be to each other and to their parents and uncles and aunts could best he worked out as a problem in Algebra. Relations multiply, as it were, cancerously."[13] She too is pointing out to the fact that the tragic potential of the situations has been affected by the multiplicity of such couples involving dilution of the theme.

Overpossessiveness verging on the abnormal is an important aspect in the theme of *A Father and His Fate*. Eliza is the possessive mother of Malcolm. Though she is extremely fond of him, she realizes the limits of her love and learns to adjust herself to the changing situations.

The sexual perversions of Hereward (*A God and His Gifts*) alone are enough to show how it disrupts the peace and harmony of the entire family. Here is a man who loves one, marries another, commits adultery with his wife's sister, incest with daughter-in-law-to-be and above all, shares an abnormal and unnatural relationship with his sister. As a result, his wife's sister is sent away from home to be out of his reach. One of his sons is afraid of getting married and bringing his wife for fear of Hereward's eye falling on her. Another son falls in love with a girl unaware of the fact that they share the same father. His innocent love is nipped in the bud as it would become incestuous if permitted to develop.

The abnormal relationships are understandable in the light of psychoanalysis of Freud. Ivy Compton-Burnett comes down heavily on free sex and consistently decrees pursuit of sex and pleasure. She emphasizes the desirability of constancy, trust and affection which should be mutual. Through Julius (*Mother and Son*) she shows that negligence and unrequited love of a wife drives the man to take to adultery and seek the comfort of companionship elsewhere as the same is lacking at home.

When love is domesticated and is legal, it is conjugal affection. The same love is adultery when it takes the form of unrestrained passion seeking satisfaction outside of the marriage bond. Miranda (*Mother and Son*) commits adultery even when her husband, Julius, remains devoted to her. When Rosebery, her son, grows up to absorb all her attention and interest, Julius takes a mistress. Miranda's withdrawal of companionship from Julius and its transfer to Robsebery drives Julius to console himself with a mistress. He tells her: "Miranda, it was the time when we grew apart, in Rosebery's early manhood. I was thrown on myself; I had to steer my course as I could, . . . I had a life apart from you, as you had one apart from me." (*MS*, 126) Julius at least admits his fault, while Miranda dies keeping it as a secret

Charlotte (*Manservant and Maidservant*), Horace's wife, plans to elope with Mortimer, her husband's uncle. The happiness and comfort of her children being her main concern, she develops intimacy with Mortimer, maybe to protect them from the cruelty of her husband.

Simon (*A Heritage and Its History*) and his incestuous son's wife, Marcia are drawn to each other. At the close of the book, there are clear hints that Marcia is destined to be his mistress.

Hereward (*A God and His Gifts*) commits adultery with Emmeline, attempts it with Trissie, the fiancee of Reuben, his third son. His love for Rosa, and his affair with the children's nurse are extra-marital affairs. Hereward's affair with Hetty, his daughter-in-law-to-be, Miles Mowbray's (*A Father and His Fate*) with Verena, Rhoda's (*A Heritage and Its History*) with Simon and Alison's (*A House and Its Head*) with Grant are examples of adultery taking the colour of incest.

Simon's wife, Fanny (*A Heritage and Its History*), is upset at his behaviour with Marcia. Ada, wife of Hereward (*A God and His Gifts*), gets her sister, Emmeline, banished, on finding that her husband is interested in her. Ada is terribly shocked when she learns the parentage of Henry. She decides to leave the house as a life with such a cheat is impossible. However, her father, Alfred, shows reluctance to take her back into his house. She is persuaded to live with him. She concedes, taking a realistic view of the situation. Solomon tells his mother that if she goes away she would lose her place as a wife and a mother. Gradually, Ada becomes mellower and finally she reaches the point where she is more sympathetic and tolerant than condemnatory as Hereward's amours are laid bare.

The novelist's views on illegal unions are expressed through Alfred in *A God and His Gifts* when he says: "we know our world. We know its limits and its laws. We know they must be followed. We do not make our own." (*GG*, 44)

Where there is adultery, there is illegitamcy; adultery itself is illegitimate. Ivy Compton-Burnett herself says that it is a common practice in those days to bring up illegitimate children along with the legitimate children.[14]

Priscilla, Susan and Lester Marlowe are the illegitimate children of Sir Jesse Sullivan (*Parents and Children*). In *Two Worlds and Their Ways*, Aldom, the butler in Sir Roderick's house, turns out to be his bastard son. Mr. Firebrace, Sir Roderick's father-in-law also has an illegitimate son in Oliver Spode, the school-master. In *Darkness and Day*, Sir Ransom's illegitimate daughter is Bridget, wife of Edmund and Mildred Hallam is Edmund's illegitimate daughter. Henry and Viola (*A God and His Gifts*) are Hereward's illegitimate children. Miles Mowbray has an illegitimate daughter born to Verena (*A Father and His Fate*). Gabriel is the love-child of Miss Rosetti and Jonathan Swift (*More Women than Men*). But he passes on his illegitimate son to be brought up by his sister, Josephine. Hamish, the illegitimate son of Simon (*A Heritage and Its History*) is brought up as the legitimate son of Sir Edwin. Francis, Adrian, Alice and Rosebery also belong to the same group of illegitimate offspring. This shows that the illegitimate children are often allowed to be brought up along with other children.

One factor that stands out very conspicuously is that the novelist does not even attempt to describe emotional aspects involved in the cases of perversions. The characters involved would certainly have undergone great mental conflicts out of the intangible web of prohibited passion they experience, but Compton-Burnett turns her face away from such delicate situations. For instance, Hereward's son's fiancee whom he seduces does not appear to batter an eyelid when she bears his father's child and later on marries the son.

Such situations were not unheard of in the Victorian age. A popular instance is that of George Lewes, who married the novelist George Eliot but had no legal sanction to this marriage. He had a first wife, who maintained a long-standing affair with Thornton, son of Leigh Hunt. She had several children through him. To save his wife's reputation and family honour, George Lewes acknowledged these children as his own. But even though he wanted to divorce his wife in order to marry George Eliot, he could not do so, since having acknowledged his wife's children as his, he could not prove his wife's adultery.[15]

The parents of these unfortunate children are more concerned with secrecy than parental responsibility. But some of them make some provision for them, as in the case of Sir Jesse Sullivan (*Parents and Children*). Bridget's mother, Mrs. Spruce, works in the household as cook and is totally devoted to her daughter. When her daughter suffers from the mistaken incest, she saves her from the trauma by revealing the secret while she herself remains anonymous.

The governess, Bridget, is revealed to be Edmund's illegitimate daughter. Yet, all that she receives is an affectionate hug from her father. She continues to be the governess for Edmund's children and as usual, works in Sir Ransom's house without any change in her status or even in her behaviour.

Adultery, as far as possible, is kept as a secret. If it is ever revealed, family members are shocked but not perturbed. Care is taken to bury the secret. They are apparently guided by the principle, 'forgive and forget.' Life continues as usual. Family is not broken. Even those illegitimate children, taken into home, are to be sent out. On the other hand, there is no change in their treatment and all behave as if nothing is amiss.

But it is found that a person like Hereward (*A God and His Gifts*) learns at last that it is dangerous to conceal facts. He tells Rose in the end, "I should not have kept the secret. I am learning the value of truth." (*GG*, 151)

Josephine, in *More Women than Men*, pretends to be an inconsolable survivor of a marriage of perfect happiness, when the truth is quite the opposite.

Harriet Haslam and Sir Godfrey (*Men and Wives*) are another unhappy couple who do not love each other. After his wife's death, he is "enchanted with the prospect of a new, fascinating companion and pleasures unknown in his life with Harriet."[16] Duncan is a monotonously amiable husband. In *A House and Its Head*, male domination is explicit and Duncan has no consideration for his wife's health. But it is only when she is dying that he shows any sympathy for her. After her funeral, he feels sorry for his inability to show Ellen how much he had loved her.

Both the marriages of Cassius Clare (*The Present and the Past*) are cases of failure. His marriage with Catherine has ended in divorce. He is unhappy with Flavia as he thinks she neglects him and leaves him to his loneliness. Cassius laments: "Alone in the morning, alone at noon, alone until night! What is the good of a wife, when you never see or hear her?" (*PP*, 32) Ultimately, he ends his life while trying to frighten her by enacting a fake suicide.

Julia and Hamish (*A Heritage and Its History*) are yet another incompatible couple. Hamish's brother, Edwin is his centre of life. Julia wishes and is contented to be a devoted wife. Another maladjusted pair is Hamish, Edwin's son and Marcia. Hamish's incestuous birth destroys their conjugal happiness. A gulf of misunderstanding yawns between the wife and husband among all the couples in this novel.

A happy marriage subsists in the case of Sir Roderick and Maria Shelley (*Two Worlds and Their Ways*) and they remain a loving and tolerant couple. The old couple, Rev. Peter and his wife Theresa (*Pators and Masters*), continue to love each other facing with equanimity and understanding the testing situations such as deprivation of his inheritance, defection of congregation and the death of his two sons.

Real and absorbing marital love is shown between Christian and Sophia (*Brothers and Sisters*) but ironically, they happen to be half-brother and sister. Deep love exists where it should not.

Brothers in her novels live as devotedly as a married couple. Usually one of the brothers, the dependent one, plays a passive role of second fiddle. In *A Family and a Fortune*, Dudley's fraternal devotion to Edgar is such that he does not want to go in for any other companionship. Dudley inheriting a fortune and Maria Sloane jilting Dudley to marry Edgar spoil the relationship. But in the end, they are reconciled proving that brotherly love does not dry up so easily.

Edwin Challoner and Hamish Challoner (*A Heritage and Its History*) is another such loving pair. Ideal fraternal love exists between them. Their devotion for each other makes Julia, Hamish's wife, realize that Sir Edwin has superseded her in her husband's heart.

Fabian and Guy, sons of Cassius Clare by his first marriage (*The Present and the Past*) love each other. On the death of the father, they have to make a choice between the real mother and the foster-mother to live with. While Fabian chooses his real mother, Guy prefers his foster-mother to his real mother. But unable to bear separation from his brother, Guy decides to go with his brother for his sake and not for his mother's sake. He tells his foster-mother: "I don't want to leave you. I don't want to go away from you. I don't want any one as much as I want you. . . . But I must go with Fabian. To live without him would be the same as being dead." (*PP*, 212-13)

The fraternal relationship begins in the nursery where children of the same age group live with their nurse. They draw affection and protection from one another. As they grow up, their bond strengthens as they have to face the oppressive attitudes of their tyrannical parents together. In the middle age, it ripens into an intimate companionship.

Miss Jane Seymour (*Daughters and Sons*) is a companion both to her brother Evelyn and her father Rowland Seymour. She is so engrossed as a companion to two grown-up men that she cannot think of any one else. The middle-aged twins, Doctor Stephen Marcon and his sister Charity (*Daughters and Sons*) is another pair of devoted brother and sister. Sarah and Julian Wake (*Brothers and Sisters*) are greatly devoted to each other. Another happy pair are Ursula and Elton Scrope (*The Present and The Past*) who are highly contented with each other. Emily (*Pastors and Masters*) does not marry William because she cannot bear the idea of deserting her brother, Nicholas Herrick.

John Ponsonby and Hetta Ponsonby (*Daughters and Sons*) are brother and sister and the love between them tends to become abnormal. Hetta finds emotional satisfaction in her companionship with her widowed brother. She keeps him exclusively to herself, not even allowing his children to claim his attention. This almost tantamounts to conjugal love. Violet Powell points out: "John Ponsonby's relationship with his sister Hetta has sailed close to incestuous shores."[17]

This kind of abnormal fraternal devotion is also discernible in *A God and His Gifts* between Hereward Egerton and his sister, Zillah. Hereward's regret that the blood-tie prevents his sister, Zillah, from being sexually accessible is remarkable in exposing the perverted relationship. Even the wife is secondary to the sister. "No relation shall supersede our own. That is the one I will not do without. Only the woman to leave it to us can be my wife." (*GG*, 38) Hereward, when he proposes to Ada, sets a condition to his marriage with her. "Share me with her, and give her a part of yourself," (*GG*, 33) and also "you must not find a way of coming between us." (*GG*, 36)

When there is a threat to their relationship by way of marriage, sisters usually resent such move. Tullia (*Elders and Betters*) is not prepared to relinquish her hold on her brother, Terence, slight though she admits it to be. When John Ponsonby announces his engagement to Edith, Hetta is shocked, When Edith gradually replaces Hetta in John's life, unable to bear agony, Hetta disappears from the house threatening to commit suicide.

In Freudianism, when the boy is sexually attracted to his mother, there is an 'Oedipus Complex'; when the girl desires her father, an 'Electra Complex' results. (Electra incited her brother to kill their mother in revenge for the latter's murder of their father.)[18]

Both these perversions can be found very conspicuously in several of Compton-Burnett's novels.

Abnormal and unnatural relationships between father and daughter are also not infrequent in these novels. It is found in its bleakest form in *The Mighty and Their Fall.* Relationship between Ninian and his eldest daughter, Lavinia, is a kind of abnormal and emotional perversion. It is widower's love for his daughter to forget the loss of his wife. After her mother's death, Lavinia has grown to be a companion, almost a wife to her father.

It may be natural for grown-up children to protest when their widowed fathers plan to marry. It may be solely due to their abhorrence of a stepmother. Justine in *A Family and a Fortune*, resents her father's marriage but later reconciles herself. But Lavinia does not. She "could not face the loss of my father. It seemed to break up my world." (*MF*, 100) After Ninian's marriage, the tension eases and Lavinia, towards the end, decides to forego her share of money only to restore her normal relations with her father. But it is not the old abnormal one.

An equally obsessive father-daughter relationship is to be found in *Elders and Betters*. Thomas is totally absorbed with Tullia. She receives a shock when he announces his engagement to Florence. She does all she can to stall this marriage when Tullia and her father are locked in an embrace of closeness, Florence sees and breaks her engagement. As she comes only next to Tullia in his heart, she has considered herself to be superfluous in his life.

In *Mother and Son*, Rosebery abstains from marriage out of his love for his mother, Miranda. His devotion to her appears to border on abnormality. Miranda concentrates on her son, Rosebery, neglecting her husband and this leads him to commit adultery for the sake of companionship. In *Darkness and Day*, the widowed mother, Selina Lovat and her bachelor son Gaunt are seen locked in a somewhat over-affectionate embrace.

Ivy Compton-Burnett does not confine herself to heterosexual relationships between man and woman. She dwells on sexual aberrations like homosexuality and Lesbianism also. Homosexuality, also called sexual inversion, is the sexual attraction of a person to one of the same sex (Greek homo-"same," and not for Latin 'homo' man). This deviation usually, but not always, leads to physical contact.[19]

It is said that Ivy Compton-Burnett was interesteed in discussing freely and academically the subject of homosexuality with some of her intimate friends.[20] In her novels some of the relationships between brothers or friends are abnormal, unnatural and perverted so that they touch the borderline of homosexuality and lesbianism, without actually developing into them.

In *Elders and Betters*, Ethel, the parlour-maid and cook are a pair of peculiar lesbian lovers. Ethel insists that, being first cousins, the intensity of thir affection is great. Yet there are hints in the novel to suspect their kinship. Anyhow they reciprocate each other's love which exceeds normal limitations.

Devotion between Miss Rosetti and Miss Luke seems to be unnatural. "That is a wonderful case of devotion" (Mrs. Chattaway) said to Miss Munday . . . "Both Miss Luke and Miss Rosetti have great gifts for intimacy." (*MWTM*, 17) The English teacher, Miss Munday, appears to have passed through an emotional relationship with both these fellow-teachers. Between Miss Rosetti and Miss Luce, Miss Rosetti is less constant. Her eyes rove over Helen's form and she herself does not deny her interest in Helen. As Miss Luke says and later events prove, she also cherishes an unconscious passion for Josephine. Rosetti herself admits her homosexual inclination. (*MWTM*, 195) Miss Rosetti nuzzling Miss Luke in the corridor on her way to Helen Keats bedroom, before finding at last a less casual gratification in Josephine's arms shows the psychological perversion.

Homosexuality is a psychological malfunctioning of the mind rather than an act of unutterable moral delinquency. It is hinted in *Pastors and Masters* where dons like Masson and Bumpus "had meant romance for each other in youth." (*PM*, 25) Homosexuality is striking in *More Women than Men*. There is the homosexual affair going on between Jonathan Swift, brother of Josephine and Felix Bacon, his lodger for twenty-two years and both of them have been happy and satisfied with each other. Even then this relationship is not explicit but implied. The novelist never mentions the word 'homosexual.' Felix constantly moves with a "dancing step" and usually sits on Jonathan's knee. Besides this there is another hint that Felix turns his eyes away from the scene when Jonathan embraces his sister and his son. These incidents indicate the kind of emotion prevailing here. When Jonathan notices that Felix's eye has fallen on his own son, Gabriel, he says: "Ah, Felix, your mind will be on Gabriel, and I shall be forgotten. . . . Felix, I ask you earnestly not to do for Gabriel what I have done for you." (*MWTM*, 44)

Finally this relationship comes to an end when Felix Bacon marries Miss Keats and Jonathan is so depressed that Felix fears he may not survive. Jonathan's feelings for Felix, as the latter describes, is a 'morbid attachment' and morbid was the 'conventional code word for homosexual.'

Oliver Shelly and Oliver Spode are two teachers in a school who are suspected to be having homosexual relationship. They are warned by the headmaster to avoid too conspicuous a friendship.

Potential incest is found in *A Heritage and Its History*. Simon commits incest with his uncle's wife, Rhoda. Simon and Rhoda consider themselves as victims of force, impulse and fate. Then comes a situation where Simon's legitimate daughter, Naomi, wishes to marry Simon's illegitimate son, Hamish who is her half-brother. Simon is forced to make the startling revelation regarding Hamish's parentage to wean Naomi from such a marriage.

In *A House and Its Head*, unrestrained desire for sensual gratification leads Grant, Duncan's nephew, to have an illicit affair with his uncle's wife, Alison, while living in his uncle's house. Violet Powell brings out the difference between Grant's and Simon's incestuous affairs. She says that Grant's seduction of Alison is the action of a practised womanizer, responding to the beauty of Alison whereas Simon's is the result of inexperience, stimulated by brooding on the sexual implications of his uncle's marriage.[21]

Josephine Napier's (*More Women than Men*) possessive love for her nephew and adopted son, Gabriel, is incestuous. She dreams of his masterfulness. Her love for him "hides behind it a perversion that kept her worrying on the blurred borderline of a jealous fondness approaching sexual love and pure affection, an instance of a frequently-noticed psychic aberration."[22] She cannot bear any one sharing his love even if it be his wife, Ruth. That is why when Ruth is in a delirious state owing to pneumonia, Josephine's murderous impulse becomes so unrestrained that she kills her by exposing her to icy draught from an open window. Hers is a perverted love, a psychic aberration. She sees her relationship with Gabriel as that which exists between a man and a woman, but not as something between an aunt-adopted mother and nephew-son. "I am not his aunt any more than any other woman." (*MWTM*, 87)

Sophia in *Brothers and Sisters* appears to be not at all troubled by it. She says: "So I am father's sister. Well, I am not troubled about that. It only seems to draw us closer." (*BS*, 209) Incest is thought to be very natural by Grant (*A House and Its Head*). "Uncle, we were thrown together. We were young. . . . The temptation to which I yielded is common to men." (*HH*, 180) Incest appears to be very casual for Simon and Rhoda also (*A Heritage and Its History*). In some days, Simon claims, "the incestuous marriage they are trying to avert "would have been lawful and right." (*HIH*, 128) Rhoda says "what Simon and I did is done in all days." (*HIH*, 128) Yet both Simon and Rhoda are ashamed of disclosing it. Rhoda says, "I would rather die than have Hamish know." (*HIH*, 127) Simon also says that he also feels in the same way. Marcia, the wife of Hamish, the incestuous son of Rhoda and Simon (*A Heritage and Its History*) regrets the knowledge of the secret. "Hamish, I wish you had not told me." (*HIH*, 127)

It is viewed as a deprivation by the children. They have only one grandfather instead of the usual two. In *Brothers and Sisters*, paternal grandfather and maternal grandfather are one and the same. Robin bitterly says, "My maternal grandfather, my paternal grandfather, my only grandmother." (*BS*, 207) In *Darkness and Day*, the father of the children himself is also the grandfather. Gaunt sums up the situation thus: "Edmund has married his daughter. . . . His children are his grand-children. Bridget is their mother and their sister." (*DD*, 106)

Mary McCarthy refers to the plight of the off-spring of incestuous relationship: "A child of incest, as one of them remarks thoughtfully, has only one grandfather; this is viewed as a deprivation. The children of Sophia Stace, thanks to her insistence on marrying her own unsuspected half-brother, are underprivileged."[23] To Ralph who argues that even Greeks allowed children of the same father to marry and there is nothing wrong in the marriage of cousins, "we are not Greek," said Simon, flushing. "And we might be no better if we were. In that way we should not be." (*HIH,* 118) Thus Simon prevents further incest.

Richard (*A House and Its Head*) born of Grant and Alison's incest, dies a premature death in a gas accident. In *Darkness and Day*, it is revealed that there is no incest at all. Emotional incest between Ninian and Lavinia, John Ponsonby and Hetta come to an end by the marriages of Ninian and John. In *A God and His Gifts*, incest is prevented by Solomon not marrying his half-sister, Viola. After *Brothers and Sisters*, no incestuous marriage takes place. Even there it would not have occurred, if only Andrew had not hidden Christian parentage.

A God and His Gifts is Ivy Compton-Burnett's penultimate novel, where the subject is touched for the last time. While Hereward represents satyriasis, Rosa Lindsay is a case of nymphomania. However, revelation of incest at the right time forewarns Hereward that Viola he has been after is but his own daughter. It also prevents Solomon from marrying Viola, who is his half-sister.

Incest figures only in five novels. In *Darkness and Day*, it is an imaginary one. In *Brothers and Sisters*, it is mistaken as such. Only in *A God and His Gifts*, *A House and Its Head* and *A Heritage and Its History*, voluntary incest is shown with ravaging consequences. Even in these novels, except perhaps in *A God and His Gifts*, where there is a hint of attempt, incest is not repeated. Those concerned learn by experience the painful consequences of it.

Incest is not a punishable crime in the last decade of the nineteenth century, the period where Ivy Compton-Burnett's novels are set. Yet, the way the novelist dealt with the problem shows that she certainly upholds moral values. Her intention is not explicit but subtle.

In spite of the revelations of their husbands' affairs, wives do not threaten to go away or divorce them. They are shocked but not perturbed. A slight revolt, again quiet resignation and submission. Life continues as if nothing has happened. They accept their positions without questioning. This is because, in the society women are not treated on a par with men. The Matrimonial Causes Act of 1857 extended the possibilities of divorce.

> After 1857, women, if they could afford it, could divorce their husbands on grounds of cruelty, desertion or rape, but it was not until 1923 that they could obtain a divorce on grounds of the husband's adultery. . . . But divorced women were considered socially beyond the pale, and it was still assumed that children belonged naturally to their father.[24]

One of Ivy Compton-Burnett's characters in *Pastors and Masters*, Miss Basden, says hopefully thus: "I think that these changes in the divorce laws still do a great deal towards equalizing the position of women." (*PM*, 111) So these poor women submit to their lot without any qustioning. When women like Ada revolt, they are not accepted in their parental homes. They have no other avenue to resort to apart from it. Lack of economic independence is the main cause for the subjugation of women. It is an age of decaying morals and every one is resigned to her fate.

Adultery or conjugal infidelity are not considered great sins or crimes. They are not punishable under the law. They are inherent in the family but pose no threat to its stability. Understanding and adjustment are invariably found for the smooth continuity of life. Their motto, perhaps, is forgive and forget. Family remains unbroken.

Ivy Compton-Burnett, a spinster, presenting mostly unhappy marriages, does not seem to be against marriages as such. It may be wrong to suggest that she deplores marriages.[25] Her opinion is voiced through Eliza Heriot (*The Last and the First*) when she says, "it will bring its changes, and they should all be welcome ones." (*LF*, 142) If she remained a spinster, it may be due to circumstances,[26] and her high ideals not to degrade herself by accepting any loveless offer that came her way. She is a believer in the marriage institution. As Robert Heriot says, "I should be glad for my son to marry and continue the line." (*LF*, 128)

Though pre-marital and extra-marital relations pose a threat to the institution of marriage, it survives as its foundations seem to be quite strong and deep. Almost all extra-marital relationships depicted are temporary. The conjugal relations alone are lasting and permanent. Only death may separate the couple. That is why in *The Mighty and Their Fall*, it is said about Miles and Ellen thus: "it is good to see you together and to know there are bonds that nothing can break." (*MF*, 184)

She desires the partners to be sensible and think properly before taking such a serious step as marriage. Indiscriminate choosing of the partners is discouraged. She asks one of her women friends to be choosy and advises against accepting a late, last proposal "Don't ever get married, unless you absolutely have to."[27]

In *The Last and the First*, her last and posthumously published novel, Ivy Compton-Burnett presents a character, Hermia, who rejects a marriage which would be materially advantageous for her. Ivy Compton-Burnett may have taken particular care to see that this novel does not have adultery, incest or abnormal relationships.

In Compton-Burnett's novels, some are found in free pursuit of sex for pleasure. Her intention is to show that sex is bound by social and moral laws and realized only in marriage for peace and happiness. Violation of such laws results in disharmony and unhappiness. She is conservative in her outlook towards love and sex. For her, love generally means conjugal affection.

She is not interested in portraying ideal love. She is a realist and likes to present how members of a family practise unlawful sex secretly. She also desires to show how these natural instincts, if absent or perverted, affect a family. She thinks sexual irregularities and perversions as highly objectionable and unpardonable. Conjugal disloyalty and betrayal are reprehensible to her.

She does not believe in the customs of the former ages where marriage is between blood-relations. She is progressive in her outlook and to emphasize the values of mutual loyalty and affection, she presents cases where they have repugnant manifestations. She evidently warns us by showing the disastrous consequences of prohibited unions.

If adultery and incest dominate her novels, if she is preoccupied with domestic misconduct and its devastating consequences, it is because, being a realist, she wants to turn the search-light onto the darker aspects of the family life in the Victorian England. She wishes to promote a system of values which would result in a healthy and happy married relationship, indispensable for a healthy family milieu. Her lurid presentation of the negative aspects of family life is only designed to lay an indirect stress on the positive aspects. She wants to show how the perversities of life-style manifest themselves to vitiate the otherwise happy and contented matrimonial lives. Her main concern is to show with a telling effect how the adulterous, incestuous, abnormal relations adversely affect the otherwise smooth-running, happy family life.[1]

Patience and resignation are the weapons with which calamities like the ruthless betrayal of conjugal fidelities are met and the home is saved from collapse and ruin. The husband and wife, in spite of sexual escapades, continue to live together and develop some sort of undefinable attachment which prevents them from separation. She shows through her novels how the family survives the shocks and tempests. A constructive view of marriage as an institution is presented underlining its resilience and usefulness.

In the novels of Jane Austen, except for the marriages between the hero and heroine, almost all other established ones are depicted as defective for reasons of incompatibility, temperamental maladjustments etc., but never for reasons of indulgence in prohibited sex, such as incest, adultery etc. which is the characteristic of the novels of Ivy Compton-Burnett.

The theme of incest has been taken up by a few earlier dramatists like Cyril Tourneur and John Ford. Tourneur's *Revenger's Tragedy* in which Duke's second wife is wooing her husband's illegitimate son, Spurio and *Atheist's Tragedy* presents this theme in all its grossness with the idea of catering to the decadent public taste. Set against the background of Renaissance in Italy, they are gloomy melodramas. John Ford's play, *'Tis Pity She's Whore* carries this theme to an illogical extreme adding horror to more horror. Annabella and her brother, Giovanni, passionately in love with each other, lead an incestuous life. When she is married to another man much against her will, Giovanni is so furious and uncontrollable in his frustration that he kills her. Ford does not stop before carrying to a point far beyond any reasonable stretch of imagination. The young man plucks her heart out, and hoists it at the tip of his sword in a mad frenzy. Havelock Ellis pays a compliment to Ford: "He is a psychologist of clear, steady and slowly progressing insight whose field is by preference abnormal conditions of the mind or unusual experiences and relations."[28] Francis Beaumont's *A King and No King* resembles Ivy Compton-Burnett's *Darkness and Day* dealing with mistaken incest. King Arbaces of Iberia and his sister Panthea are the characters involved. Philip Massinger's play *The Fatal Dowry* deals with adultery.

But Ivy Compton-Burnett's handling of the theme appears to have a social purpose beyond the vicarious pleasure of exposing the dirt as Tourneur and Ford did. The civilized and refined British society with its veneer of sophistication has the undercurrent of evil, lurking there and restively waiting for an opportunity to raise its ugly head. Very often the truth remains hidden. The sense of refinement or image-building is so strong in society that most of such skeletons remain safely hidden in cupboards which may never be opened at all.

Louise Bogan's observation on *Darkness and Day* is applicable to several other novels: "Sex, in this closed universe, keeps cropping up in terms of comedy. A prevalent background of illegitimacy exists; so that masters are frequently faced with the results of their early 'stumbles' in the form of butlers who are their natural sons and housekeepers who are their natural daughters."[29] Ivy Compton-Burnett tried to handle the isolated passion of individuals finding outlets without legal sanction, several of them existing only in imagination. V. Ramakrishna Rao sums up the novelist's views: "Though she has no religious leanings, she never preaches against the sanctions of the church in matters of sex. Incest, restricted to human beings, is an abnormal area of human experience."[30] He quotes Mary Douglas, an anthropologist: "It would be wrong to interpret the great mythologies of antiquity which depict the horror of brother/sister incest as merely enacting the emotions of childhood. The magnifying and glorifying social dimension gave the relation of brother to sister its special hold on poetic imagination. For us, the brother/sister theme has lost its poignancy as a great literary and dramatic symbol because the social tie has lost its central significance."[31] Finally, V. Ramakrishna Rao would have us believe that "Her exploration and judgment of incestuous love should perhaps warn us not to assume too easily that our property-oriented morality is conducive to our cultural health."[32]

INDEX

1. Jenni Calder, *Women and Marriage in Victorian Fiction* (London: Thames and Hudson, 1976), p. 10.
2. Calder, p. 18.
3. *Ibid.*, p. 31.
4. *Ibid.*, pp. 30-33.
5. Charles Dickens, "Sketches of Young Couples," qtd in Calder, p. 107.
6. Calder, p. 131.
7. Pamela Hansford Johnson, *I. Compton-Burnett* (London: Longman, 1951), p. 31.
8. Kay Dick, *Ivy and Stevie* (London: Allison and Busby, 1983), p. 29.
9. Johnson, p. 19.
10. Dick, p. 33.
11. *The New Encyclopaedia Britannica* (Chicago: Encyclopaedia Britannica, 1974), p. 322.
12. *Ibid.*, pp. 12-14.
13. Mary McCarthy, "Inventions of I. Compton-Burnett," *Encounter* 27:5 (1966), p. 20.
14. Hilary Spurling, *Secrets of a Woman's Heart* (London: Penguin, 1984), p. 274.
15. Calder, p. 123.
16. Violet Powell, *A Compton-Burnett Compendium* (London: Heinemann, 1973), p. 32.
17. Powell, p. 75.
18. *Britannica,* 7, p. 486.
19. *Ibid.*, 5, p. 107.

20. Spurling, p. 116.
21. Powell, p. 202.
22. Rabindranath Sarkar, *Ivy Compton-Burnett: A Trend in English Fiction* (Calcutta: Firma KLM, 1979), p. 96.
23. McCarthy, p. 20.
24. Calder, p. 120.
25. Spurling, *Secrets*, p. 263.
26. *Loc. cit.*
27. *Ibid.*, p. 264.
28. Havelock Ellis, "Introduction to Ford's Plays," qtd. in *The Jacobean Drama*, Una Ellis-Fermor (London: Methuen, 1977), p. 234.
29. Louise Bogan, "Childhood's False Eden," *Selected Criticism* (New York: 1955), p. 189.
30. V. Ramakrishna Rao, *Ivy Compton-Burnett: A Critical Study* (Waltair: Andhra University Press, 1974), p. 51.
31. *Loc. cit.*
32. *Loc. cit.*

Technique

An examination of the different aspects of technique adopted by Ivy Compton-Burnett in her novels becomes imperative in a study which seeks to place her in the mainstream of English Domestic novel. The tradition which can be considered to have had its proper beginning with Goldsmith's *The Vicar of Wakefield*, and developed with substantial contributions from novelists like Fanny Burney, Elizabeth Gaskell and Jane Austen maintained its claim to have an identity of its own through the common features of the art of such veterans in the field, not confined exclusively to the choice of themes, but to the detailed execution of the basic ideas through careful handling of the technical aspects. The individual proponents differed in several details which testified to their originality as well as to the demands made by the specific themes. Technical aspects like dialogue, plot, characterization and style contribute to the building up of the right atmosphere for domestic novels. The background, the setting and the 'mood' generated are as much essential for the domestic atmosphere as the plot and the characters are. The images evoked by the word 'domestic' should be conjured and produced by the art of the novelist. It is in this context that Ivy Compton-Burnett's literary technique is being analyzed with a view to examining how the use of the technique enriches the Domestic novel, and how she differs from the other major proponents of this form. She follows the broad, general aspects of the technique while establishing her originality in handling some aspects which are very crucial in a work of fiction. All the same, her points of deviation, in effect, become her individual contribution to the Domestic Novel which had to face new challenges in the decades ahead.

Among the salient features of Compton-Burnett's technical achievement, the very first point that strikes a reader is the way the author retreats, as it were, to the background without assuming the role of the omniscient narrator. R.N. Sarkar compares her stand with regard to her characters as similar to that of a shepherd to his flock of sheep: "She is related to her world in the way a shepherd is related to his flock. The shepherd sits apart from his herd playing upon his pipe, and allows the sheep to browse as long as they do not stray away from the flock.[1]

In a typical Victorian novel, a reader is guided through it by its omniscient author. He is very rarely left to his own free interpretation. The author is always there to elucidate and interpret what the reader perceives. John Galsworthy, Arnold Bennett and H.G. Wells adopted this accepted tradition. Some of the novelists of the post-war period deviate slightly from the accepted tradition. In the novels like E.M. Forster's *Passage to India* and D.H. Lawrence's *St. Mawr*, the relationship is retained between the reader and the author, but it is not so intimate as in the Victorian novels. They too, like Victorian writers, tend to be personal in influencing the readers' understanding.

Some of the writers like James Joyce and Virginia Woolf choose the subjective technique of presenting the narrative, in which the narrative proceeds along the current of the character's thoughts instead of the author's narration of the story. In contrast to the subjectivity, there is objectivity sans personal element. There is no participation of the novelist as narrator or interpreter. Neither does he project himself indirectly as one of the characters.

Ivy Compton-Burnett's method of narration is unique as she "has stripped the Victorian novel of everything but its essentials. . . . Her interest is in its logic, which she applies anew."[2] Discarding the traditional techniques in vogue, she introduces a purely objective method which leave little room for the mediatory role characteristic of the Victorian authors. In spite of her making use of the omniscient point of view, she recedes to the background as a narrator and maintains an objective aloofness from her characters. This prompts Mario Praz to comment thus: "Compton-Burnett, the most impersonal of narrators, does not comment, she is not even concerned to draw full-length portraits of her characters; she lets them speak, records their conversation with the impartiality of a tape-recorder; the comments of the chorus are provided by governesses, servants, relations. And the result is that the exploration made by Compton-Burnett with her dungeons of the family is the most complete."[3] It is this 'exploration' which has made her novels some of the richest and the most original specimens of Domestic Novels in English. Instead of the day-to-day surface details, the novelist probes into the very recesses of the characters' minds to bring out reality in its shocking and crude form.

Commenting on this aloofness, a reviewer observes: "Miss Compton-Burnett has, in fact, discovered a convention, a means of standing away from her characters and avoiding the limitations of reporting."[4] Such aloofness, however, does not imply any negative attitude or lack of concern for her characters. Brian McFarlane's words throw light on this point: "While she appears to be the most objective of writers, seeming to withdraw herself completely from the lives she presents, offering no comment on them, yet this very approach seems to me to reveal the profound nature of her commitment to them."[5]

The novelist herself wanted the story to develop through conversations among the characters: "in reading novels, I am disappointed if a scene is carried through in the voice of the author rather than the voices of the characters."[6]

It is but briefly that she describes her characters and when she does so, sometimes the reader can at once measure them up even before they talk. "By making them reveal themselves in their own words, she is as able to penetrate the darkest recesses of the human mind as any of the most skilful third-person analysts among English novelists."[7] Without a semblance of intervention, Ivy Compton-Burnett seems to be judging her characters simultaneously. Explaining how it is possible, Charles Burkhart says: "The truth-telling people in the novels examine clichés to explode them; the people less than sincere reveal their insincerity by their reliance on clichés."[8]

She relies on the dialogue and refrains from comments or interpretations. Such refraining, as Brian McFarlane observes, may be seen "as an austerely humane withholding of direct judgment on the more vicious possibilities of man."[9] Yet the pattern of the story, particularly the denouement, shows the unmistakable omnipresence of the author, though invisible and indirect. R.N. Sarkar comments on this aspect: "Her unseen hand works as the Creator's will works in His creation, she only sets the track but leaves the wheels free. No definite indication of the author's presence is to be found in her novels, not even in the last phase of the story (denouement), yet everything occurs as she may have wished."[10]

Her summaries, usually brief and few, are descriptive in nature rather than narrative. When compared to other novels, only *Brothers and Sisters*, her third novel, has long and large summaries. However, the two-page introduction to the story and the detailed description of Andrew Stace's manor house do not contribute to the action. The action starts from the second chapter onwards. The summary found in the first chapter of the novel performs expository, interpretative and informative function. The summaries present in the other novels also hardly ever contribute to the action. They mainly serve informative purpose giving a brief account of the characters. Age, occupation, physical features and other important particulars are given in bare outline. The two brothers, Edgar and Dudley (*A Family and a Fortune*) are clearly differentiated with the aid of a brief half-page summary:

> The two brothers who entered were tall, lean men in the earlier fifties, the elder . . . bad thick, straight, speckled hair, speckled, hazel eyes, vaguely speckled clothes, a long, solid nose and chin, a look of having more bone and less flesh than other men, a face and hands which would have been called bronzed. . . . The younger brother, Dudley, was of the same height and lighter build, and was said to be a caricature of the elder, and was so in the sense that his face was cast in a similar mould and had its own deviations from it. His nose was less straight; his eyes were not entirely on a line . . . his skin was rather pale than bronzed. (*FF*, 11-12)

As Ivy Compton-Burnett leaves action out of the scope of the summaries, they mainly serve the purpose of illustrating character and situation. So it is rightly observed that "Compton-Burnett had already mastered her special technique of stating simply the initial predicament of her characters, reserving their own thoughts and speech for later phase of the story, when hearts are opened and confidences come to painful birth.[11]

In *Dolores*, her first novel, she employed a narrative art with a very liberal use of commentary and summary and a sparingly little dialogue. Though it does not fall in line with her subsequent novels, it gives "an opportunity to understand the strong technical discipline by which Compton-Burnett achieved her later purity of narrative style."[12] It may be noticed that, even in *Dolores*, the last chapters are characterized by less narrative and total absence of authorial comment. After a gap of fourteen years, she published her second novel, *Pastors and Masters*, in which she began to experiment with a new narrative technique. Stevenson rightly comments: "during the interval a transformation occurred in both her technique and her attitude. In place of excessive exposition there was now an extreme reliance upon dialogue."[13] However, these dialogues appear to have been arranged rather loosely about the plot. Very few descriptive passages are there and she seldom interposes her comments between persons and scenes. This novel marks only the seed time and after that she has been completely the mistress of her unique style which she has used to increasing perfection in the novels to follow.

Though *Brothers and Sisters* opens with a narrative and also abounds in descriptive passages, it marks the end of the experimental phase of her novels. After choosing her right medium of narration in dialogue, she never abandoned or even modified it. Robert Liddell points out: "Miss Compton-Burnett has freed herself from all irrelevancies in order to write the pure novel. And like Miss Austen, she has a dislike for merely descriptive writing, which she uses with even greater economy."[14]

In spite of the brevity of description in her novels, there is no difficulty for the reader to understand the background. "Using our detective commonsense . . . we can in fact piece together a lot more background details than at first appear."[15] In *Parents and Children*, for example, the nurse-maid Mullet's romantic tales about her tragic childhood reveal the fact of her upbringing in a very ordinary village home. Absence of adequate descriptions is invariably compensated by the dialogue that helps to evaluate the characters. The dialogue carries the entire burden of action.

Ivy Compton-Burnett innovated the dialogue method by peeling away superfluous descriptions so that there is only the dialogue to cover the skeletons of the story. "It is a dialogue of a power and brilliance unmatched in English prose fiction."[16] This occasioned the comment that Ivy Compton-Burnett's novels "consist of conversation to the extent that a water melon consists of water."[17] Despite the technical difficulty of heavy reliance on dialogue, Ivy Compton-Burnett rarely wearies or falters. Novel after novel has the same formula. That is why "opening a new novel by Miss Compton-Burnett is like resuming a conversation that had temporarily ceased but had not ended."[18] It may not be an exaggeration to say that any novel by Ivy Compton-Burnett is one long continuation of dialogues. 'Tirelessly penetrating and immaculately written dialogue' appears on page after page in each of her novels. All signs of movement are auditory. A character's presence is known only when he joins in the conversation.

Like Ivy Compton-Burnett, Henry James too experimented once with this dialogue technique in *The Awkward Age*. But Ivy Compton-Burnett is more successful in the conversational method because, unlike James, she allows her characters to usurp authorial omniscience and to speak with clarity and precision.

Henry Green, Ivy Compton-Burnett's contemporary novelist, observes that more and more importance is being given to dialogue. He predicts that it will be "the principle support of the novel for a long time to come."[19] Replying to a question on her choice of dialogue method, Ivy Compton-Burnett says that it has been 'just natural' to her. She adds that she is neither desirous of nor has ever attempted to write a different kind of book. "I don't know why I write so much in dialogue. I think it must just have been my nature. It just came like that."[20] The power of dialogue in her novels is such that "the author has vanished behind the words of her characters, declining to comment or to explain, and so we are deprived of any background save the utterances of the characters themselves."[21] By replacing the usual practice of explanation of the thought of the characters by their conversations, the novelist does not face the problem of how to expose the characters because, "Her conversational method creates, as it were, an external stream of consciousness, in which the characters overtly voice what the traditional novelist usually explains about them. Consequently, we see what they are—there is nothing to hide, for the very nature of their communication forces complete disclosure of their thoughts."[22]

The dialogue technique preferred by the author perfectly coordinates with her choice of family themes. In her novels, two or three families are brought together to represent the whole of society and their interplay, the sum of all essential forces in the world. Dialogue is the weapon with which the novelist punctures vanity, cruelty and affection.

As a means of communication, dialogue is highly suggestive and flexible. It replaces the kind of interior analysis so vital to the novels: "this supremely sensitive stylistic instrument records every nuance of hypocrisy or irony, stupidity or sentimentality."[23]

The dialogue method enables Ivy Compton-Burnett to achieve ultimately what she intends to. Arnold Kettle makes an apt observation: "Her conversationalised dialogue makes possible . . . a sharpness of conflict, verbal, moral and psychological, of sometimes almost terrifying force and a fundamentally down-to-earth situation, unexaggerated in its essential qualities which pins the conflict to reality and prevents . . . abstraction."[24]

Ivy Compton-Burnett's conversational device is often a theatrical one. "In flight from the novelist's freedom to wander into minds, Miss Compton-Burnett is logically driven to embrace the restrictions of a dramatist."[25] This prompts Grylls to observe: "In approaching the novels we must accept certain conditions as we would at a play."[26]

Character revelation through dialogue and very little scope for authorial comment make her technique essentially dramatic. In this aspect she resembles Jane Austen who too preferred dramatic method, and *Pride and Prejudice*, the most dramatic of her novels, has been analyzed into five acts. Ivy Compton-Burnett's novels may be said to be closer to plays for the effective use made of dramatic devices like misplaced documents, overheard conversations and the revelation of secrets. She too considers every novel of hers as "something rather between a novel and a play."[27] Talking to John Bowen, she affirms the same fact, "my books seem to me to be something between a novel and a play."[28] Commenting on the dramatic quality of her novels, Lord Horder points out: "Miss Compton-Burnett is by instinct a playwright and once more offers us, whatever its outward appearance, not a novel but a play. Her chapters are the static acts of a drama, in which the characters discuss at length a new set of circumstances disclosed on the first page of each."[29]

Her novels abound in situations and incidents with very high dramatic potential. The son killing the mother in *Men and Wives*, Anna committing psychological murders, manipulating the will, and bringing round the marriage between her cousin and herself, a father seducing the fiancé of his son, Sybil conspiring to kill her father's child and so on would be intensely effective and appealing in the theatre. Handled by Aeschylus, Sophocles, Shakespeare or even Webster, such themes would have produced masterpieces on the stage with dramatic conflict, suspense, horror, tense anticipation and even final sense of catharsis. The modern dramatists like Ibsen and Chekhov have constructed great masterpieces like *A Doll's House* and *The Cherry Orchard* on much lighter themes and simpler incidents. Even though Ivy Compton-Burnett claims that her novels come in between a novel and a play, her novels fail to have a genuine dramatic appeal. The impact such situations should have created is almost totally lost in the overflowing dialogue submerging the effect. Nor are the situations as effective as in the case of Thomas Hardy's novels. Simpler incidents such as the seduction of Tess in *Tess of the D'Urbervilles* or the tragedy of Henchard in *The Mayor of Casterbridge* create very deep impact on the readers. The little bird dying in Henchard's cage, Arabella killing the pigs, and Little Father Time 'helping' his parents by getting rid of his siblings in *Jude thee Obscure* have passed into world literature due to the intensity of their appeal. From this perspective, Ivy Compton-Burnett's narrative, relying too much on the strength of dialogue, can be said to have had a stifling effect on the emotional appeal which such situations should have normally generated. Passions get weakened.

However, it should not be wrongly interpreted as her fascination for play-writing. She has no penchant for a play as, in her view, it does not offer her as much scope as a novel does. She thinks that the dialogue novel suits her best. Interviewed by Michael Millgate, she said: "It gives me more range and a little more length, and it doesn't subject me to the mechanical restrictions of a play."[30]

Ivy Compton-Burnett can be said to have refined and perfected the dialogue-dominated technique that began with *What Maisie Knew* (1897) and the *The Awkward Age* (1899) by Henry James.

Of the significant difference between Ivy Compton-Burnett's novel and a play, Joanne Hutchinson says: "Strictly speaking there are not appearances, we see nothing except words. As in the theater we listen, but without the help of the actors. Compton-Burnett obliges her readers to do the work of both actor and director and to help even with the conventional writing chores."[31]

Though her novels bear some resemblance to Greek drama where events, happening off the stage, are deduced by the reader through what the characters talk on the stage, Brian McFarlane seems to disagree with this comparison. He says: "the books never read like plays: there is something too measured and too abstract in the dialogue to carry the sort of dramatic action a play requires."[32] Wolfgang Iser finds some subtle but substantial difference between the dramatic dialogue and the dialogue in her novels. He says that in her novels, "the form of conversation seems rather to diffuse than to bring out the situation of the characters in Victorian society. Even though the atmosphere of the Victorian family and home does pervade the whole novel, the words and actions of the individual members of that family continually exceed the limits of what was considered to be proper in that particular society . . . the function of the dialogue in the drama—communicating different positions and throwing emphasis on the common ground underlying the conversation—is here quite transformed. Now the dialogue means the common ground—i.e., Victorian convention—dwindle into insignificance, blotting it out with the unfathomableness of human actions and reactions."[33]

But there is no denying the fact that a typical page in any of her novels reads like the script of a play. Ivy Compton-Burnett had a gift for producing dramatic effects and *Daughters and Sons, A Heritage and Its History* and *A God and His Gifts* are her novels where such situations abound. The form, content and structure of *A House and Its Head* make it look more like a play than as a novel, with about four thousand short, three-line speeches. *A Heritage and Its History* is another which has been successfully adapted for stage.

In her novels, soliloquies, asides and stage directions are also present. Asides are never overheard in plays but not so in her novels. Some of the asides are ironical:

> "Spoiling people does not make them happier," said Anna, voicing a theory that Jenney always thought a strange one.
>
> "It only exalts them in their own estimation," said Claribel, as if this were indeed a thing not to be done." (*EB*, 10)

The refinement of the dialogue comes from the stage directions. Robert Liddell identifies "about two hundred and fifty of the different ways in which the characters may speak, and there may be nearly as many ways more."[34]

In her later novels, Ivy Compton-Burnett curtails the use of stage directions. The characters come and go unannounced. They break into conversations suddenly and somewhat unexpectedly. Sean O'Faolain says: "She writes much as if she were writing the script of a play or radio play, with most of the stage-directions omitted, or cut to the bone, or expressed in words that do not evoke a picture: 'quizzical,' 'off hand,' 'neutral,' 'parenthetic,' and the like."[35]

Ivy Compton-Burnett gives utmost importance to linguistic precision. Her style of conversation is extremely formal. Even the children are made to talk rather formally. She justifies this when she tells Frank Kermode: "children, you know, do really talk rather formally if you listen to them. Colloquialism comes later. It is what people pick-up."[36] Abbreviations like 'don't' for 'do not,' 'it's' for 'it is,' 'that's' for 'that is' or 'I'll be' for 'I will be' are conspicuous by their absence in all her works. The extreme formality of style seems to fit in while depicting ceremonious and artificial behaviour. Maybe it is a sort of parody designed to expose the darker side of the culture and ethos of the Victorian era.

Though colloquialism is generally avoided, slang expressions seem to have been sparingly employed with a definite purpose. Besides formal utterance and slangy speech, the convention employed by the novelist is that of speech either half-meant to be heard or to be silent. Most of the speeches in the later novels may be taken as silent thoughts. In *Men and Wives*, one of her early novels, Godfrey Haslam's soliloquy is not meant to be heard by any. It is like interior monologue. In her other early novels, there are speeches that are half-meant to be heard, for example: "'We have hushed enough things up,' said Nance under her breath." (*HH*, 268) Another is from *A Family and a Fortune*:

> "Justine now shows tact," murmured Aubrey.
> "I love a conversation between Father and Jellamy," said Justine in an undertone. (*FF*, 15)

Silent speeches figure in her later novels. In *Manservant and Maidservant*, George and Miss Buchanan speak silently. George, to a question about his stealing food: "'Because I am so plainly fed, that the dining-room pudding was irresistible,' said George, but only in his heart." (*MSMS*, 47) "These silent speeches, definitely so described, make us conjecture that many speeches not specifically described as silent, may be unheard—I believe the author works within an almost Elizabethan convention, which gives her the liberty to pass at will from ordinary spoken dialogue to soliloquy heard only by the reader."[37] In the talk between Sophia and Robin (*Brothers and Sisters*), the speech made by Sohpia is audible but there is no indication of Sophia having heard of what Robin says.

> "Do take your hands out of your pockets, Robin," said Sophia. "I told you that just now. Can't you find something to occupy them? Or must you stand about all the evening because other people are in trouble?"
>
> "Yes, of course I must be about at people's service, when things are amiss, and they might have a use for me" said Robin. "I hope you will do the same when you get down to father. To do you justice, I believe you will. And I discover something to employ my hands in opening the door for you. You are doing harm up here."
>
> Sophia went out, without looking at and almost without thinking of her son. (*BS*, 99-100)

The dialogue is used to conceal the feelings as well as to communicate them. It helps to understand the discrepancy between the surface manners and the withheld feelings. "Ivy Compton- Burnett's concern had always been less with conversation than with subconversation, the things left unsaid while somebody is speaking."[38] Because of this technique, the readers get an impression of the things that are said in normal conversation and also the things that are consciously suppressed. Arnold Kettle writes: "What is new in Miss Compton-Burnett's novel is the continuous tensioning the dialogue between what is actually said and what is expressed but only thought and the consequent ruthlessness in the exposure of the underlying issues and implications of a scene."[39]

Occasionally, certain facts are revealed by indirect expressions as in the case of Julius who confesses a secret of his past life to his wife thus:

> Miranda, it was the time when we grew apart, in Rosebery's early manhood. I was thrown on myself; I had to steer my course as I could, you will remember how things were. My life took on a second thread, as the first one went away. I had a life apart from you, as you had one apart from me. (*MS*, 126)

Sometimes Ivy Compton-Burnett employs diagonal technique, answering the unexpected part of a question.

> "It is certainly odd that civilized people should have it on their tables."
>
> "Do uncivilized people have things on tables?" (*FF*, 10)

At some other times, Ivy Compton-Burnett's style becomes heightened by use of poetry and alliteration. As Robert Liddell says: "A tendency to verse, perhaps not altogether intended . . . seems to mark some of the later books."[40] In *Darkness and Day*, Edmund tells Bridget:

> Yes, that is the sadness in our sorrow, that it takes the guise of shame. That is what I would spare you, if you would be spared. Shame is no less, that it is helpless, and pity may carry much that destroys itself. And we shall face it in its hardest form, the form that carries self-pity. We shall have to give pity ourselves. (*DD*, 101)

For the poetic quality of style, Ivy Compton-Burnett can be compared to T.S. Eliot. Arnold Kettle says: "Miss Compton-Burnett's method is essentially the method of the poetic dramatist (T.S. Eliot's dialogue in *The Family Reunion* is technically not at all unlike a Compton-Burnett novel, though not nearly so closely integrated?"[41] Endorsing this opinion, D.S. Bland comments: "It is apparent that her mature style, tight, clipped and oracular, as it often is, comes very close at times to the heightened and exact language of poetry."[42]

Her prose is intensely disciplined and regimented. Richard McLaughlin, an American reviewer, deservedly praises her for this thus: "Miss Compton-Burnett's conversation pieces will come as a refresher in an era of stale and laboured prose."[43]

Rhythmic prose is another feature not uncommon in her novels. In *Men and Wives*, Sir Godfrey says to his butler:

> "This is a day that is good to live and breathe in, that makes a man feel in his prime . . . "
>
> "What aged man would you take me to be, as I step as it were casually into your view? . . ."
>
> "I'll wager not fifty-six. But that is what I am . . ." (*MW*, 7)

Regular rhythm characterizes her dialogue and this fact makes Elizabeth Bowen say: "an icy sharpness prevails in their dialogue. In fact, to read in these days a page of Compton-Burnett is to think of the sound of glass being swept up, one of these London mornings after a blitz."[44]

To many like Brian McFarlane, Ivy Compton-Burnett's dialogue produces a stylized effect. But Robert Liddell argues, "While we must still call much of the dialogue stylized, it is not so much stylized as many people seem to think."[45] The novelist herself says, "My writing does not seem to me . . . 'stylized.'"[46]

Wolfgang Iser appears to defend Ivy Compton-Burnett's statement when he says: "if one defines stylization in terms of those preconceptions necessary in the novel for a presentation of reality, then it must be said, paradoxically, that Ivy Compton-Burnett's novels contain an absolute minimum of such preconceptions. There is no confusion or identification of means of presentation and thing presented. The reader is made constantly aware of the distinction, for the author does not stylize the reactions of her characters, as she renounces any form of coordination that might join the dialogue into a coherent whole."[47] Usually the speech of children is not stylized. Simple characters, even though adults, do not use stylized speech. "How do you do, Mrs. Napier? I have come back to-day because the term begins to-morrow." (*MWTM*, 9)

Robert Liddell has his own reservations on the quality of Ivy Compton-Burnett's style. He says: "While we must still call much of the dialogue stylized, it is not so much stylized as many people seem to think. Nevertheless stylization is there and, like any language that is at all remote from living speech, that of Miss Compton-Burnett does not escape occasional clumsiness and woodenness. It is too exact a transcription of thought, while speech is both more and less than that."[48]

Brian McFarlane, however, agrees that her speech is highly stylized, arguing, at the same time, that it is not unreal: "if it is not naturalistic dialogue, it is equally not 'unreal' in so far as it reveals with remarkable precision the true modes of thought, the essential selves of the characters who speak it."[49]

Ivy Compton-Burnett displays a unique skill in describing things with carefully chosen words and phrases. At times, she prefers a phrase to a bare statement. 'Broke into weeping' is her phrase to describe the grief of a younger child and for an older child, her phrase is 'sank into tears.' In the same way, when children laugh, she says 'they broke into mirth' or 'going into mirth.' When an elder brother kicks his younger brother, she says: "he lifted his foot and gave him a blow." To suggest that a woman saw a man going to be her possible husband, the phrase is 'threw her eyes over his face.' 'She speaks flashing her eyes over his face' suggests that she is angry with him. These phrases describe the situations more aptly and eloquently than bare statements.

Ivy Compton-Burnett's reluctance to use words and phrases readily available forces her to go in for rare and unfamiliar ones. In *Manservant and Maidservant*, Magdalene brings a 'restorative' to her tutor brother, Gideon, when he comes home tired. 'Restorative' is a drink but she prefers to use rather that unfamiliar word. In her early works, she used words that have almost passed out of normal speech. In *Brothers and Sisters*, after describing a house where the Slangs lived, the garden is described thus:

> The garden did not even do as well, unless the purpose of a garden is to accommodate a moderate quantity of potsherds, and a considerable one of properties the neighbourhood finds dispensable. (*BS*, 67)

The word potsherds, meaning rubbish dump, was archaic even when Ivy Compton-Burnett used it.

Ivy Compton-Burnett's dialogue is stringed with epigrams, one after the other. One rude remark is followed by the perfect rejoinder producing a flow of aphorisms. These increase in number and brilliance from novel to novel. Her subjects speak in saws and proverbs, such as:

> "To know all is to forgive all."
> "To thine own self be true."
> "It is more blessed to give than to receive."
> "Where there is smoke, there's fire."

But these aphorisms are not used to convey their usual meanings. Ivy Compton-Burnett, like Oscar Wilde, tends to invert the proverbs. Mary McCarthy observes: "Compton-Burnett's own work often has a paradoxical air, which is the result, however, of her empiricism: her interest in seeking how an idea or a verbal structure would behave if subjected to certain slight' changes. Moreover, in the angular geometry of her mind forms imply their complements; a form of words prompts her to find its opposite and its converse, without prejudgment as to the outcome."[50]

A familiar maxim, turned upside down, holds an unexpected truth and attains new meaning contrary to its common meaning. The reversal of an accepted notion may result in a discovery and her characters make bland and devastating assumptions. "To know all is to forgive all" becomes "To forgive, it is best to know as little as possible."

'To thine ownself be true' is to be false to everyone else. The characters like Clement (*A Family and A Fortune*) and Anna Donne (*Elders and Betters*) who are true to themselves prove to be villains.

> "It is more blessed to give than to receive" said Latimer.
> "Ha, ha! There is something in that," said Peter.
> "We have to have things before we can give them." (*BS*, 44)

Her style is marked by a perfect balance. There is a "perfect balance of synthesis and antithesis, comparison and contrast."[51] Cicely Greig thinks that one of Ivy Compton-Burnett's innovations is balance. She writes thus: "action and re-action, climax and anti-climax, a general questioning and answering, so perfect that there is nothing like it in the history of the novel in England, and one must go back to the strophe and anti-strophe of a Greek chorus for comparison. This balance makes for a wonderful architechtonic effect."[52]

There is a continuing distinctive pattern in Ivy Compton-Burnett's dialogue: "a gradual undercutting of ironies and frivolous remarks, a conversation that seems to come nearer the truth, a brief lapse into platitude . . . and then the whole matter crumbles into mock tautology. . . . The result is that by having her characters speak with complete logic and frankness Miss Compton-Burnett achieves an effect of absolute disingenuousness: when nothing is held back, everything seems kept in reserve. It is the absurd dead pan comedy of Joseph K and Alice."[53] This pattern is illustrated in a dialogue from *A God and His Gifts*. Morton greets his father, Hereward Egerton, sarcastically when he comes to know that he fathered the child of his wife:

> "And shall I do and say likewise?" said Morton, in a tone of self-mockery. "Am I also to retract my hasty words? I will try to be a son to you, Father. Better perhaps than I have been. If I had not failed you, you yourself might not have failed. Let us learn from each other."
>
> "I am glad, Merton," said Hereward, as if accepting the literal words. "I will not say more. Again it need not be said." (*GG*, 122)

Most of Ivy Compton-Burnett's speeches prove ironic as the story unfolds. Sophia, angry with her father for ordering her life, comments, "I would not stoop to use absolute power like that. It shows how degrading absolute power can be."[54] Ironically, she proves to be a much greater tyrant than her father.

"Miss Compton-Burnett is the wittiest of living writers and her wit, like all true wit, is not a matter of superficial smartness or a cunning ornamentation of style. It springs from deep in her observation of life, from her critical consideration of the standards and values of the society, she is presenting."[55] Complimenting Ivy Compton-Burnett for her humour, Burkhart says: "She is read for her comedy. Surely these twenty novels constitute the most brilliant and sustained verbal comedy in English."[56] Brian McFarlane says: "With her, wit is the vehicle of truth. At her wittiest, she is giving us the truest things about her characters."[57] It is "witty, acid, malicious, mordent, stinging, it frequently corrodes to the bone."[58] Her description of life may be brutal and grim but it is also essentially comic. "There is an energy behind Miss Compton-Burnett's wit which is exhilarating as well as destructive."[59] She is a postmaster in tempering her work with a sublime sense of wit. "She can create and sustain an impression of wit and profundity as forcibly as any novelist"[60] as seen in a simple sentence like this: "'I suppose this is a thing I should not say,' said Madeline, as she prepared to say it." (*LF*, 53)

Brian McFarlane pays the greatest tribute to her when he says: "It is not too extravagant a claim, I think, to say that Ivy Compton-Burnett achieves the highest order of sustained wit to be found anywhere in the English novel."[61]

This may be the conscious wit of the intelligent characters or that made use of to reveal the obtuseness of the dull ones. The author uses wit to such advantage as delineating the moral or cultural attributes of her characters.

The first effect of her wit is to provoke laughter even though it does not reveal anything strange or unusual. The second is the shaping of the conversation which bristles with unassailable logic and unbeatable repartee. The third is in respect of the masterly presentation of the true nature of her characters and their interaction.

Ivy Compton-Burnett is a literary adventurer. She shows great enthusiasm for the inclusion of her name in the book. Cicely Greig is writing to trace the history of adventurous writing in prose and poetry in English literature.[62] Regardless of any scruples about speech, she makes her characters say unhesitatingly and bluntly what exactly is passing through their minds.

Her technique in the first novel, *Dolores*, is entirely different from that of her subsequent works. The style of *Dolores* "is crude, bare and rather alarming. It is not like real English: it is like the language or translation."[63] Lionel Stevenson finds "laborious exposition, the harsh elliptical style and the prevalence of long, abstract words,"[64] in the novel. However, irony and wit bring liveliness to the otherwise drab narrative and conversational passages. Surprisingly, the turgidity of style clears up towards the end of the novel.

Pastors and Masters, her second novel, "is but a Compton-Burnett novel in embryo—the witty conversations lack the bone foundation of the works that follow."[65] Unlike the first two novels, her third novel, *Brothers and Sisters*, is a fully realized one with a well-developed plot and skilfully woven narration and conversation, complementing each other in bone and flesh relationship. Later on, she switches over completely to the dialogue method with the barest minimum of description. One has to remember that "Miss Compton-Burnett is not concerned with simple 'verisemblance.' She is attempting a direct translation of thought and feeling, and anything which she considers an obstacle to this direct apprehension is as far as possible eliminated . . . just as no loose phrase is ever allowed by her characters to escape without its implications being probed and exposed, she will not allow the imperfect expression that verisimilitude demands to interfere with the penetrating economy of her exposition of a human situation. She makes many of her characters speak, not colloquially, but with the language of the understanding, formulating for them the perceptions that lie behind words."[66]

Even as Ivy Compton-Burnett relies almost entirely on the dialogue methods for the denouement of her story, she also adapts her own technique in the portrayal of character which is strikingly different from the descriptive or dramatic methods then in vogue. The former is the traditional method based on the description of the physical traits of the characters. Dickens and Hardy working on the physical realism belong to this traditional class. Charlotte Bronte excels in combining both the descriptive and dramatic methods whereas Jane Austen uses the dramatic method to best advantage in character portrayal. In depicting her characters, she very rarely introduces herself. She conveys her impressions and opinions by the direct record of dialogue and action. At times, however, the task of interpreting people and events is shared by certain of her intelligent characters and the anonymous, impersonal, omniscient narrator. The writers using stream of consciousness technique work on the psychological realism and present the though of a character. But Ivy Compton-Burnett innovates her own method through a fine blend of both the physical and the psychological realms for the description of character. "Ivy Compton-Burnett successfully combines physical and psychological realism and evolves a new technique of her own by which she makes character consciousness external. She does not take us directly into the inner-self of her characters. But the very words they utter and the slightest movements they make reveal how the minds of her characters are working."[67]

Almost all Ivy Compton-Burnett's characters are initially given an apt but brief description and are then left to reveal themselves by their conversations. Another method of characterization is through deeds. It is merely mentioned that Sophia Stace (*Brothers and Sisters*) is beautiful but no attempt is made to substantiate it by describing her looks etc. But one detail repeatedly mentioned in the book is an aural image of Sophia's dress rustling as she moves in the house.

"What? What is this?" said Sophia, rustling in. (*BS*, 47)

Sophia's rustle sounded on the stairs as if she meant it to be heard. (*BS*, 103)

She left them, and they heard on the stairs the familiar rustling that seemed as if it should be different. (*BS*, 139)

Mary Dolton Rowsell remarks: "This rustling is suggestive of Sophia's character: the connotations of snake and queen hint at the warring aspects within."[68]

Mary McCarthy discovers a hidden touch in making Sophia develop cancer. Against the background of the relations multiplying cancerously, the critic elaborates: "And now a new hidden fact emerges: Sophia has cancer. Sophia *is* cancer, the disease at the centre of the novel. . . . Her will is a parasite on her family, like a choking organism."[69]

Robert Liddell, one of Ivy Compton-Burnett's admirers, thinks that the novelist's personal descriptions tend to be perfunctory in that they do not help proper conception of the character. He says: "One is inclined to wonder if much would be lost by the suppression of such passages."[70] Talking to Margaret Jourdain, Ivy Compton-Burnett herself answers this criticism thus:

> I should have thought that my actual characters were described enough to help people to imagine them. However detailed such description is, I am sure that everyonc forms his own conceptions, that are different from everyone else's, including the author's.[71]

She seems to think that profuse descriptions would only be a sheer waste of effort. In her opinion, what the readers need is a little guidance to catch the picture.

She also denies the charge that her characters are faceless. In a spirited defence to John Bowen, she says: "I shouldn't have thought my characters were faceless. I always describe their faces once, which I should have thought would be enough. I know some people describe a face again and again and again, but I should have thought one description was enough."[72] However, R. Glynn Grylls opines thus: "the features thus catalogued do not contribute anything to the part their owners play later to the story. . . . Such details may have been useful to Dame Ivy to keep the character before her own eyes while writing, for looks were important to her, but she does not make her readers feel their relevance."[73]

Naming her subjects so as to be suggestive of their essential character is another facet of Ivy Compton-Burnett's technique. The names of the tyrants like Harriet (a home ruler), Miranda (admirable), Matilda (a battle maid) and Sophia (wisdom) are examples of such pattern of naming. A ruthless old woman is named Sabine and another who savagely loves her own family is called Regan. A powerful, despotic father is christened Duncan meaning chief. Horace Lamb is like a lamb before the bull-like butler, Bullivant. In some cases, ironical effect is intended in the choice of names. Eleanor means 'light' but she does not shed light either for herself or for others. Anna means 'grace,' but she is devoid of any grace. Illustrious names are sometimes given to ordinary persons. Jonathan Swift, Chaucer, Bunyan, Blake, Hallam, Keats, Bacon, Herrick, Edgeworth, Donne and Marlowe are present in her novels without reflecting the virtues or talents of the writers whose names they adorn. Duplication is another feature. Hallam is, perhaps, suitable for spinsters working as governesses. Hence it is repeated in *Darkness and Day* after *Daughters and Sons*. In the same way, Reuben appears in both *Elders and Betters* and *A God and His Gifts*.

When it comes to exposing the inner conflicts of a character, Ivy Compton-Burnett makes use of narration too, though not as freely as Jane Austen does. In *More Women than Men*, Josephine's murderous instinct is narrated thus:

> Josephine sprang to prevent her, but stopped and stood with an arrested look, that seemed to creep across her face and gather to a purpose. She moved with a soft step to the bed, where Ruth had fallen. . . . Josephine lifted Ruth to her feet, and stood with here arm about her, but did not guide her forward. It was as if she felt some security in nearness to the bed. The girl leant against her, falling but for the support, and made no further movement. Josephine glanced from the open window to the door, and contracted her shoulders in the draught between them. . . . She [Ruth] shuddered, and indeed the draught seemed stronger. (*MWTM*, 158-59)

Ivy Compton-Burnett's characters reveal themselves at the very commencement of their speech. In *A Family and a Fortune*, the dialogue between the crippled Matilda Seaton and her father Oliver on arrival at the small but pleasant gate-lodge, so kindly made for them by her sister Blanche, illustrate this point:

> "Is this a house or a hutch? It is meant, I suppose, for human habitation," said Blanche's father. ". . . it is well that I shall soon be gone and leave you alone in it. For it is better for one than for

two, as I cannot but see."
"Come, Father, pluck up heart. You are an able-bodied man and not a crippled woman. I must not be given any more to bear. You must remember your poor invalid, though I never remind you that I am that." (*FF*, 37)

The very first words spoken by Matty and Oliver betray their sense of mental depression. The cottage provided with great financial loss to Blanche's family is greeted with a sneer. In the words of Pamela Hansford Johnson, "This is character-drawing in the most cheese-paring economy; but the cheese is pared with such precision that nobody goes short."[74]

The variance in the notes struck in the conversation is significant. Brian McFarlane comments: "One judges the characters, as she does, through the tone of the voices in which she creates them. Any deviation from the truth, whether sentimental cliche or deliberate lie, is caught and measured by this tonal control."[75]

"Is that fire smoking?" said Horace Lamb.
"Yes, it appears to be, my dear boy."
"I am not asking what it appears to be doing. I asked if it was smoking."
"Appearances are not held to be a clue to the truth," said his cousin. "But we seem to have no other."
Horace advanced into the room....
"Good morning," he said in a preoccupied tone....
"It does seem that the fire is smoking?"
"It is in the stage when smoke is produced. So it is hard to see what it can do."
"Did you really not understand me?"
"Yes, yes, my dear boy. It is giving out some smoke. We must say that it is." (*MSMS*, 5)

The conversation looks rather dull and pointless. One of the speakers chooses to be humorous, but the other refuses to be amused. More than this, a reader can recognize the respective tones of the voice. He understands that Horace is going to be a stern character while cousin Mortimer is witty and wise but weak.

Though, to a certain extent, all characters speak alike, certainly differences are found in idiom between servants and masters, elders and children. Certain characteristic remarks enable the reader to distinguish the voices. There are plenty of conversational 'bromides.' Villains are usually fond of banal phrases.

Some characteristic form of expression or pre-occupation always identifies the speaker.

> "Why do all gates have different fastenings?" said Anna. "A standard one might bring a fortune to somebody."
>
> "I suppose each one was to have been that one," said Thomas.
>
> "And I wonder it was not. Latches are so very clever," said Terence. (*EB*, 63)

These remarks hint at Anna's interest in fortunes and Thomas' indifference to politics. Terence's remark catches his effeminate tone.

A person's character is sought to be reflected in the style of speech. Peter Bateman and Edward Dryden are fond of clichés and platitudes revealing their pompous and hypocritical nature. Peter's choice of exotic expressions like 'Skinnamajinks,' "Snarling snippet" and "Phiz and Squeak" in striking contra-distinction from the restricted vocabulary of other characters, is a sure enough clue to his overbearing nature.

Different moods of a character are indicated by changing speech rhythms. Pamela Hansford Johnson affirms that "when we become used to her speech rhythms . . . we never fail to catch the slightest nuance in the speaker's voice."[76]

Sophia, when she learns that her husband is dead, bursts into grief:

> What is it? What is it, Peter? Is he gone from me? He is gone from me! Why did you not fetch me? Did he ask for me? Was he in here alone? What was he in here for? Tell me. Why can't somebody tell me? Why can't somebody tell me? Tell me.[77]

Sophia's grief-stricken mind is effectively conveyed with the short, repetitive sentences. After some time, Sophia regains her equilibrium: "Come with me, my dears. We three will go away and be together. We are at this solemn moment of our lives, a moment we shall always remember."[78] The changed rhythm in the above with sonorous modulations of voice deftly conveys that Sophia has cushioned her initial shock. She settles down to mourn, bringing a part of her sorrow to bear on her children.

Stilted or unmeaning language helps understand bad and insincere characters. Faults of expression usually spring from faulty character. Moral lapses like vanity, insincerity, cowardice and so on are reflected by faulty speech. *Dulcia Bode in a House and Its Head* is an example.

Jane Austen will be recalled when Ivy Compton-Burnett's use of dialogue is discussed. But the comparison will not be fully justified since Jane Austen's novels do not depend on dialogues alone for the planning of the theme. In fact, a better literary ancestor for Ivy Compton-Burnett in the matter of dialogue will be Elizabeth Gaskell whose use of dialogue is highly stylized and elaborately worked out as in the case of her novels. Gaskell's *Wives and Daughters* bears close comparison with the novels of Ivy Compton-Burnett even though the latter does not acknowledge any such resemblance or conscious influence. Edward Sackville-West points out the obvious similarity: "It need not be supposed that this remarkable invention owes nothing to former novelists; but those who seek its origin in an obvious place (e.g., Henry James) will return empty-handed. The true hiding place, I suggest, is perhaps rather an unexpected one. No one would be surprised to discover a resemblance between the Compton-Burnett milieu and that of *Cranford*; but a finer, less known novel by Mrs. Gaskell—*Wives and Daughters*—another kind of resemblance too startling to be accidental."[79]

Walter Allen observes that Ronald Firbank is the only exception as far as the use of dialogue is concerned. He explains: "The manner of Miss Compton-Burnett's novels exists in the strongest possible, contrast to the matter. Miss Compton-Burnett conducts her novels, to a degree beyond any other novelist with the exception of Firbank, through dialogue, though there is rather more description than is sometimes recognized."[80]

The reference to Firbank, the author of novels like *Valmouth* (1919), *The Flowery beneath the Foot* (1923) and *Concerning the Eccentricities of Cardinal Pirelli* (1926), is strictly based on one point, the exclusive dependence on dialogue for the development of the theme. The themes of the novels or the detailed aspects of the dialogue have virtually nothing in common. In the words of Walter Allen, "Decadent, frivolous, trivial—the adjectives come hopping off the typewriter—Firbank creates an artificial world."[81] The normal structure of the novel has been left out. The dialogue is full of flippant, affected and overtly obscene words. The sole dependence on conversation is the common factor.

Pamela Hansford Johnson points out that Ivy Compton-Burnett "draws, in fact, not the character of the individual but of the type; and when she has finished with this type, stripped it, gutted it, and laid it nearly out in pieces, we recognize its appalling universality."[82] Emphasizing the same view elsewhere, she finds fault with Ivy Compton-Burnett for "her inability to draw character in the round. She cannot, in a full sense, create character. What she does create, magnificently, is the character-type. Like Dickens . . . she makes her people symbolize various virtues and vices. . . . They are not complex . . . each character is basically a study in the fullness, not of a human personality, but of a vice or a virtue in one particular manifestation."[83]

Glynn Grylls agrees with Pamela Hansford Johnson in that Ivy Compton-Burnett's characters are often types or humours but argues that they are mainly "individuals, so that although they may recur, there is something new each time."[84] Lionel Stevenson refuses to consider Ivy Compton-Burnett's characters as individuals. He argues: "Miss Compton-Burnett's characters, though very strongly marked, remain types rather than becoming individuals. The impression is intensified by the recurrence of the same basic types in most of her novels, so that many readers find it hard to remember which names and actions belong to which persons."[85]

This criticism is somewhat uncharitable. The novelist introduces a character giving particulars of his role, position in family and society. In spite of being introduced as a social being, he is primarily treated as an individual. This rouses Mary Dalton Rowsell to come to defend: "characters are nonetheless individuals possessing differing qualities and interpreting their roles in vastly different manners; the contrasts between Dinah and Sophia as daughters and Andrew and Christian as fathers illustrate this."[86]

E.M. Forster uses the terms 'Round' and 'Flat' to differentiate various kinds of characters. Flat character is one which centres about a single idea or quality. It is also called a 'type' or 'caricature' for it can be summed up in a single sentence. It never surprises as it lacks complexity. The advantage of this type is that it is recognizable immediately and remembered afterwards. Characters who reappear in novel after novel are types. On the other hand, a 'Round' character is capable of surprising a reader in a convincing manner. An author's achievement lies in creating round ones: "The test of a round character is whether it is capable of surprising in a convincing way. If it never surprises, it is flat. If it does not convince, it is flat pretending to be round."[87] If Ivy Compton-Burnett's characters are judged as per the definition of E.M. Forster, most of the characters in a single novel like *Manservant and Maidservant* are round as they never fail to surprise us by their deeds failing which, by their brilliant speech. If we take E.M. Forster's test for flat characters namely, "In their purest form, they are constructed around a single idea or quality; when there is more than one factor in them, we get the beginning of the curve towards the round,"[88] none of the characters in any novel of Ivy Compton- Burnett passes the test for flat characters. All the characters including the minor ones like Peter

Bateman and his children are multifaceted, capable of different reactions to different situations.

Mary McCarthy finds many of Ivy Compton-Burnett's characters 'two-faced,' and feels a kind of dependence of multiplicity of the same type can be traced in her works. She elaborates: "The child of incest has only one grandfather; in *Pastors and Masters*, a semblance of three manuscripts, where there is actually only one, is produced by theft and lying. The same with the pair of earrings in *Two Worlds and Their Ways*, which go their separate ways, criss-cross, and seem at one point to be three. Duplicity is a moral case of doubling; many or most of Compton-Burnett's characters are two-faced. Coincidence, which plays such a part in these novels, is a sort of incest in the household economy of narrative: a simple grandfather (a place or time or person) serves two families of events."[89]

The author describes Dinah (*Brothers and Sisters*) thus: "Dinah was like her father as her mother had been to hers, with a touch of extra comeliness owed to Sophia, and more than a touch of humour that was her own. Her broad, young face, with its nervous features and deep-set eyes was older than age in repose." (*BS*, 25-26) Dinah's humour, perception and resignation enable her to bear the unbearable tyranny of her mother. "There is Sophia, calling to us not to lag and loaf and chatter. Three unlawful things is a large proportion for so early in the day. Sophia is reasonably struck by it." (*BS*, 34) This is Dinah's characteristic humorous tone. The author conveys Dinah's grief in a superbly evocative sentence: "Dinah was sitting on a chair, near to nothing else in the room, and looked up blindly at her mother." (*BS*, 144) Dinah can be angry, contemptuous and capable of scathing rebuke at the scornful behaviour of Edward. When he asks her as to what she says to Andrew's suggestion that the engagements be broken, she reacts very sharply:

> "I do not say anything," said Dinah. "You are better at saying than I am. I won't say I will be your sister, because in our family that seems to lead to marriage. Why didn't you deal with cousin Peter for making the truth public, as you did through us with Sophia? A strong man doing it on purpose, to other people's harm, and a very sick woman helplessly, to her own." (*BS*, 234)

Dinah's capacity for strong affection is proved by her breakdown when Patty longs for a word of recognition from the dying Sophia.

These fragments prove that Dinah is no symbol or flat character. She is a three-dimensional character. As Edward Dryden, her one-time fiancé points out, "Dinah is always herself, quite different from other people." (*BS*, 60)

It will thus be seen that even all the minor characters are not types. In Cicely Greig's opinion: "Like Dickens she magnifies their faults and virtues and peculiarities; unlike him she stops short of caricature."[90] Bentley in *Pastors and Masters*, is not merely a 'Psychopathic Nagger' but more than that. He is a good example of "Miss Compton-Burnett's ability to give the illusion of depth and complexity to even the most caricatured of her characters."[91]

Jane Austen's major characters are 'three-dimensional' or 'round' and developing ones. However, her minor characters are fixed. They are not capable of improving or degenerating. On the other hand, there is a criticism that Ivy Compton-Burnett's characters are for the most part static; they do not grow and develop. Edward Sackville-West finds fault with Ivy Compton-Burnett in that "Her chief characters do not develop in the course of the book, they only loom larger or dwindle, according as the author lengthens or shortens her opera-glass."[92] True, there is little growth in her characters but this is so because her characters are already fully developed when the story begins. Admitting that her characters are static, Ivy Compton-Burnett thinks that it is because the essence of a person usually remains the same.[93] She also views that it requires a long time for a person to change. "The action of my books, on the whole, covers a short time, so that it is hardly possible for a character to grow. It takes a long time for a human being to change."[94] In accordance with this argument, Simon's change in *A Heritage and Its History* is attributed to the long duration of the story.

Everyone agrees that one of Jane Austen's achievements in character-drawing is immense vitality and variety. She has given us a multitude of characters, all commonplace, but perfectly discriminated from each other.

In Ivy Compton-Burnett's case, however differently characters are conceived, the apparent repetition, if any, cannot be avoided: "if they are people of the same kind, produced by the same mind, and carried out by the same hand."[95] Each of her characters talks with maximum clarity and self-revelation and in a polished way. Thus they are alike and differ from the characters created by any other writer. Ivy Compton-Burnett emphasizes her view to Millgate: "I've never conceived two characters in the same way. I think sometimes some of my characters have turned out more alike than I meant them to be, and too like people in my other books."[96]

Ivy Compton-Burnett employs two methods which make her characters, though superficially alike, substantially differ from one another. The first one is character imitation method in which if a character tries to imitate another, the reader is instantly aware of the imitation. This is possible because both the characters are very distinct in his mind. Thus a reader is not deceived when Latimer imitates Julian (*Brothers and Sisters*) and Kate imitates Rachel Hardisty (*Men and Wives*). The second method is family resemblance syndrome which is successfully implanted in her later novels. For instance, in *A Family and a Fortune*, Aubrey combines peevishness of his maternal grandfather, Oliver Seaton, with the clear-headed fineness of his paternal uncle, Dudley Gaveston. Robert Liddell pays the novelist a glorious tribute: "this sort of achievement is perhaps unique—it is much more than mere technical virtuosity, it is real character creation."[97] Burkhart endorses Liddell's view: "No two characters in the novels are ever quite the same; what other novelist has quite Dame Ivy's range and multiplicity of types? The characters which most attract us for their comedy in *The Last and the First* are both like and different from her earlier people."[98]

Lotus Snow thinks that Ivy Compton-Burnett's leading characters range themselves into two groups. Glynn Grylls categorizes them into three groups: the tyrants, friends and employees. P.H. Johnson divides them into eight groups. Robert Liddel classifies them into three broad groups with sub-groups.

One may entirely agree with Burkhart when he says: "Each book contains characters so different, so completely life-like that any attempt, like Mr. Liddell's, to categorize them into tyrants or victims tells us nothing of any importance about them. Matty Seaton, cruel, brutal, that occasional real life person who is larger than life, clever and understanding, refuses to be categorized as a tyrant, and she certainly has nothing to do with the other tyrants, Harriet Haslam or Sophia Stace or Miranda Hume or Duncan Edgeworth or Sir Jesse Sullivan."[99]

Ivy Compton-Burnett at times shows a tendency to model her characters after her close relatives or acquaintances. For instance, the Compton-Burnetts' beloved nurse, Minnie, is a prototype for Miss Patmore (*Brothers and Sisters*), the governess-cum-housekeeper in the Staces' household. Sophia is patterned after Katharine Compton-Burnett, her mother. Something of her brother, Noel, crept into the drawing of Jesse Sullivan (*Parents and Children*). She passes on her uncle, Robert Blackie's feature to Sir Godfrey Haslam (*Men and Wives*). Glimpses of her father may be traced in the characters of Christian Stace (*Brothers and Sisters*) or Justine (*A Family and a Fortune*).

It is only in her early novels that Ivy Compton-Burnett had this tendency of taking people of real life as models for her characters. This prompted Hilary Spurling to comment: "All her books are sewn with retrospective allusions, but only the first three show a demonstrably closer connection with her early life."[100]

But Ivy Compton-Burnett denies that she has drawn upon people. 'No, not really!' is her reply about this aspect while talking to Millgate.[101] She even denies to have taken any hints or suggestions from her friends or acquaintances. She says: "I think that actual life supplies a writer with characters much less than is thought. . . . People in life hardly seem to be definite enough to appear in print."[102]

In this respect she differs from Samuel Butler, whom she admired, as he vividly and mercilessly caricatured his family members in *The Way of All Flesh.* Though Ivy Compton-Burnett does not strive for realistic exactitude, her characters, like Jane Austen's, are realistic. However, Jane Austen shows much more capacity in creating living characters. Commenting on Ivy Compton-Burnett's characters, Ramakrishna Rao observes: "Her novels are full of people that are life-like. The gallery of the various portraits, no doubt, seems to be unreal and non-representational; yet it is realistic and presents a juxtaposition of truth in art and truth in life."[103] Mrs. Gaskell and Charlotte Bronte too create life-like characters. But they take note of people's mannerisms. Fanny Burney used to maintain a diary in which she recorded all interesting conversations.

Mary McCarthy admires the novelist's portrait of Hereward Egerton, the "creative" writer, in a *A God and His Gifts*. She reads a great deal of significance in the character: "Being an immortal, the author is manifestly a god, just as God is an immortal fictional character (perhaps Compton-Burnett's favourite villain) described in the Good Book. Such an author, Hereward Egerton, is the epic hero of her latest novel, *A God and His Gifts*. He is named after Hereward the wake—an allusion to Charles Kingsley's novel and to an early literary forgery. The "creative" writer has figured in a minor way in many of the novels, but he has usually been a failed writer or a failing one. . . . Here he expands into a cosmic joke, filling the whole sky."[104]

In *Pastors and Masters*, the novelist shows lukewarm interest in characterization. In her next novel, *Brothers and Sisters*, characters are fairly developed. Her sixth novel, *A House and Its Head* is rich both in the depth of its study of character and emotion. She started giving importance to child characters with *Daughters and Sons*. In *Manservant and Maidservant*, though characters are often repetitions of earlier types, the roles they play are very different. From now onwards, Ivy Compton-Burnett gives importance to children and servants as well and attempts to integrate minor characters into the plot. In *Present and the Past*, the character of Cassius is painted in full colour. In *A Father and His Fate*, the supporting characters are less fully developed than in other books. In *A Heritage and Its History*, minor characters help in the development of the story. Characters in the later novels, whether major or minor, are found brilliantly drawn up.

Finally it may be said that "the variety and richness of these characters, together with the resource and inventiveness of the plots in which they are involved, that make the novels of Dame Ivy Compton-Burnett a living monument to other creator."[105]

NOTES

1. R.N. Sarkar, *Ivy Compton-Burnett: A Trend in English Fiction* (Calcutta: Firma KLM, 1979), p. 114.
2. Elizabeth Bowen, "Elders and Betters," ed. Charles Burkhart, *The Art of I. Compton-Burnett* (London: Victor Gollancz, 1972), p. 61.
3. Mario Praz, "The Novels of Ivy Compton-Burnett," ed. Burkhart, pp. 126-27.
4. "Analysis by Dialogue," *The Times Literary Supplement*, 10 Apr. 1937, p. 273.
5. Brian McFarlane, "Ivy Compton-Burnett's *A House and Its Head:* Truth and Wit," *Southern Review, II* (1978), p. 160.
6. "I. Compton-Burnett and M. Jourdain: A Conversation," ed. Burkhart, p. 21.
7. McFarlane, p. 160.
8. Charles Burkhart, *I. Compton-Burnett* (London: Victor Gollancz, 1965), p. 38.
9. McFarlane, p. 160.
10. Sarkar, p. 115.
11. Violet Powell, *A Compton-Burnett Compendium* (London: Heinemann, 1973), p. 11.
12. Powell, p. 1.
13. Lionel Stevenson, *The History of the English Novel* (New York: Barnes and Noble, 1967), vol. 6, p. 266.
14. Robert Liddell, *A Treatise on the Novel* (Jonathan Cape, 1965), p. 148.
15. "Fact or Fiction," *The Times Literary Supplement*, 7 Oct. 1960, p. 645.
16. Liddell, p. 149.
17. "An Autocraft at the Tea-Table," *Time*, Vol. 52, 19 July 1948, p. 112.

18. "Talking points," *The Times Literary Supplement*, 18 Sep. 1959, p. 529.
19. Nathalic Sarraute, "Conversation and Sub-conversation," qtd. in *I. Compton-Burnett*, Charles Burkhart, p. 38.
20. Kay Dick, *Ivy and Steve* (London: Allison and Busby, 1983), p. 31.
21. Wolfgang Iser, "Patterns of Communication in Prose Fiction from Bunyen to Beckett," *The Implied Reader* (The Jones Hopkins University Press, 1974), p. 153.
22. Frederick R. Karl, "The Intimate World of Ivy Compton-Burnett," *A Reader's Guide to the Contemporary English Novel* (London: Thomas and Hudson, 1972), p. 209.
23. McFarlane, p. 156.
24. Arnold Kettle, *An Introduction to the English Novel* (London: Hutchinson, 1974), Vol. 2, p. 168.
25. "A God and his Gifts," *New Stateman*, Dec. 1963, p. 168.
26. R. Glynn Grylls, *I. Compton-Burnett* (London: Longman, 1971), p. 4.
27. Frank Kermode, "The House of Fiction," *Partisan Review*, 1:30 (1963), p. 72.
28. John Bowen, "An Interview with Ivy Compton-Burnett," *Twentieth Century Literature*, 25:2 (19799), p. 165.
29. Lord Horder, "Glittering Tide of the Peculiar," *Time and Tide*, 17 Oct 1959, p. 1134.
30. Michael Millgate, "Interview with Miss Compton-Burnett," *Review of English Literature*, 3:4 (1962), p. 101.
31. Joanne Hutchinson, "Appearances are all we have," *Twentieth Century Literature*, 25:2 (1979), p. 188.
32. McFarlane, p. 155.
33. Iser, p. 154.
34. Robert Liddell, *The Novels of I. Compton-Burnett* (London: Victor Gollancz, 1955), p. 92.
35. Sean O'Faolain, "New Novels," *The Listener*, 3:1355 (1955), p. 307.
36. Kermode, *The House*, p. 71.
37. Liddell, pp. 102-3.
38. Elizabeth Sprigge, *The Life of Ivy Compton-Burnett* (London: Victor Gollancz, 1973), p. 148.
39. Kettle, p. 168.
40. Liddell, p. 110.
41. Kettle, p. 168.
42. D.S. Bland, "T.S. Eliot's Case-Book," *Modern Language Notes*, 75:1 (1960), p. 24.
43. Richard McLaughlin, qtd. in *The Life*, Sprigge, p. 122.

44. Elizabeth Bowen, "Parents and Children," ed. Burkhart, *The Art*, p. 55.
45. Liddell, p. 96.
46. Burkhart, ed., p. 22.
47. Iser, p. 252.
48. Liddell, pp. 96-97.
49. McFarlane, pp. 155-56.
50. Mary McCarthy, "The Inventions of I. Compton-Burnett," *Encounter*, 27:5 (1966), p. 23.
51. Cicely Greig, *Ivy Compton-Burnett: A Memoir* (London: Garnstone, 1972), p. 12.
52. Greig, p. 52.
53. Renata Adler, *The New Yorker*, 2 May 1964, p. 184.
54. McCarthy, p. 16.
55. Kettle, p. 166.
56. Charles Burkhart, "A Critical Epilogue," Ivy Compton-Burnett, *The Last and the First* (London: Victor Gollancz, 1971), p. 158.
57. McFarlane, p. 155.
58. "Family Dialogue," Rev. of *A Family and Fortune* and Ivy Compton-Burnett, *The Times Literary Supplement*, 4 Mar. 1939, p. 133.
59. Kettle, p. 171.
60. "Live Dissection," *The Times Literary Supplement*, 27 March 1953, p. 201.
61. McFarlane, p. 162.
62. Greig, pp. 52-53.
63. Liddell, p. 149.
64. Stevenson, p. 149.
65. Mary Dalton Rowsell, "Brothers and Sisters: A Most Complex Relation," *Twentieth Century Literature*, 25:2 (1979), p. 207.
66. Bernard McCabe, "Ivy Compton-Burnett, An English Eccentric," *Critique*, 3:2 (1960), pp. 52-53.
67. J. Bhagya Lakshmi, *Ivy Compton-Burnett and Her Art* (Delhi: Mittal, 1986), p. 5.
68. Rowsell, p. 217.
69. McCarthy, p. 20.
70. Liddell, p. 148.
71. Burkhart, ed., p. 25.
72. Bowen, p. 166.
73. Grylls, pp. 20-21.
74. Pamela Hansford Johnson, "Three Novelists and the Drawing of Character: C.P. Snow, Joyce Cary and Ivy Compton-Burnett," *Essay and Studies*, 3 (1950), p. 96.

75. McFarlane, p. 155.
76. Johnson, *Essays*, p. 83.
77. McCarthy, p. 135.
78. *Ibid.*, p. 138.
79. Edward Sackville-West, "Ladies Whose Bright pens are," *Art*, Burkhart, p. 106.
80. Walter Allen, *Tradition and Dream* (London: Phoenix, 1964), p. 189.
81. *Ibid.*, p. 39.
82. Johnson, *Essays*, p. 83.
83. P.H. Johnson, *I Compton-Burnett* (London: Longman, 1951), p. 20.
84. Grylls, p. 6.
85. Stevenson, pp. 268-69.
86. Rowsell, p. 214.
87. E.M. Forster, *Aspects of the Novel* (London: Penguin, 1981), p. 81.
88. Forster, p. 73.
89. McCarthy, p. 21.
90. Greig, p. 25.
91. Stanley B. Greenfield, "*Pastors and Masters,* the Spoils of Genius," *Criticism*, 2:1 (1960), p. 75.
92. Sackville West, p. 113.
93. Dick, p. 41.
94. Millgate, p. 105.
95. Burkhart, ed., p. 31.
96. Millgate, p. 104.
97. Liddell, p. 162.
98. Burkhart, *Critical*, p. 155.
99. Angus Wilson, "The Novels of Ivy Compton-Burnett," *Art*, ed. Burkhart, p. 134.
100. Hilary Spurling, *Ivy when Young* (London: Allison and Busby, 1983), p. 124.
101. Millgate, p. 105.
102. Burkhart, ed., pp. 27-28.
103. Ramakrishna Rao, *Ivy Compton-Burnett: A Critical Study* (Waltair: Andhra University Press, 1974), p. 95.
104. McCarthy, p. 30.
105. Powell, p. 233.

Summing Up

A study of Ivy Compton-Burnett's novels from the specific perspective of her contribution to the form of Domestic Novel in English is bound to lead more to the recognition of the points of her deviation than to those of similarities. 'Pure' as Robert Liddell declares, her novels, as irony would have it, concentrate on the impure aspects of personal relations within the domestic confines, polluting the entire atmosphere. An iconoclast in the sense that she attempts to explore the ugly side of the sophisticated and respectable British families instead of glorifying conventional virtues by creating ideal men and women with the promise of a happy life ever after, Ivy Compton-Burnett presents a world difficult to recognize in its strangeness, but as unavoidable as naked truth itself. Mary McCarthy describes this portrait: "Felix Culpa, an androgyny bookworm, is in the schoolroom, curled up with a popular novel, the Book of Job. His sister, Maxima Culpa, is in the library; a sulphurous smell of will-burning proceeds from the grate."[1]

The culpable deeds of the socially 'high' individuals form the core of Compton-Burnett's novels. Having turned the Victorian novel "inside out" to expose the maggots breeding underneath the veneer of sophistication, she deserves compliments for having dared into an area which has been left rather untouched by her predecessors. She is, therefore, more true to the traditions of Domestic Novel than it is generally taken to be. She has shown what 'home' really means. It is "the law of the jungle" with the motto of "survival of the fittest" which operates at this level. Frederick Karl explains: "how does one sustain himself in what amounts to a predatory jungle? . . . Neither side is restricted to gentleman's weapons. Nagging is raised to an art, and each side dogs the other, looking for an advantage, trying to thrust in a verbal dagger. For in the destruction of the other person, whether actual or figurative, the individual gains his own life."[2]

Her novels come very close to Domestic Drama in England, especially in the hands of Heywood. Dramatic situations abound in her novels even though they have not been exploited to the full advantage. Passions die down while presented by her cold, impartial touch. Yet, the themes of personal relations, especially those between married couples, frequently marred by instances of adultery, incest and such other aberrations, carry the theme onwards to a tragic or nearly tragic denouement.

Arden of Feversham and *A Woman Killed with Kindness* maintain the serious tempo throughout. Even where violent death is not introduced, solemn and serious tone suit such an ending, elevating the character of tragic dignity. The best example is *Brothers and Sisters* where the ending is in perfect keeping with the traditions of the Domestic tragedy. The parents are rid of the problem, they are dead. But the survivors, especially Andrew and Dinah Stace, are presented with high tragic potential, reminiscent of Oedipus who determines to live on while Jocasta kills herself. O'Neill's *Mourning Becomes Electra* ends on a similar note. Domestic tragedy lends itself to several adaptations of the classical themes, the Greek Drama having been domestic at the core.

"In Miss Compton-Burnett's world there is no repentance, no Christian charity which will reward the good person, no Christian revenge which will punish the bad."[3] This is so because Ivy Compton-Burnett believes that evil is not punished in this world. She says: "I don't think guilty people meet punishment in life. I think it is a literary convention."[4] With an eye on realistic presentation of life, she wants to do away with poetic justice. In this regard, Lionel Stevenson has this to say: "Miss Compton-Burnett's rejection of the sacred literary canon of just retribution is an inevitable consequence of the new morality of scientific determinism."[5]

Bernard McCabe records his assessment on Ivy Compton-Burnett's novels thus: "The material of these novels is tragic or at least pessimistic."[6] The prosperity of the wicked, the oppression of the good, the bleak chances of marital happiness may make some people think that Ivy Compton-Burnett is a pessimist. She depicts adultery or incest in her novels as an accidental occurrence, but never as a calculated, deliberate way of life of her characters. Tyranny is never made to triumph in the end. She is thus neither a pessimist nor a cynic. "The forces of good and evil are displayed without sentimentality in true balance; there is no cynicism."[7]

She depicts life as she sees it. In the picture she draws, there is "not hope or despair about human life, but the way it is as she sees it. . . . To accept this stoical vision implies a commitment to truth of an unusually clear-eyed kind; and she never falters into sentimentality."[8] Lotus Snow rightly says, "Far from a chilling view of human nature, as Miss Compton-Burnett reviewers have so often called it, it is compassionate."[9]

In her first novel, *Dolores*, Ivy Compton-Burnett portrayed a dutiful daughter in Dolores who sets duty before her personal wishes. But later, after *Pastors and Masters*, her outlook underwent such a sea-change that she came to regard such sacrifices as horrible. Commenting on this change of outlook, Pamela Hansford Johnson says: "the thesis is this: that to sacrifice for oneself for the good of others is beautiful and ennobling. Fourteen years later, the thesis had altered—and this new thesis, either dominant or subsidiary in every novel Miss Compton-Burnett has written since, is as follows: that to sacrifice oneself for the good of others is splendid for others but horrible for oneself."[10]

Ivy Compton-Burnett is neither didactic nor reformative. She says, "it's very difficult to alter people. . . . The essence of people remains what it is."[11] She neither condemns nor pronounces any judgment but "says that that is how it is: people and societies are like that."[12] Walter Allen calls her view of life as "implacable and intransigent and she offers no comfort, nothing beyond a stoical acceptance of things as they are."[13]

It is usually believed that Ivy Compton-Burnett was influenced by Jane Austen. Both the novelists confine themselves to the upper middle-class society, to the exclusion of both the aristocracy and the lower strata. They are not didactic and do not preach morals. However, unlike Ivy Compton-Burnett, Jane Austen shows how virtue is rewarded.

Robert Liddell feels that both think in unison. Adverting to Ivy Compton-Burnett, he says: "She is writing the pure novel, as Jane Austen did, concentrating upon human beings and their mutual reactions. So rare is such concentration in the English novel that any writer who conscientiously practises it is almost sure to be accused of 'imitating Jane Austen' whether their minds are alike or not: and the minds of Miss Austen and Miss Compton-Burnett are in many ways alike."[14]

Arnold Kettle too finds many similarities between them. He writes: "Like Jane Austen, she examines with very little illusion and from a humane and critical basis a limited society and the quality of her novels, like Jane Austen's, lies in their concrete revelation of human relationships and behaviour in very precise contexts. Like Jane Austen she is materialist and skeptical and like Jane Austen she eschews the generalized symbol. We are not offered a comment on the nature of life as such."[15]

Frank Kermode thinks that the comparison should not be carried too far. He says: "People compare her with Jane Austen, one can see why; but in the end this is as absurd as comparing Hobbes with Hooker."[16] Bernard McCabe seems to caution the readers against comparing these two writers when he says, "Members of the Compton-Burnett cult do not hesitate to place her beside Jane Austen, a dangerous comparison to risk."[17] Writing on their differences, Fraser rightly says:

"Jane Austen's world is one in which the soul can breathe, and, in its miniature range, it gives one a Shakespearean sense of life's gravity, order, and fullness. Miss Compton-Burnett's world is not sane and rich in that sense; it is a narrow, enclosed, obsessed world and though its flavour is very distinctive, a little of it is enough at a time."[18] Unmistakably Ivy Compton-Burnett's is a shrunken world when compared with that of Jane Austen. However, as Harvey Curtis Webster says, "she is not, as some have implied, a Jane Austen turned cynical by the twentieth century."[19]

Ivy Compton-Burnett's world is all her own and so is her way of treading upon it. Lionel Stevenson says: "Ivy Compton-Burnett has sometimes been compared to Jane Austen. . . . Actually she has a closer affinity with a very different writer, Ann Radcliffe. Drafty country-houses have been substituted for medieval castles and dungeons, bland gentlemen for brutal nobles, stupid clergymen for depraved monks, but the nightmare horror of imprisonment and torture has merely been transferred from the physical to the psychological plane, and the recurrent incest motif is a further link with the Gothic romances."[20]

If any, who reads Ivy Compton-Burnett's novel for the first time, thinks that he has come across another Jane Austen, according to Joanne Hutchinson, he will soon realize his mistake. She writes: "For Jane Austen's recurring theme is that we live and, if we are the right sort, we learn that appearances are deceptive but that experience teaches us to get beneath them to the truth. . . . Compton-Burnett's theme, on the other hand, is that we live, that we learn very little, and that experience teaches the wary to be a bit warier. With luck and good parts our perceptions become sharper."[21]

Ivy Compton-Burnett herself clinches the issue when she says: "I have read Jane Austen so much, and with such enjoyment and admiration, that I may have absorbed things from her unconsciously. I do not think myself that my books have any real likeness to hers. I think that there is possibly some likeness between our minds."[22]

There are some who believe that Ivy Compton-Burnett's novels are akin to Greek plays and, as such, she is influenced by Greek playwrights. Mario Praz, who believes that Ivy Compton-Burnett has affinities with Jane Austen, also links her to Greek tragedians. He says: "in Compton-Burnett there is something profoundly sinister that you would search for in vain in Austen or Gaskell . . . that you certainly find in Greek plays."[23] Anthony Powell also makes a similar observation that the novelist "saw life in the relentless terms of Greek tragedy, its cruelties, ironies, hypocrisies—above all its passions—played out against a background of triviality and ennui."[24] To Raymond Mortimer, her novels appear "like hearing the plots of Aeschylus and Sophocles recounted in the cool detached tones of Miss Austen."[25]

Ivy Compton-Burnett is highly objective and aloof like Greek dramatists. "Just as Sophocles and, still more, Aeschylus, dealing with the most immense of themes, set a deliberate barrier between themselves and the heroic events of which they treated, so Miss Compton-Burnett, formidably arrayed on the drawing-room floor, prefers to keep both people and events at a certain distance in order to use just what she wants of them and no more."[26] *Two Worlds and Their Ways* has the pattern of the classical Greek drama. "Like Sophocles' Oedipus, struggling to gauge the future and discovering that it twists horribly back into his own past, the characters in *Two Worlds and Their ways* march blindly to their fate, doomed from the start but always demanding, with the eloquence and dignity of Aeschylean heroes, their right to respect as well as humiliation."[27] *Brothers and Sisters* too has unmistakable overtones of Greek tragedy. As in *Oedipus Tyrannus*, happiness is suddenly transformed into misery due to the unexpected discovery of a shocking secret. At the same time, it differs from the Sophoclean play insofar as there is no divine power to order things.

As in Greek plays, there is a choric commentary throughout in her novels. Ainger, the butler, at the end of *The Mighty and Their Fall*, makes a comment like chorus on the entire household. "Some people are put too high. They fail in their own sphere. The master and Miss Lavinia, the old master and Mr. Hugo: and the old mistress in a way. Ah, I have heard, and said to myself: 'How are the mighty fallen.'" (*MF*, 220)

Robert Liddell finds analogy between Greek chorus and the dialogues in Ivy Compton-Burnett's novels. However, he shows one main point of difference. "They mass, like a chorus, to form an audience for family scenes but they do not speak like a chorus—each witness has his own clear voice."[28]

In Greek plays, the Furies avenge blood. In Ivy Compton-Burnett's novels, all is worked out and quietly hidden within the family circle. Pamela Hansford Johnson says that the novelist's strong and compelling themes "bear some relation to the themes of Greek tragedy, if we could conceive Greek tragedy with the Furies impotent or non-existent."[29]

When asked whether she was conscious of Greek influence, Ivy Compton-Burnett once told an interviewer, "I'm not conscious of it but I was classically educated both as a child and at college, and it would not be unnatural if something had come through."[30] Thus she herself has admitted about there being some unconscious and diffused influence of Greek learning on her work.

In the initial stage of her career, Ivy Compton-Burnett was almost wholly unoriginal in her writings. They bear unmistakable traces of having been influenced by others. One such influence was from George Eliot: "it is seldom that one finds one major author submerged so completely in the personality of another as I. Compton-Burnett, at the start of her career, in George Eliot."[31]

The original title of *Dolores* 'unhistoric Acts' comes from the last sentence of George Eliot's *Middlemarch. Dolores* opens with the episode of the burial of the Reverend Cleveland Hutton's wife. This resembles the funeral scene which comes at the end of 'The Sad Fortunes of the Reverend Amos Barton,' the first story in George Eliot's first book, *Scenes of Clerical Life*. Both the scenes are identical in personnel, tone and treatment.

Ivy Compton-Burnett acknowledges her debt to George Eliot in *Dolores* thus: "there may be, because I read a good deal of her then. I haven't read her nearly so much for a good many years."[32]

Ivy Compton-Burnett's views on the evils besetting the family life are similar to those of Samuel Butler. But it will be uncharitable to her to suggest that she came heavily under the influence of Butler. It may well be that her views and the views of Butler on the contemporary family life were almost identical. At best her views might have received a touch of refinement on reading Butler. "He had . . . sharpened her humour, improved her morals, confirmed her dislike of religion."[33] To this extent at least Butler's influence, howsoever negligible, must have been there on her.

Denying any direct literary influence on her work, Ivy Compton-Burnett says: "People who do the same work naturally have some of the same qualities. When I hear people say that someone is indebted to somebody else, I often think he may not even have read him. It may be that people who are in the same line have the attributes that led them to it."[34]

Whether Ivy Compton-Burnett exercised literary influence on other writers, there seems to be no unanimity of opinion. R. Glynn Grylls writes: "If Dame Ivy acknowledged no influences, she is also unlikely to prove an influence herself. There are scenes in contemporary novels which recall some of hers, and phrases . . . which are 'post-Ivy' . . . but these are minor matters: in essentials no attempt to imitate her . . . is likely to be sustained beyond a very faint echo."[35] Martha Duffy, however, thinks differently when she says: "Dame Ivy Compton-Burnett . . . has often been called a 'writer's writer.' This is a handy term to describe such authors . . . whom other writers often cite as important influences but who seldom stay in print . . . and each passing decade brings Dame

Ivy new disciples."[36]

Robert Liddell draws an interesting parallel when he acknowledges Ivy Compton-Burnett's influence on T.S. Eliot. He writes: "It is not surprising that the only successful, living writer of English verse tragedy should show signs of Miss Compton-Burnett's influence both on the situation and the dialogue of *The Family Reunion* —though its action is more diffuse and less tragic than the greater moments in her novels. Perhaps it is not entirely fanciful to see Mr. Eliot acknowledging the influence when he names one of his characters Ivy, gives another an invitation to stay at 'Compton-Smith's place in Dorset.'"[37]

Living death characterizes the life with its cramping routine and an over-hanging curse, both in Moreton Edge (*Brothers and Sisters*) and the Wishwood (*The Family Reunion*). Amy is a matriarch in *The Family Reunion* and Harriet Haslam occupies a corresponding position in *Men and Wives*. Matthew (*Men and Wives*) kills his mother, Harriet, and Harry (*The Family Reunion*) also suffers from a delusion or a dream of wish-fulfilment that he has murdered his wife, Mary, by pushing her overboard during a voyage.

D.S. Bland has this to offer: "Each of these resemblances, taken in isolation, might be mere coincidence. Together they amount to a seeming affinity . . . even the very 'feel' of a typical Compton-Burnett country house is similar to that of Wishwood."[38] An affinity of technique, of language and overmuch reliance on the dialogue form are discernible as common enough features between the two. T.S. Eliot believes that good will ultimately prevail, but Ivy Compton-Burnett has no such faith. About a dominating parents' ill-doing escaping retribution, as it happens in T.S. Eliot's *The Family Reunion*, D.S. Bland says: "at this point in his work Eliot is very close to Miss Compton-Burnett, whatever the ultimate difference in their beliefs may be."[39]

Apart from T.S. Eliot, no other writer bears even a remote resemblance to Ivy Compton-Burnett. Bass Yarling sums this up when he says: "This irrationally gifted English woman has had a few parodists but no really hopeful imitators."[40] R. Glynn Grylls sounds realistic when she writes: "The novels are 'suigeneris': nothing quite like them before or to come after. Attempts to find them a literary ancestor or some relation in a modern movement have always proved abortive."[41] In short, as Frank Kermode says, "she is literally inimitable . . ."[42]

Commenting on the "sameness' of Ivy Compton-Burnett's novels, Mary McCarthy remarks that the 'sameness' is a conscious formula, deliberately cultivated: "A Compton-Burnett is a reliable make, as typical as British Isles workmanship as a tweed or Tiptree or an Agatha Christie. . . . She produces Compton-Burnetts, as someone might produce ball bearings (Dickens produced Dickenses, but Flaubert did not produce Flauberts). Hence the uniformity of labelling in her titles and the open stock patterns of her incidents and dialogue. The author, like all reliable old firms, is stressing the *sameness* of the formula: Senior service. . . . She has no imitators. The formula is a trade secret."[43]

Ivy Compton-Burnett is not without adverse criticism. "With Ivy one is either an addict or an abstainer"[44] says Cicely Greig. While some are addicts, there are others among the reading public who are averse to certain features of her writing.

Her melodramatic plots are condemned and labelled as 'chill and claustrophobic.'[45] Some reviewers call them baffling, morbid, neurotic, unpleasant and unnatural. Edward Sackville-West enumerates her 'fallings' with great precision. He refers to the perfunctory way in which she describes her characters, her inability to 'manage' masculine men, and the similarity of her plots making it difficult for readers to distinguish them easily. He adds that her subsidiary characters are often 'flat' and dim, and that even the chief characters do not develop in the course of the book. "They only loom larger and dwindle, according as the author lengthens or shortens her opera glass."[46] She "skates over action" and fails to exploit the potential of the situations.

P.H. Johnson comments, "Miss Compton-Burnett's writing appears so strange to the reader who comes upon it without warning . . . a coil of vipers in a sewing-basket."[47] A reviewer in *Time* blames the novelist that "the people in her novels talk all the time but never talk naturally."[48]

Homogeneity of her work is also often assailed. Since almost all her novels possess identical titles and deal mostly with unhappy families, she is accused of "immersing her readers in the same unmoving pool."[49] A reviewer of *A God and His Gifts* says: "the author has varied neither her ways nor her pace. She is where she was decades ago."[50]

This deliberate and uniquely uniform nature of her novels should have appeared rather curious to Edward Sackville-West who says: "like a sculptor obsessed by the human figure, she recommences the same task in each successive book."[51]

Burkhart reacts sharply when the uniformity of her novels is labelled as a stigma. He says: "It is true that her books are more alike one another than those of any other great writer, but I do not see how this can be called a defect. . . . They stand one after the other in their own brilliant integrity, their glittering intelligence, insight, and wit."[52]

Most of the critics are of the opinion that the demands her novels make on the readers are rather severe. "There is nowhere to relax in her novels: apart from the invariable account given at each character's first appearance, there is almost no description; there are no reminders for the reader who has missed a small important detail in the dialogue. The dialogue is virtually all there is, and not to catch its changes of tone and rhythm is not to read her at all. To many, even dedicated novel-readers, she can seem repellingly odd."[53]

C.P. Snow is blunt when he takes the novelist to task: "In order to read this novelist at all, much more to get the maximum out of her work, the reader has to perform a creative act himself; . . . No novelist has ever asked so much from her readers; I think it is too much."[54] It is true that the novelist makes stiff demands on the attention of her readers. But she is not the only writer to do so. Huxley, Waugh and Rose Macaulay also demand a certain degree of education and effort from their readers. So do Virginia Woolf and Elizabeth Bowen who ask for an ear sensitive to the cadences of their writing.

Brian McFarlane says: "Almost a decade later, nine years after her death . . . the problem with her novels remains the same: not that they are under-valued but that they are under-read. While the addicted have always been ready to ascribe to her a very high place indeed in the twentieth century English novel, their number has remained small."[55]

The reason for dwindling reader patronage is the need for deep concentration on his part. If a single line is missed, the whole thing will become unintelligible. "It is absolutely essential to read every line of a Compton-Burnett novel, because to miss a single line one turns the whole book to gibberish."[56] What is required is intense concentration and Raymond Mortimer is not far from the truth when he says: "the difficulty of Miss Compton-Burnett's books comes . . . from concentration: they require very slow and attentive reading."[57] The readers are not allowed to drift. But Christine Brooke-Rose speaks defensively of the novelist when she remarks: "the effort demanded of the reader is one of concentration. . . . And the effort is rewarded."[58] Edward Sackville-West, in his spirited defence of Ivy Compton-Burnett, says that it is "difficult to decide where to put the book down, when it becomes necessary to attend to something else. Once launched on the stream one must attend completely to every word until the end is reached. But although these difficulties render her work no light undertaking for the reader, the reward is proportionate—not only in the illumination of so much in life . . . but in irresistible laughter."[59]

Ivy Burnett's 'Austenite'[60] canvas receives severe attack. Her classic economy and self-imposed limitations seem to Arnold Kettle "rather a retreat that may be tactically discreet but which nevertheless prevents Ivy Compton-Burnett . . . from being regarded as a major novelist."[61]

Much more disparaging is G.S. Fraser's remark: "Miss Compton-Burnett's world . . . is a narrow, enclosed, obsessed world and though its flavour is very distinctive, a little of it is enough at a time. One cannot read two Compton-Burnett novels in succession."[62] It is quite uncharitable to Ivy Compton-Burnett to deride her for the somewhat narrow and restricted ambit of her novels. This is of her own volition in order that her probe into human nature way be thorough, purposeful and revealing. "By choosing not only the family . . . but the family of the past . . . Miss Compton-Burnett can . . . concentrate entirely on measuring the depths of human motives and reactions."[63] Fascinated by the richness, variety and complexity of the family, she chooses this for thorough exploration, and by going about her task with missionary zeal, she succeeds in unravelling several freaks of human nature that endanger the peace and harmony in the family circle. Walter Allen comments: "she achieves a perfection in her work beyond anything reached by her contemporaries; and she does so because, like Jane Austen, she knows her limits and never transgresses them."[64]

As it always happens, Ivy Compton-Burnett arouses mixed reaction in her critics, some extolling her for her outstanding literary output and others decrying her for not holding a mirror to real life in all her novels. A reviewer in *Time* writes: "All Compton-Burnett's novels . . . appear at first glance to be out of this world, artificial, aimless."[65] But the truth is otherwise. The so-called artificiality about her work stems from a hasty assessment on first encounter. One has to go a little deeper for the refreshing revelation that her world is very real and organic. "If her characters are totally unlike any others in fiction, they are not all that unlike some of those that we come across in real life."[66] While discussing family life with Janet Beresford, Ivy Compton-Burnett defends her works by saying: "People say that things don't happen like they do in my books. . . . Believe me, Janet, they do."[67] On some other occasion, she herself tries to give the lie to the raging controversy about the restricted scope of her works. She says: "I don't think my work is narrow—some people say it is, although I agree the scene is narrow."[68]

"No other novelist writes quite, or even remotely, like Miss Compton-Burnett, and no other characters in fiction are quite like those in her books."[69] She is refreshingly unique with a style of her own characterised by incessant dialogue, little or no description and almost devoid of narrative. She laid bare the domestic oppression and exploitation with subdued wit but forthright and devastating insight. Though a sense of homogeneity pervades through all her novels, they nevertheless provide an absorbing and fascinating reading. But she is by no means everyone's taste. She appeals to a considerable number of discriminating readers. There are also others whom she wearies and bores. Elizabeth Sprigge affirms that "those who have tired of superficial and sentimental family sagas will be ready to give this author her due, which is considerable."[70]

R.C. Churchill refers to Ivy Compton-Burnett as an "eccentric" or "mannered" novelist, and places her in a class along with Ronald Firbank, "with no great pejorative implications."[71] The terms could refer only to the peculiar oddities in the choice of themes and the excessive dependence on dialogue. The individual stamps are so unmistakable that they are termed 'mannered.'

Among the twentieth century novelists, May Sinclair bears close similarity both to Samuel Butler and to Ivy Compton-Burnett. The themes of her masterpieces, *Mary Olivier* (1919) and *The Life and Death of Harriet Frean* (1922) are reminiscent of Compton-Burnett's domestic world with its decadent atmosphere with undercurrents of the perverted, the abnormal and the tyrannical. *Mary Olivier* introduces a "ferociously intelligent" young heroine from a family where there is an Oedipal situation between her mother and one of her brothers. A jealous father and the other characters including Mary are victims in different ways, expediting the total defeat and destruction of the family. May Sinclair was a student of psychology and philosophy, and it has influenced her a great deal in the delineation of characters. *Mary Olivier* and *Harriet Frean*, rich in the character delineation of young women against the modern domestic background, have "the foreshadowing of the matter, though not the manner, of the fiction of Ivy Compton-Burnett."[72]

Elizabeth Bowen has a relatively wider scope which includes various cities in Europe and references to the ravages of war. Yet her central interest is in domestic themes against a larger backdrop. She has a lyrical quality, essentially visual and pictorial. *The Death of the Heart* (1938) introduces adultery and other acts of breach of faith against the background of love and the crisis of war. *The Heat of the Day* (1949) concerns a domestic aspiration of conjugal fulfilment fettered by the atmosphere of war.

Ivy Compton-Burnett was never a best-seller and this fact remained a source of disappointment and vexation to her. Rose Macaulay, the best-selling author of the time, recognised the all-time quality of Ivy Compton-Burnett's books and said: "My books won't live. Yours may, Ivy."[73]

Considering the question "How would you place Ivy Compton-Burnett?" Francis King refers to a Major/Minor Symposium on this issue and mentions that most people might consider her "a minor and peripheral figure but of a kind that often survives long after 'major' and 'central' figures have been swept into oblivion by the winds of time."[74] He says she had absolutely refused to believe in God and therefore her works were not meant for the manifestation of His glory. "But it was certainly created for the manifestations of both the glory and the vileness, the power and the weakness, and the wisdom and the folly of the human race as a whole." He concludes, "Yes, certainly a great writer; but one who is, alas, unlikely ever to command a great readership."[75]

All said and done, she is an "unusual novelist, who has, in her own well-tilled field, no rival and no parallel."[76] A writer of superb originality, Ivy Compton-Burnett occupies a position of unequalled excellence among the twentieth century women novelists.

NOTES

1. Mary McCarthy, "The Inventions of I. Compton-Burnett's, *Encounter*, 27:5 (1966), p. 19.
2. Frederick Karl, *A Reader's Guide to the Contemporary English Novel* (London: Thomas and Hudson, 1972), p. 202.
3. Karl, p. 205.
4. Michael Millgate, "Interview with Miss Compton-Burnett," *A Review of English Literature*, 3:4 (1962), p. 108.
5. Lionel Stevenson, "Yesterday and After," *The History of the English Novel* (New York: Barnes and Noble, 1967), Vol. 11, p. 270.
6. Bernard McCabe, "Ivy Compton-Burnett, An English Eccentric," *Critique*, 3:2 (1960), p. 53.
7. "Aeschylus and Austen," *The Times Literary Supplement*, 22 Sep. 1961, p. 625.
8. Brian McFarlane, "Ivy Compton-Burnett's *A House and Its Head:* Truth and Wit," *Southern Review*, 10 (1956), p. 276.
9. Lotus Snow, "Good is Bad Condensed: Ivy Compton-Burnett's View of Human Nature," *Western Humanities Review*, 10 (1956), p. 276.
10. P.H. Johnson, *I. Compton-Burnett* (London: Longman, 1951), p. 25.
11. Millgate, p. 110.
12. Mary Brown, *Twentieth Century Fiction* (Macmillan, 1983), p. 156.
13. Walter Allen, *Tradition and Dream* (London: J.M. Dent, 1974), p.

191.

14. Robert Liddell, *A Treatise on the Novel* (London: Jonathan Cape, 1965), p. 147.
15. Arnold Kettle, *An Introduction to the English Novel* (London: Hutchinson, 1974), Vol. 2, pp. 166-67.
16. Frank Kermode, "Fiction Chronicle," *Partisan Review*, 27:3 (1960), p. 554.
17. McCabe, p. 62.
18. G.S. Fraser, *The Modern Writer and His World* (London: Penguin, 1967), pp. 151-52.
19. Harvey Curtis Webster, "A Visit with Ivy Compton-Burnett," *Saturday Review*, 40:2, Mar. 1957, p. 14.
20. Stevenson, Vol.11, p. 271.
21. Joanne Hutchinson, "Appearances are all we Have," *Twentieth Century Literature*, 25:2 (1979), p. 91.
22. Margaret Jourdain, "I. Compton-Burnett and M. Jourdain: A Conversation," *The Art of I. Compton-Burnett,* ed. Charles Burkhart (London: Victor Gollancz, 1972), p. 23.
23. Mario Praz, "The Novels of Ivy Compton-Burnett," *The Art*, ed. Burkhart, p. 124.
24. Anthony Powell, "Three Obituaries," *The Art*, ed. Burkhart, p. 187.
25. Raymond Mortimer, "A House and Its Head," *The Art*, ed. Burkhart, p. 52.
26. "A Series of Delicate Keys," *The Times Literary Supplement*, 11 Feb. 1955, p. 88.
27. "Future in the Past," *Time*, 13 June 1949, p. 42.
28. Robert Liddell, *The Novels of I. Compton-Burnett* (London: Victor Gollancz, 1955), p. 68.
29. Johnson, p. 37.
30. Millgate, p. 100.
31. Hilary Spurling, *Ivy when young* (London: Allison and Busby, 1983), p. 167.
32. Millgate, p. 100.
33. Spurling, *Ivy*, p. 270.
34. Millgate, pp. 100-1.
35. Glyn Grylls, *I. Compton-Burnett* (London: Longman, 1971), p. 27.
36. Martha Duffy, "Household Tyrants," *Time*, 98, 16 Aug. 1971, p. 51.
37. Robert Liddell, *A Treatise*, p. 159.
38. D.S. Bland, "T.S. Eliot's Case Book," *Modern Language Notes*, 75:1 (1960), p. 25.
39. Bland, p. 26.
40. Bass Yarling, "Miss Ivy's Tobacco Road," *The New Republic*, 4

Mar. 1957, p. 20.
41. Grylls, p. 3.
42. Kermode, *Fiction*, p. 554.
43. McCarthy, p. 19.
44. Cicely Greig, *Ivy Compton-Burnett: A Memoir* (London: Garnstone Press, 1972), p. 12.
45. Greig, p. 71.
46. Edward Sackville-West, "Ladies whose bright pens are," *The Art*, ed. Burkhart, p. 113.
47. P.H. Johnson, p. 10.
48. Futures, p. 42.
49. Stuart Hampshire, "The Art of a Moralist," *Encounter*, 9:5 (1957), p. 79.
50. "With a Shiver and a Laugh," *New York Times Book Review*, 2 Feb. 1964, p. 5.
51. Sackville-West, p. 111.
52. Charles Burkhart, "I. Compton-Burkhart, The Shape of a Career," *The Art*, p. 159.
53. Brian McFarlane, "Ivy Compton-Burnett's *A House and Its Head:* Truth and Wit," *Southern Review*, 2 (1978), p. 154.
54. C.P. Snow, qtd. in *Ivy*, Greig, p. 50.
55. McFarlane, p. 154.
56. Johnson, p. 42.
57. Mortimer, pp. 51-52.
58. Christine Brooke-Rose, "A God and his Gifts," *London Magazine*, 3 (1964), p. 85.
59. Sackville-West, pp. 113-14.
60. Anne Freemantle, "Tragedy in Tea cups," *Saturday Review*, 41 (1958), p. 23.
61. Kettle, p. 166.
62. Fraser, p. 152.
63. "Fact or Fiction," *The Times Literary Supplement*, 7 Oct. 1960, p. 645.
64. Allen, p. 191.
65. "An Autocrat at the Tea-Table," *Time*, 52 (1948), p. 112.
66. "Family Feeling," *The Times Literary Supplement*, 16 Aug. 1957, p. 493.
67. Cited in Hilary Spurling, *Secrets of a Woman's Heart* (London: Penguin, 1984), p. 117.
68. John Bowen, "An Interview with Ivy Compton-Burnett," *Twentieth Century Literature*, 25:2 (1979), p. 172.
69. "Family Feeling," p. 493.

70. Elizabeth Sprigge, *The Life of Ivy Compton-Burnett* (London: Victor Gollancz, 1973), p. 94.
71. R.C. Churchill, *A Concise History of English Literature* (Cambridge: C.U.P., 1972), p. 899.
72. Allen, p. 15.
73. Cited in Spurling, *Secrets*, p. 133.
74. Francis King, "Major/Minor Symposium," *Twentieth Century Literature*, 25 (1979), pp. 128-29.
75. King, p. 128.
76. "The Unhappy Family Game," *The Times Literary Supplement*, 22 Mar. 1947, p. 126.

Bibliography

(a) Primary Sources

Dolores. London: William Blackwood, 1971.
Pastors and Masters. London: Victor Gollancz, 1965.
Brothers and Sisters. London: Victor Gollancz, 1961.
Men and Wives. London: Victor Gollancz, 1972.
More Women than Men. London: Eyre and Spottiswoode, 1951.
A House and Its Head. London: Penguin, 1982.
Daughters and Sons. London: Allison and Busby, 1984.
A Family and a Fortune. London: Penguin, 1983.
Parents and Children. London: Victor Gollancz, 1951.
Elders and Betters. London: Victor Gollancz, 1964.
Manservant and Maidservant. London: Victor Gollancz, 1964.
Two Worlds and Their ways. London: Victor Gollancz, 1964.
Darkness and Day. London: Victor Gollancz, 1960.
The Present and the Past. London: Victor Gollancz, 1953.
Mother and Son. London: Victor Gollancz, 1955.
A Father and His Fate. London: Victor Gollancz, 1969.
A Heritage and Its History. London: Victor Gollancz, 1979.
The Mighty and Their Fall. London: Victor Gollancz, 1979.
A God and His Gifts. London: Penguin, 1983.
The Last and the First. London: Victor Gollancz, 1971.

(b) Select Critical Works

(i) Journals

Adler, Renata. *The New Yorker*. 2 May 1964.
"Aeschylus and Austen." *The Times Literary Supplement*, 22 Sep. 1961.
"A House and its Head." *The Times Literary Supplement*, 25 July 1935.
"A Series of Delicate Keys." *The Times Literary Supplement*, 11 Feb. 1955.
Amis, Kingsley, "One World and Its Way." *The Twentieth Century*, Aug. 1955.
"Analysis of Dialogue." *The Times Literary Supplement*, 10 Apr. 1937.
"An Author and her Aberration." *The Times Literary Supplement*, 21 Nov. 1963.
"An Autocrat at the Tea-Table." *Time*, 52, July 1948.
"An Extra Grudge against Life." *Time*, 83, Feb. 1964.
Baro, Gene. "With a Shiver and a Laugh." *New York Times Book Review*, 2 Feb. 1964.
Bland, D.S. "T.S. Eliot's Case Book." *Modern Language Notes*, 75:1 (1960).
Bowen, John. "An Interview with Ivy Compton-Burnett." *Twentieth Century*

Literature, 25:2 (1979).

Brooke Rose, Christine. Review of *A God and His Gifts*. *London Magazine*, 3, Mar. 1964.

"Brothers and Sisters." *The Times Literary Supplement*, 9 May 1929.

Burkhart, Charles. "A Critical Epilogue to *The Last and the First*." London: Victor Gollancz, 1971.

"Comic Tragedy." *Time*, 28 Jan. 1957.

Coxe, Louis O. "A Tyrant's Little World." *New Republic*, 132, 4 Apr. 1955.

Coxman, Max "Manners and Morals." *The Commonweal*, 5 Feb. 1960.

Crane, Milton. "Dialogue on a Dark Theme." *Saturday Review*, 2 Mar. 1957.

"Dolores," *The Times Literary Supplement*, 2 Mar. 1941.

Duffy, Martha. "Household Tyrants." *Time*, 98, 16 Aug. 1971.

Dunbar, Olivia Howard. "Neglected Novelist." *New Republic*, 22 Apr. 1940.

"Elders and Betters," *The Times Literary Supplement*, 12 Feb. 1944.

"Fact or Fiction." *The Times Literary Supplement*, 7 Oct. 1960.

"Family Attitudes." *The Times Literary Supplement*, 17 May 1941.

"Family Dialogue." *The Times Literary Supplement*, 4 Mar. 1939.

"Family Feeling." *The Times Literary Supplement*, 16 Aug. 1957.

Faolain, Sean O. "New Novels." *The Listener*, 53:1355 (1955).

Fremantle, Anne. "Tragedy in Teacups." *Saturday Review*, 41, 19 Apr. 1958.

Furbank, P.N. "Butlers and Beliefs." *Encounter*, 42, June 1974.

"Futures in the Past," *Time*, 13, Jan. 1949.

Ginger, John. "Ivy Compton-Burnett." *The London Magazine*, 9, 1970.

Greenfield, Stanley B. "Pastors and Masters: The Spoils of Genius," *Criticism*, 2:1 (1960).

Hampshire, Stuart. "The Art of a Moralist." *Encounter*, 9:5 (1957).

Hansen, Marlene R. "The Victorianism of Ivy Compton-Burnett." *English Studies*, 55, 1974.

Hicks, Granville. "The Laconic Words, A Revolution." *Saturday Review*, 45, 10 Feb. 1962.

"Home and Away." *The Times Literary Supplement*, 17 Jan. 1949.

Hutchinson, Joanne. "Appearances are All We Have." *Twentieth Century Literature*, 25, 1979.

"I. Compton-Burnett." *The Times*, No. 21, 1963.

Johnson, Pamela Hansford, "Three Novelists and the Drawing of Character." *Essays and Studies*, New series III, 1950.

______. "Pity for the Mouse." *New Statesman*, 54, 10 Aug. 1957.

Kermode, Frank, "Fiction Chronicle." *Partisan Review*, 27:3 (1960).

______. "The House of Fiction," Interview with Seven English Novelists, *Partisan Review*, 30, 1963.

King Francis et al. "Major/Minor: A Symposium." *Twentieth Century Literature*, 25, 1978.

Lehman, John. "Review of the Present and the Past." *Listener*, 69.

Lewis, Constance. "Manservant and Maidservant: A Pivotal Novel." *Twentieth Century Literature*, 25, 1979.

"Live Dissection." *The Times Literary Supplement*, 27 Mar. 1953.

Marsden-Smedley, Hester, "Ivy . . . Friend of the Family." *Twentieth Century Literature*, 25:2 (1979).

McCabe, Bernard. "Ivy Compton-Burnett: An English Eccentric." *Critique,* 3:2 (1960).

McCall, Lois. *Western Humanities Review*, 20, 1960.

McCarthy, Mary. "The Inventions of I. Compton-Burnett." *Encounter*, 27:5 (1966).

McFarlane, Brian. "Ivy Compton-Burnett's *A House and Its Head:* Truth and Wit." *Southern Review*, 2, 1978.

Millgate, Michael. "Interview with Miss Compton-Burnett." *Review of English Literature*, 3:4 (1962).

"More Women Than Men." *The Times Literary Supplement*, 7 Sep. 1933.

Muir, Edwin. Review of *Mother and Son. Observer,* 6 Feb. 1955.

______. Review of *The Present and the Past. Observer*, 22 Mar. 1953.

"New Fiction." Review of *A God and His Gifts. The Times*, 21 Nov. 1963.

"Of Human Bondage." *Time*, 4 Apr. 1955.

Potter, Lois, "Show and Dumbshow in *A Family and a Fortune.*" *Twentieth Century Literature*, 25:2 (1979).

Preston, John. "The Matter in a Word." *Essays in Criticism*, 10, 1960.

Review of *A God and His Gifts. New Statesman*, Dec. 1963.

Rowsell, Mary Dalton. "Brothers and Sisters: A Most Complex Relation." *Twentieth Century Literature*, 25:2 (1979).

Snow, Lotus. "Good is Bad condensed: Ivy Compton-Burnett's view of Human Nature." *Western Humanities Review*, 19, 1956.

Spurling, Hilary. "I. Compton-Burnett: Not one of Those Modern People." *Twentieth Century Literature*, 25:2 (1979).

Sykes, Christopher. "The Reign of Tyranny." *The Listener*, 85:2185 (1971).

"Talking Points." *The Times Literary Supplement*, 18 Sep. 1959.

Talking to Dame Ivy: Interview. Ed. K. Dick, *Harper's Bazaar*, 103, May 1970.

"The Hells of Ivy." *Time*, 75, Feb. 1960.

"The Unhappy Family Game." *The Times Literary Supplement*, 22 Mar. 1947.

"The Work-A-Day World that the Novelist Never Enters." *The Times Literary Supplement*, 9 Sep. 1960.

"Two Households." *The Times Literary Supplement*, 20 Apr. 1951.

"Vulture and Cat." *Newsweek*, Apr. 1955.

Waugh, Evelyn. Review of *A Father and His Fate. Spectator*, 6 Aug. 1957.

Webster, Harvey Curtis. "A Visit with Ivy Compton-Burnett." *Saturday Review*, 40, 2 Mar. 1957.

"When an Age is Ended." *The Times Literary Supplement*, 5 Feb. 1971.

Wilde, Alan. "Surfacings: Reflections on the Epistemology of Late Modernism." *Boundary*, 8:2 (1980).

Yarling, Bass. "Miss Ivy's Tobacco Road." *The New Republic*, 4 Mar. 1957.

Young, Kenneth. "A Novelist and her style." *Time and Tide*, 28:34 (1957).

(ii) Books

Adams, Henry Hitch. *English Domestic or Homiletic Tragedy*. 1575-1642.
Allen, Walter. *The English Novel*. London: Penguin, 1954.
______. *Tradition and Dream*. London: Phoenix House, 1964.
Allott, Miriam. *Novelists on the Novel*. London: Routledge and Kegan Paul, 1959.
Armstrong, Nancy. *Desire and Domestic Fiction*. Oxford: Oxford University Press, 1987.
Baker, A. Ernest. *The History of the English Novel*. New York: Barnes and Noble, 1967, 6 Vols.
Barnhart, L. Clarence, ed. *The New Century Hand Book of English Literature*. New York: Appleton Century Crofts, 1967.
Beach, J.W. *The Twentieth Century Novel*. New Delhi: Kalyani, 1965.
Beckson, Karl and Granz Arthur. *A Reader's Guide to Literary Terms*. London: Thames and Hudson, 1972.
Bhagyalakshmi, J. *Ivy Compton-Burnett and Her Art*. New Delhi: Mittal, 1986.
Blake, Nevius. *Ivy Compton-Burnett*. Columbia U.P., 1970.
Burkhart, Charles. *I. Compton-Burnett*. London: Victor Gollancz, 1965.
______, ed. *The Art of I. Compton-Burnett*. London: Victor Gollancz, 1972.
Butler, Sir James. *The History of England 1815-1939*. Oxford: Oxford University Press, 1960.
Calder, Jenni. *Women and Marriage in Victorian Fiction*. London: Thames and Hudson, 1976.
Compton-Rickett, Arthur. *A History of English Literature*. New Delhi: Universal Book Stall, 1983.
Cross, Wilbur L. *The Development of the English Novel*. Ludhiana: Lyall, 1968.
Daiches, David. *A Critical History of English Literature*. London: Secker and Warburg, 1969.
Dick, Kay. *Ivy and Stevie*. London: Allison and Busby, 1983.
Elton, Oliver. *A Survey of English Literature*. London: Edward Arnold, 1948. 2 Vols.
Encyclopaedia Britannica. Chicago: William Benton, 1968. 16 Vols.
Forster, E.M. *Aspects of the Novel*. London: Penguin, 1981.
Fraser, G.S. *The Modern Writer and His World*. London: Penguin, 1967.
Gentile, Kathy. *Ivy Compton-Burnett*. London: Macmillan, 1991.
Gillie, Christopher. *Longman Companion to English Literature*. London: Longman, 1977.
______. *Movements in English Literature 1900-1940*. London: C.U.P., 1975.
Gilmour, Robin. *The Novel in the Victorian Age*. London: Edward Arnold, 1986.
Glynn, Grylls, R. *I. Compton-Burnett*. London: Longman, 1971.
Greig, Cicely. *Ivy Compton-Burnett: A Memoir*. London: Garnstone Press, 1972.
Hoggett, Brenda M. "Parents and Children." *Social Work and Law*. London: Sweet and Maxwell, 1977.
Iser, Wolfgang. *The Implied Reader*. The Johns Hopkins University Press, 1974.
Jack, Ian. "English Literature 1815-1832." *Oxford History of English Literature*, ed. Allott Kenneth and Norman Davis. Oxford: O.U.P., 1963.

Janet, Godden. *Ivy Compton-Burnett*. London: Macmillan, 1993.
Johnson, Pamela Hansford. *I. Compton-Burnett.* London: Longman, 1951.
Karl, R. Frederick. *A Reader's Guide to the Contemporary English Novel*. London: Thomas and Hudson, 1972.
Kelley, Gary. *The English Jacobean Novel 1780-1805*. Oxford: O.U.P, 1976.
Kettle, Arnold. *An Introduction to the English Novel.* London: Hutchinson, 1974. 2 Vols.
Laslett, Peter. *Household and Family in Past Time*. Cambridge: C.U.P., 1974.
Legouis, Emile. *A Short History of English Literature*. Oxford: The Clarendon Press, 1953.
______ and Louis Cazamian. *A History of English Literature*. London: J.M. Dent, 1965.
Liddell, Robert. *A Treatise on the Novel*. London: Jonathan Cape, 1965.
______. *The Novels of I. Compton-Burnett*. London: Victor Gollancz, 1955.
______. *Some Principles of Fiction*. London: Jonathan Cape, 1961.
Meyer Spacks, Patricia. *The Female Imagination*. London: George Allen and Unwin, 1976.
Neill, S. Diana. *A Short History of the English Novel*. London: Jarrolds, 1954.
Pandeya, Shiva M. *Studies in Modern Fiction*. New Delhi: Vikas, 1983.
Phelps, William Lyon. *The Advance of the English Novel.* New York: Dodds, Mead, 1917.
Pollard, Arthur, ed. *Webster's New World Companion to English and American Literature*. New York: Compton Russell, 1973.
Powell, Violet. *A Compton-Burnett Compendium*. London: Heinemann, 1973.
Rao, Ramakrishna. *Ivy Compton-Burnett: A Critical Study*. Waltair: Andhra University Press, 1974.
Rathburn, Robert C. and Martin Steinmann, Jr. ed. *From Jane Austen to Joseph Conrad*. Minneapolis: University of Minnesota Press, 1958.
Saintsbury, George. *A Short History of English Literature*. London: Macmillan, 1953.
Sampson, George. *The Concise Cambridge History of English Literature*. London: The English Language Book Society and C.U.P., 1972.
Sarkar, Rabindranath. *Ivy Compton-Burnett: A Trend in English Fiction*. Calcutta: Firma KLM, 1979.
Shroff, Homai J. *The Eighteenth Century Novel*. New Delhi: Arnold-Heinemann, 1978.
Skilton, David. *The English Novel*. London: David and Charles, 1977.
Sprigge, Elizabeth. *The Life of Ivy Compton-Burnett*, London: Victor Gollancz, 1973.
Spurling, Hilary. *Ivy When Young*. London: Allison and Busby, 1983.
______. *Secrets of a Woman's Heart*. London: Penguin, 1984.
Stapleton, Michael. *The Cambridge Guide to English Literature*. Cambridge: C.U.P., 1983.
Tillotson, Kathleen, *Novels of the Eighteen-Forties*. Oxford: O.U.P., 1956.
Tom Linson, T.B. *The English Middle-Class Novel*. London: The Macmillan, 1978.

Ward, A.W. and A.R. Waller. *The Cambridge History of English Literature*. Cambridge: C.U.P., 1953. 12 Vols.
Watt, Ian. *The Rise of the Novel*. London: Chatto and Windus, 1957.
West, A. *Principles and Persuasions*. London: Eyre and Spottiswoode, 1958.
Williams, Merryn. *Women in the English Novel 1800-1900*. London: Macmillan, 1984.
Williams, Raymond. *The English Novel*. London: Chatto and Windus, 1971.
Woodcock, George, *Twentieth Century Fiction*. London: Macmillan, 1983.

Index